Airship of Dreams

Valiant Heart Trilogy

Book 1: Airship of Dreams
Book 2: The Call to Arms
Book 3: Blood and Fire

AIRSHIP of DREAMS

C.M.S. Thornton

Copyright © C.M.S. Thornton 2024

The right of C.M.S. Thornton to be identified as author of this work has been asserted by her in accordance with the Copyright, Designs and Patents Act, 1988.

All rights reserved. No part of this book may be reproduced or transmitted by any person or entity (including Google, Amazon or similar organisations) in any form or by any means, electronic or mechanical, including photocopying, recording or by any information storage and retrieval system, without prior permission in writing from the publisher.

No AI training: Without in any way limiting the author's and publisher's exclusive rights under copyright, any use of this publication to "train" generative artificial intelligence (AI) technologies to generate text is expressly prohibited. The author reserves all rights to license uses of this work for generative AI training and development of machine learning language models.

A catalogue record for this book is available from the National Library of Australia.

Author: Thornton, C.M.S., author.
Title: Airship of dreams : the doomed flight of the titanic of the skies / C. M.S. Thornton.
ISBN: 9781923212008 (hardcover)
ISBN: 9781923212015 (paperback)

Series: Thornton, C.M.S. Valiant heart ; 1.
Notes: Includes bibliographical references.
Subjects: Biography--Non fiction.
Genre: Non fiction.

www.leavesofgoldpress.com
ABN 67 099 575 078

AIRSHIP of DREAMS

The Doomed Flight of the Titanic of the Skies

Squadron Leader William Palstra M.C., B.A.

1891 - 1930

First World War soldier and airman

~ Salvation Army ~

~ 39th Battalion, Australian Imperial Force ~

~ Australian Flying Corps ~

~ University of Melbourne ~

~ Royal Australian Air Force ~

'Nobody would have guessed—least of all himself—
that beneath the waistcoat of this humble office clerk
there beat the heart of a leader of men
and a conqueror of the skies . . .'

"—Shades of 1913—what a difference between then and now, and so there should be,
for you have set yourself to it as a Greatheart."
~ *Commissioner Wiebe Palstra in a letter to his son, 24 February, 1930.*

*This book is dedicated to the families of the Australians and New Zealanders
who took part in the Great War 1914-1918;
also to the Palstras, the Holdaways,
and my sisters.*

W & K   R101 THE WORLD'S LARGEST AIRSHIP No 199.

On *Airship of Dreams*:

". . . an emotional read. . . a heartfelt tribute to those lost in this national tragedy seen from the other side of the world including much new material not previously published."
~ Peter Davison, BA(hons) AMRAeS. Independent Consultant at the Airship Heritage Trust, UK.

"I found the story of a man who started out a Salvation Army officer and ended up a RAAF Squadron Leader, and his family, a fascinating read."
~ C.P. Hall, book reviewer for the US Naval Airship Association.

CONTENTS

Introduction xv
Prologue 1
Background 13
    Book #2: The Call to Arms 13
    Book #3: Blood and Fire 14

PART I: 1919 17
    Homecoming 18
    Application to join the air force 19
    The fairy glasses 24
    Courting & betrothal 28
    Setting the wedding day 34

PART II: 1920 37
    Wedding and house 38

PART III: 1921	45
Airships	50
Types of airships	51
Zeppelins	52
Airships R33 and R34	53
Airships—the hope of the empire	55
Drawbacks of airships: hydrogen	57
Ashbolt's Imperial Air Company	60
The R38 airship	63
PART IV: 1922 and 1923	75
The Burney Scheme	75
Airship enthusiasm wanes	77
The family in Surrey Hills	79
PART V: 1924	85
The Golden Age of Airships	87
PART VI: 1925	91
Australia's air force	93
Everyday life	94
PART VII: 1926	109
The progress of the Imperial Airship Scheme	112
PART VIII: 1927	115
PART IX: 1928	123
Over the sea	133

PART X: 1929 137
Life in England 137
    An English spring 142
1929: The Imperial Airship Scheme 150
    The design of the R101 158
    Airship construction materials 162
    The R101 takes to the skies 164
    The R100 comes to Cardington 172
Pride and joy 173

PART XI: 1930 175
The Empire's airship 175
Road trip to Wales 177
Road trip to Scotland 179
The Hendon Air Display 188
A ticket to ride the R101 195
The trip to France 196
Extreme modifications to the R101 208
Plans for the future of airship travel 209
The pressure for haste 211
The single test flight 212
Preparations for the flight to India 214
    Will's feelings about the trip 216

PART XII: STEPPING ABOARD THE R101 217
Stepping aboard the R101 219
    The dawning of the day 219
    The weather forecast 221
    Baggage and last letters 221

- The passengers and crew 226
  - Lord Thompson's luggage 227
- The airship 228
  - The engine cars 230
  - The control car 232
  - Living quarters 233
  - The mooring mast and its lift 234
- The weather 235
- The dignitaries arrive 235
- The onlookers 239
- To ride the storm 240
  - Inside the airship 240
  - Passenger cabins 241
  - Imagine: 246
  - The Passenger Lounge 247
  - The Promenade Deck 250
  - The Dining Saloon 252
- The Smoke Room 256
- The Galley 258
- A visit to the Control Car 259
- In the engine cars 260
- The flight 261
  - 7.30 pm to 8.30 pm 265
  - 8.40 pm 267
  - 9.30 Crossing the English coast 268
  - 11 pm 269
  - 11.30pm 270
  - Midnight 271
  - Approaching Beauvais 272
  - 2am change of watch 272

The fall 273
    Allonne Wood 273
    Time: 02:07 + 24 seconds: The first dive 275
    Time: 02:07 + 37 seconds: recovery 277
    Time: 02:07 + 40 seconds 278
    The Second Dive and Landing 279
    Time: 02:08 + 32 seconds 280
Catastrophe 285
    Wreckage and survivors 292
    Recovery of bodies 299
    The News Travels 306
The French pay tribute 309
    Allonne 309
    By farm cart to Allonne 309
    Vigil at Allonne 312
    The Memorial at Allonne 312
    Allonne Village School Monday 6 October 1930: 313
Strange finds, four days later 315
Reactions to the worst aviation disaster in history 315
Squadron Leader Palstra's brilliant career 320
Allonne to Beauvais 324
    Beauvais 326
    The last salute at Beauvais, 7 October 326
Beauvais to Boulogne 338
    The railway journey to Boulogne 340
Return to England 345
Victoria Station 351
Westminster Hall and St Paul's Cathedral 354
    Lying-in-state 355

The Memorial Service at St Paul's Cathedral	368
The common grave	374
London to Cardington	374
Funeral procession through London	374
Euston Station to Bedford Station	379
The funeral at Cardington	384

PART XIII: AFTERMATH ... 391

Will's Family	391
The endless grief of May and Margaret	400
The Enquiry	400
The Effect on Airship Development	403
The Fading of the Age of Airships	403
Zeppelins	405
Vale R101	406
Memorials	406
The Years that Followed	407
Eternal Love	407
Down the years: What happened to the family afterwards	409
Charles Palstra	410
Paranormal claims	411
Voices from the past	414
The legacy	420

MEMORIES ... 421

Bibliography ... 426

INTRODUCTION

The house of my childhood was haunted.

History permeated our family life, for it had soaked into the very fabric of the walls. It seeped from the antiques and curios brought back by our globe-trotting ancestors—the Chinese and Dutch ornaments, and the Māori artefacts. The past lurked, too, in the photograph albums, the wooden aeroplane propeller in the hall cupboard, the shoe-boxes filled with slightly tarnished AIF 'rising sun' buttons and badges, the handful of shrapnel, the old upright piano, the derelict chicken coop at the bottom of the garden, the old wooden sea-trunk in my bedroom, plastered all over with faded P&O steamship luggage labels that hinted at long-ago journeys to exotic places...

Ghosts, nameless and silent, were central to that history, emanating from memories that were not our own. Throughout the years, as my sisters and I grew up, these wraiths walked among us, pervading the waking hours and dreams of the adults. With every solemn tick of the vintage clock on the mantelpiece, they gradually increased their power over us, too.

The adults were unable to escape the influence of the past, let alone shield the children. There was nothing deliberate on their part; they did not intend to transmit the hauntings that bled into our young bones, but it happened. They were not conscious of it, and nor were we. The trauma has passed from the injured generation to the next, then halted.

We children did not yet understand it, but one 'present absence' in particular was the focus of unspeakable, long-buried anguish and longing. His legacy continues to affect our family to this day, almost a hundred years after his death.

A massive bureau, or chest-of-drawers, stood in the hallway of my childhood home. Made of age-darkened mahogany, it contained a hidden compartment; a long, low, deep drawer with no handles, which appeared, to the uninitiated, to be part of the decoration. Only those who were aware of its existence knew the trick of opening it. Within that drawer, known only to members of the immediate family, a multitude of old letters and diaries lay concealed for decades.

These faithfully preserved letters and diaries were written by, and to, my mother's father. For it was he whose terrible absence was the vortex into which the threads of our young lives were being drawn, and the burden we were destined to bear.

For as long as I can remember, an irresistible need to do the impossible, to bring him back to life, has ridden on the shoulders of me and my loved ones, like some demon. We each coped in our own way.

When I reached adulthood, my way of coping was to use the letters and diaries concealed in that secret drawer to tell his story. I was also able to include many of the intriguing sepia photos from the well-preserved family albums.

My mother's profound, repressed and lasting trauma drove me to document his life almost day-by-day, extrapolating to fill the gaps in the first-hand material. This gave me around 632,000 words. Having condensed them into three more concise volumes, I have finally completed the duty that seemed to be laid upon me at birth. In the only way possible I have (I hope), after decades of work and longing, immortalised my grandfather, William Palstra.

C. M.S. Thornton

PROLOGUE

Every event has consequences. Those consequences can ripple far across the universe, far into the future. In truth, they never really fade, even when we are no longer aware of them. After the primal event has passed out of human knowledge, still the effects flow inexorably on.

When His Majesty's airship R101 fell out of the sky in 1930, her terrible ending seemed to herald the fading of the most far-reaching empire the world has ever known. It caused other effects, too—powerful enough to impact the lives of generations. Effects that, to this day, continue to reverberate through time and space . . .

On the evening of October 4th, 1930, rain-clouds were piling up in the skies over Bedfordshire, England.

At the Cardington Air Base, the British Empire's new airship, the largest object ever to fly, hovered two hundred feet above the ground, looking like some surreal deep-sea fish. She was tethered by the nose to the top of her mooring mast. A dazzling beam from a flood-lamp pierced the gathering dusk. Against the darkening skies, the massive hull of the cigar-shaped dirigible shimmered silver-grey. She floated parallel to the fields below, where a large crowd milled about, their faces upturned, marvelling at the sight. Surely this this improbable machine was too huge, too cumbersome to be suspended magically in the air, trembling slightly in the breeze, like a leaf!

The R101 being hauled to her mooring mast. Image: airshipsonline.com

With a length of 237 m (777 ft) the R101 airship was longer than three Boeing 747s. That is more than twice the length of an international soccer pitch, or 2 ½ times the length of an American football field.

Though she was built to float, her gross weight is estimated to have been 158,25 tons. Her hydrogen was capable of lifting 158.75 tons. Her motors, carried in five egg-shaped gondolas supported beneath the hull, were compression ignition engines developing five hundred and eighty-five horsepower each, and burning heavy oil. The R101 was indeed a spectacular sight; a leviathan looming against the rain-clouds like some flying monster from an alien world.

Thousands of spectators lined the roads bordering the Air Base, whose gates were closed to the general public. Rows of parked motor-cars, head-lamps blazing, helped to illuminate the scene.

The R101 at Cardington mooring mast. Image: www.liveinternet.ru

At 7.36 p.m. (1836 hrs, GMT) the great airship cast off from her mooring mast and began to rise.

'Hurrah! Hurrah!' chorused the spectators. 'God speed! Good luck!'

To the roar of enthusiastic cheering from the cap-waving crowd below, she slowly gained height, buoyed by the 5.500,000 cubic feet of hydrogen gas sealed within her envelope. The crew of the airship evidently heard the cheering, and responded by flashing their lamps.

This was the beginning of the R101's first international voyage, and she was bound for India. Her first stop was to be Ismailia, on the Suez Canal in Egypt, for re-fuelling. The 54 men on board—48 crew members and six passengers—were preparing to enjoy a long, comfortable flight.

On completion, the R101 boasted luxurious passenger accommodation and service to rival that of the greatest ocean liners. Her sumptuous outfitting could be compared to the ship *RMS Titanic*. Potted palms and Axminster carpet adorned the elegant dining room. The dinner service had been specially commissioned, and bore her insignia. The airship officers wore dark blue uniforms. Their caps bore the blue and gold badge embroidered with 'Airship R101', topped by a crown representing King George V.

Dining room of the R101 with the chief steward, Albert Savidge. Alamy ID:TA26BC

Passengers in the lounge room of the R101. Image: www.airshipsonline.com

The R101 was to be among the first of a fleet of commercial dirigibles, 'liners of the skies', capable of carrying huge numbers of passengers back and forth across the globe.

The huge volumes of hydrogen gas carried in bags inside the airship's envelope made her lighter than air. It also made her highly flammable. Officers and crewmen had to wear shoes without nails in the soles, lest the steel strike sparks. Smoking was forbidden, except in the specially fire-proofed 'smoking room'.

The R101 had been carefully trimmed before leaving the mast, and she slipped her mooring cable without lurching or dipping. A report from the meteorological office had warned Captain Irwin to expect winds of up to forty to fifty miles per hour, worse than any conditions a British airship had experienced over land in the past.

The airship swung easily clear on an almost level keel, and very slowly wheeled away to gain height. Moving steadily south, she sent out regular radio messages so that her course could be followed. She circled around the nearby town of Bedford before rising to a thousand feet, then to fifteen hundred feet as she moved towards London.

Soon after she left Cardington, rain began to fall.

The R101 in flight. Image: www.britainfromabove.org.uk

As the R101 passed across England heading for the coast, householders peered out of their upper storey windows, eager to see the famous dirigible they had read about in the newspapers. They could see her huge bulk passing by, above the tree-tops. Her lights illuminated the surrounding landscape, glinting on silver spears of rain that stabbed through the darkness. Had the householders been able to look through the airship's windows into the interior, they might have glimpsed the passengers and officers gathered on the promenade deck, enjoying the view of the ground below.

The experienced crew on board expressed no concerns about the airship's performance in their wireless messages. At 9.21 p.m. the airship reported, 'Over London, All well. Moderate rain . . . course now set for Paris.' The message also gave the wind speed as 25 miles an hour—less than anticipated.[1]

A moderately serious engine problem occurred before the airship reached London. Being so heavily laden with passengers, luggage, fuel and water ballast, the airship continued to gain altitude slowly. She was still flying quite low when she passed over the capital city, and

---

1   Note: Published records of wireless messages are unreliable.

her own radioed description of her manoeuvre before crossing the hills to the south was, 'Gradually increasing height so as to avoid high land'.

Near Hastings she left the English coast.

So vast was her envelope that the pounding of millions of raindrops on the fabric would add considerably to her weight. It was raining hard over the English Channel and, burdened beneath the weight of the downpour, the great silver dirigible fought her way with some difficulty, a thirty-five mile an hour sou-wester hammering on her starboard beam.

Navigator Johnston ordered the R.101 to be brought down from 1,000 ft. so that he could see the flares he'd dropped on the water to estimate wind speed and drift.

As she passed over the sea, the winds picked up and she slowly lost height until she reached the alarmingly low altitude of about seven hundred and fifty feet. Those on board could see the white caps of the foaming waves below.

At 10 p.m., the height coxswain, whose sole responsibility was maintaining correct altitude, received a visit from the watch officer, Lieutenant Commander Atherstone. As airship officers often did, he took over the wheel himself for a while, until he had managed to raise the airship to the 1,000 ft. designated cruising altitude. Then he handed back the controls to the coxswain, warning him not to let the R101 go below a thousand feet again.

By the time the R101 had reached the French coast the engineers had corrected the mechanical problem. She made France over the Point de St Quentin and set a course direct for Paris. Strong winds were pummelling her vast envelope, and rain poured down in torrents.

At midnight, the airship sent out a further message. In spite of the rough weather conditions and serious trouble in maintaining height, its words betrayed no real fears on the part of the airship's guests and crew—

> After an excellent supper our distinguished passengers smoked a final cigar and having sighted the French coast have now gone to bed to rest after the excitement of their leavetaking.

> All essential services are functioning satisfactorily. The crew have settled down to watch-keeping routine.

R101 sent out a regular position report at 1.28 am. At 1.30 she passed over the village of Saint-Valery-sur-Somme, appearing so low that the inhabitants scrambled from their beds, certain she would scrape the rooves off their houses. Slowly the airship thundered away into the pitch-dark night.

She sent another routine wireless transmission at 1.51, by which time she was approaching Beauvais, north of Paris. As she passed slightly to the east of the town, the roar of her engines awoke the townsfolk and frightened the children. People rushed to the windows to catch a glimpse of this historic sight; the majestic dirigible flying over their heads with her red and green warning lights twinkling, buffeted by rain and storm clouds.

After 2.07 a.m. there were no more messages from the R101. Just outside Beauvais, with no warning at all, she went into a steep dive. She tilted so sharply that the engineers manning the ship were thrown off balance, and furniture shot forward across the decks. The height coxswain pulled hard on his wheel in an effort to right the airship, and managed to get her on an even keel once more. Within seconds, however, she plunged down again and this time the cox could do nothing to pull her out of the dive.

The officers in command could see what was coming. They ordered all engines to reduce power—although in the confusion, one engineer may not have received the signal—and warning bells were rung throughout the airship.

It is difficult to imagine, but there was no panic. Airship flight is normally so smooth and buoyant, and altitude changes so much a part of the pattern, that few people would leap to the idea of 'crashing' in the way that modern aircraft passengers might. The professional men on board were trained to remain calm in dangerous situations; besides, it was just not 'the thing' to panic in front of one's peers. Perhaps also their faith in God and the British Air Ministry held firm.

The chief coxswain had time to go aft, where the crew members were sleeping, to announce quite matter-of-factly, 'We're down, lads.'

With a great grinding noise of engines ceasing and metal grating on metal, the airship lumbered to the earth and slid several yards along the ground.

Then, less than a minute after her last wireless transmission, she exploded into flames. A crashing roar swept through the valley as 5.5 million cubic feet of hydrogen ignited.

It shook the nearby village of Allonne to its foundations, and shattered windows. Sheets of flame towered into the sky. The furnace that was once an airship lit up the countryside with a ghastly yellow light, like some nightmarish sun. Night had turned into day.

People in the vicinity of Beauvais were awakened by the thunder. On rushing to their windows, they saw streaks of light soaring across the sky.

Next day, all that could be seen was a massive tangle of scorched metal. The twisted, burnt and charred framework was all that remained of the glorious R101. She had been completely destroyed by fire. Forty-eight men perished out of a total of fifty-four passengers and crew.

That tragedy finished the British airship industry and was counted among the worst disasters of the twentieth century.

One of those aboard was Squadron Leader William Palstra, M.C., B.A.

This is his story.

William Palstra in AIF uniform with swagger stick (date unknown). Image: family archives

PALSTRA FAMILY TREE

Wiebe PALSTRA (b. 4 March 1867 Harlingen, Friesland, Netherlands d. 1944) married **Jacoba Christina Hendrika ENGELBERT VAN BEVERVOORDE** (b. 29 December 1858 Deventer, or Hasselt, Overijssel, Netherlands. d. 1935). Their children:

- William (b. 8 October 1891 Zwolle, Overijssel, Netherlands. d. 5 October 1930, France)
- Henrietta Christina Alberdina (b. 10 October 1892 Amsterdam, Netherlands. d. 23 July 1969 USA?)
- Charles Engelbert (13 January 1893? 94? Amsterdam, Netherlands. d. Australia) Probably born in 1893.
- Frank Elwyn (b. 5 October 1896 St. Jean, Belgium. d. 23 September 1957, Australia)
- Blanche Evangeline (b. 14 October 1898 Brussels, Belgium. d. November 1978 Melbourne, Australia)
- James Victor (b. 26 October 1900 Belgium.)
- John Bernard Philip (b. 7 September 1904 Johannesburg, South Africa. death date unknown, possibly September 24 1957 Australia)

'Only time, not space, separates us from the past.'

~ Author unknown ~

Background

Airship of Dreams is Book 1 in the Valiant Heart trilogy. Books 2 and 3, *The Call to Arms* and *Blood and Fire*, deal with William Palstra's life before 1919. In other words, they tell his life story leading up to the events recounted here, in Book 1. Reading them is optional; *Airship of Dreams* can stand alone.

Here's an overview of the other two books in the series. They explain Will's journey from a humble office clerk plugging away at typing and shorthand, to a dare-devil air force pilot decorated with the Military Cross.

Book #2: The Call to Arms.

Twenty-two-year-old office clerk William Palstra, the eldest of seven siblings, travels by steamship to Melbourne, Australia, to join his missionary family, who have been posted there by the Salvation Army. He is a rather shy and self-effacing young man, but resourceful and conscientious. Lean and lithe, he stands 5 foot 9 inches tall (69 inches or 1.75 metres), his eyes are blue-green and his brown hair is worn short, as is the style of the times.

It is 1914, and the British Empire has just declared war on Germany. When Britain is at war, her dominions are automatically at war too. In 1914 British dominions include Canada, New Zealand, South Africa, Newfoundland and Australia. By the time Will arrives in Melbourne his younger brother Charles, aged 21, has already enlisted in the Australian Imperial Force (AIF).

On the 25 April 1915, Australian and New Zealand soldiers form part of the Allied expedition that disembarks on the shores of the Gallipoli peninsula in Turkey, and Charles Palstra is one of them. He is wounded at Gallipoli, but survives the carnage—physically, at least.

Back in Melbourne, Will leaves his job as a clerk working for the Pianola Company and enlists in the Australian Imperial Force (AIF) on 3rd January 1916, at the age of twenty-four. He becomes a private in the 39th Infantry Battalion AIF (Tenth Brigade).

In May 1916 the battalion voyages to England to complete its training on Salisbury Plain. It is here that Will sees biplanes flying above the ancient megaliths of Stonehenge, and vows to become a pilot if he can.

After being selected to study for a commission in a course based at Oxford University., he graduates as a Second Lieutenant. In April 1917 he crosses the English Channel to join his battalion, which is already fighting on the Western Front.

Book #3: Blood and Fire.

At the Battle of Messines in West Flanders, Belgium, Lieutenant Palstra distinguishes himself by his courage. For a while he finds himself commanding the entire battalion when all the other officers are gassed, wounded or killed. On the 12 December 1917, in recognition of Will's "dash and determination", King George V personally invests him with the Military Cross medal at Buckingham Palace.

Lieutenant Palstra and the 39th continue to fight in the trenches. They play an active part in several deadly conflicts. On 26 October, 1917, Will receives a telegram informing him that he has been selected for training with the Australian Flying Corps (AFC).

He leaves the 39th Battalion and returns to England, where he learns how to fly biplanes. On 10 September 1918 he returns to the thick of the fighting in France, now as a pilot with No. 3 Squadron, AFC. From then until the end of the war he performs daring and dangerous stunts in flying-machines, supporting Australian, British and American troops, while dodging anti-aircraft fire, often over enemy lines.

Germany signs an armistice agreement with the Allies and Associated Powers on 11 November, 1918 and the Great War finally ends. The global "Spanish Influenza" pandemic then proceeds to kill at least 50 million people worldwide.

On 7 May 1919, Will returns home to Melbourne, having been away for three years. During that time he has transformed himself from an unassuming office clerk to a confident leader of men, a medal recipient and an aircraft pilot.

What an adventure it has been!

Now it is over. What does the future hold for this 27-year-old war veteran, returning to his family in Australia?

PART I: 1919

"I look at the moon and say to myself, I wonder when the first Hun bomber will come over tonight. But all is silent, no guns, no searchlights, no gasmasks, no tin hats. It's wonderful, it is a new world. Let us hope it will be a better one."
~ William Palstra, on the Western Front, 1918

'Rule Britannia,' played in England to the sweet tunes as of old;
And our Allies, they have fought like men, have proven true and bold;
They played their part, straight from the heart, as anyone can see,
To protect the little countries, whether on the land or sea.
'Marseillaise' they played all over France, the first time since the war;
When they played 'Australia Will Be There' the boys began to roar!

Chorus: Now the boys in khaki, they are coming home,
To their H.O.M.E., home, home, sweet home;
They are worth their weight in gold, that is what the world's been told,
The Australian boys in Khaki coming home.

~ The Australian Boys in Khaki Coming Home.
Music: JE Dodd. Words: Wm. W Forscutt. 1918

HOMECOMING

Lieutenant William Palstra departed from England at Devonport on the 21 March 1919 on the *SS Kildonan Castle*, arriving home in Australia on 7 May. After disembarking at Station Pier, Will was greeted as a hero by the Salvation Army community of Melbourne. His parents and siblings welcomed him with the utmost enthusiasm, and brought him in triumph to their new home, 'Carrigmore', in the Melbourne suburb of Surrey Hills. So celebrated was Will, that his arrival—along with that of his friend Lieutenant V. Knight—was reported in Melbourne's most influential daily newspaper, *The Argus*.

```
The Argus (Melbourne, Vic. : 1848 - 1956)
Saturday 10 May 1919 page 20
Officers Welcomed Home

A public welcome was given to Lieutenant W. Palstra
M.C., and Lieutenant Knight, both of the Flying Corps
on their return to Australia after an absence of three
and four years respectively. A large crowd attended
the Salvation Army citadel at Camberwell [a Melbourne
suburb] where the welcome took place. Lieutenant Palstra
is the son of "Colonel"[2] Palstra, chief secretary of the
Salvation Army in Australia, and Lieutenant Knight is
the son of "Colonel" Knight, principal of the Salvation
Army Training College.
```

---

2   Since the war, newspaper reporters had taken to enclosing Salvation Army quasi-military titles in quotation marks to distinguish them from military ranks.

APPLICATION TO JOIN THE AIR FORCE

It was probably at one of the Salvation Army welcome-home celebrations that Will first set his heart on May Holdaway, the daughter of a well-respected Salvation Army family. His family had mingled with hers in the past, and indeed, Will's father "Colonel" Wiebe Palstra had spoken at the funeral of her father, "Brigadier" Ernest Holdaway. However, as May's brother Allan wrote, "So far as I can recall, we did not have a great deal to do with the Palstras until Will and Charles Palstra and my brother Arthur came home from the War."[3]

At the time of Will's homecoming May was 23 years old, slender, five feet eight and a half inches tall (174cm). She worked as a typist with the international news agency, Reuters, in the Melbourne central business district. Her smile was radiant smile and her cascade of corn-silk hair abundant. Photographs taken around that time show her to be a beautiful young woman.

In later days, when asked about their meeting, May Holdaway would explain how glamorous Will seemed to her. An airman in 1919 was not only rare but also a hero, a knight of the skies, a man of dash and daring.

For Will, did the days following his arrival seem to drag like an anti-climax for him, or fly past in a whirlwind of activity? There was always a lot to be done, so perhaps there was little time for dwelling on awakening love. His appointment as an officer of the AFC would be terminated in a few weeks' time—in Melbourne, on 21 June, 1919. Once more he would be a civilian. He had to consider his future career.

It took about a year to repatriate the Australian armed forces. Week by week, newspapers reported their departures from the northern hemisphere and arrivals in the southern.

At this time, also, the Australian government was discussing the future of the newly-fledged AFC, which had distinguished itself so courageously during the war.

---

3   Allan Holdaway, Memoirs, 1967

Will's love of flying remained strong. Faced with the prospect of being "grounded" in the immediate future, he applied for a position in the Australian Air Force which, at that time, had been proposed to replace the A.F.C., but had not yet been formed.

On 15 May 1919 he wrote to The Secretary of Defence, Victoria Barracks, Melbourne, saying, "Sir, I hereby make application for appointment to commissioned rank in the Australian Air Force to be formed. My military history and qualifications are as follows—" Among other information, he listed the following:

- Enlisted 3 January 1916 as a private.
- Sailed 27 May 1916 as a corporal in the 39th Infantry Battalion Australian Imperial Force (A.I.F.).
- Promoted to sergeant and transferred to headquarters of the 10th Infantry Brigade, 25 August 1916.
- Completed four months' Infantry Officers' course at No. 6 Officer Cadet Battalion Oxford, November 1916 to March 1917.
- Appointed Second Lieutenant in A.I.F. as from 28 March 1917
- Posted to 39th Battalion A.I.F.
- Awarded Military Cross (Messines 7 June 1917)
- Promoted to lieutenant 28 July 1917. Appointed Battalion Lewis Gun Officer. Attended three weeks L.G. course at Le Touquet, France.
- Seconded for training with Australian Flying Corps (AFC) 7 December 1917.
- Graduated as pilot 2 May 1918, Pilot Certificate No. 13002 C.F.S. Royal Air Force. and transferred to A.F.C.
- Posted to No. 3 A.F.C. France 10 September 1918 to "Contact" Flight (flying an R.E.8 aircraft). Specialised in low flying, including ground strafing, ten successful contacts, spotting of three enemy counter-attacks and oblique photography. Brought down one enemy aircraft (officially credited).

- Seconded for duty with "O" Flight R.A.F. (Special Bristol Fighter Flight). Long distance low oblique photography and reconnaissance.
- Transferred for duty as Instructor with No. 8 Training School A.F.C. and to command "A" Flight, 25 February 1919.
- Sailed for Australia 23 March 1919.
- Age: 27 (8 October 1891) Single
- Previous occupation: Assistant accountant, The Pianola Company 252 Collins Street Melbourne.

"I should be very much obliged if you could give me some idea of the time it will still take for the Air Force scheme to mature. If this is not likely to come to pass for some time will Pilots be provisionally accepted? Your advice on this subject would be greatly appreciated and would enable me to fix definitely my plans for the future.

Thanking you,
I have the honour to remain,
Sir,
Your obedient servant,
W. P."

After dropping this letter in one of the red letter-boxes that stood on so many street corners, Will must have felt impatient for a reply. After the non-stop action of the war years, he yearned to be up and doing, to be achieving, and to be following his chosen path with a vengeance. It was not in his character to be idle.

It was hard for returned servicemen to settle down to civilian life, but if Will shared in the sense of anti-climax experienced by so many returned soldiers, there is no mention of it in his papers.

The war had stimulated rapid technological advances. When it ended, the fervent desire to pursue these new technologies blossomed not only throughout the British Empire and the USA, but also in Germany. Aeroplanes had played a spectacular part in the conflict; new aeronautical inventions were being unveiled at a fast pace, and aviation was hot news. Newly designed aeroplanes could fly further and faster than ever before, although distances were limited by how much fuel they could carry. Private companies and governments were eagerly considering alternative forms of international aerial commuting; in particular, airships.

```
The Western Argus (Kalgoorlie, WA : 1916 - 1938)
  Tuesday 14 January 1919:


AERIAL NAVIGATION
Before the war was dreamt of except at Berlin, American
aeronautic enthusiasts were meditating a trans-Atlantic
airship. One did in fact start from South Carolina,
was buffeted about by storms for several days, and with
disabled engines drifted northward till abandoned off
the New England coast. But the airship of to-day is a
vast improvement on that of seven years ago; and when
the upper air currents and their zones are thoroughly
known a commercial Zeppelin should have no more difficulty
in crossing the Atlantic in two or three days than has
the albatross or frigate bird, which simply spreads his
wings and allows the aerial drift to carry him faster
than he could fly. . .
. . . But, most significant of all, Germany — which wails
so plaintively that the allies have ruined and are
starving it — is busily but quietly embarking on a new,
and comprehensive aerial campaign. Her war machines are
being organised for internal service, and she is con-
structing a model over-ocean aeroplane, to cost over
£100,000. The new Teutonic cry is —"The future of Germany
is in the air."
```

```
Britain is at present more concerned in the restoration of
her mercantile marine tonnage than in aerial navigation,
but is nevertheless awake to the fact that provision
must be made for the airships of the future. . . .
```

Will's fellow Victorian aviator, Harry Hawker, was making his mark on history by attempting to win the Daily Mail newspaper's £10,000 prize for the first flight across the Atlantic in "72 consecutive hours".

Larger aeroplanes were also being designed at this time. The most modern of these was able to carry ninety-two people, but on long journeys it would have to travel in short "hops" between refuelling stations.

```
The Advertiser (Adelaide, SA : 1889 - 1931)
Saturday 24 May 1919 page 8
AIR ENTERPRISE.
WORLD'S LARGEST PLANE.
CARRIES 92 PEOPLE.
LONDON. May 14.

The largest aeroplane in the world has been finished at
Farnborough. It was originally intended to bomb Berlin.
There are three principal planes [meaning sets of wings]
and it has six 450-horsepower engines. The machine is
capable of attaining a speed of 100 miles. The fuselage
is 80 ft. long and it will carry 92 persons.[4]
```

Exciting schemes like Hawker's must have thrilled Will. He must have hoped that the new Air Force would be formed with all speed, so that he could take to the skies once again. His wait, however, would turn out to be a long one.

---

4   The Tarrant Tabor was a British triplane bomber designed towards the end of the First World War and was briefly the world's largest aircraft. It crashed, with fatalities, on its first flight.

THE FAIRY GLASSES

The Salvation Army carried on their work, helping the poor and sick, marching through the streets with their brass bands, holding their regular meetings.

At some of these meetings, six grown-up children of the Holdaway family performed. Photographs show them playing a glittering array of bells and water-glasses[5]; instruments that produce ethereal, fairy-like music. The Holdaways also sang Maori songs, their voices blending in harmony. These occasions were recorded in the Army's newspaper, the War Cry, and they were certainly witnessed by Will Palstra and his family.

In 1911, Ernest and Agnes Holdaway had voyaged to Australia from New Zealand, (not for the first time), with six of their eight children. Ernest had been promoted to Brigadier and appointed Provincial Commander for Tasmania.

May's father had been, from all accounts, a remarkable man. The War Cry had once reported, 'Adjutant Holdaway is a magnificent man, no two ways about it. He stalks along in Maori garb, six and a half feet high, his every movement picturesque and telling. As a speaker he has held every assemblage.'

The Maori people gave Ernest the title of honorary chief, and called him 'Enata Horowe'. The ceremonial spear which accompanied this title is treasured by his descendants to this day. In New Zealand the Holdaway children had learned to sing Maori songs and to dance the famous 'haka'.

They gave famous musical performances at Army meetings.

The Salvation Army in Melbourne, it must be remembered, was a small and tightly-knit community in those days; the population of the whole of Australia was less than six million.

The fame of the Holdaways had preceded their arrival in Australia. By means of the War Cry and the Army grapevine, the Palstras had been hearing about them for years. Salvationists were interested in the work of Ernest and Agnes Holdaway as missionaries among the

---

5 Sets of musical glasses are sometimes called a 'glass harp', a 'glass harmonica' or 'fairy glasses'. Such instruments, in one form or another, were favoured by European monarchs of old. Even Marie Antoinette took lessons on the glass harmonica as a child. The Russian composer Tchaikovsky composed a piece specifically written for the instrument. Dance of the Sugar Plum Fairy became popular throughout Russia after the Nutcracker ballet's first performance, though the glasses were later replaced by the celesta.

Maori people. Ernest was renowned as a singer and musician. His musical band attracted tremendous crowds at Army meetings all over New Zealand, and also at the first Salvation Army International Congress in London.

All over the world, in those early days, there were people who objected to the Army's activities, especially their bans on drinking and gambling. In the 1890s, when Ernest Holdaway was just a young officer in New Zealand, the mission often met with suspicion, derision and violence. Salvationists holding open-air meetings or marching through the streets were often heckled, or suffered injury from thrown objects. The same persecution was happening in England.

The New Zealand War Cry reported on the Saturday night 'battle' when, as the Salvationists were marching up the main street to the tune of 'Onward Christian Soldiers', four men came out of a hotel, mounted their horses and charged the band in the rear at a gallop, scattering the Soldiers in all directions, knocking the torches out of their hands and even trying to kick in the drumhead (the skin of the bass drum).

In Australia, some local councils passed by-laws forbidding Army street processions, and the police were liable to arrest the Soldiers. Undaunted, the Army flaunted the new by-laws and continued to march and hold street meetings. Their people went to jail, or were fined, rather than turning away from their sworn duty to spread the word of God.

No matter how many by-laws they passed, however, the councils couldn't stop people joining the movement. In spite of it all, the number of members and corps in Australia and New Zealand grew at an amazing rate in those early years.

By the turn of the century there were more than thirteen hundred Corps and Outposts across both countries, administering to hundreds of thousands of members. In 1903, 0.082 percent of Australia's population of almost 4 million had joined the Salvation Army—around 320,000 people.

The strain of 28 years of strenuous Salvation Army activity under difficult conditions in New Zealand had taken its toll on May's father. Ernest Holdaway died of pernicious anaemia in Melbourne on 18 September 1913. Five hundred Salvationists walked in his funeral procession, following the flag bearers, the full brass band and the coffin on its horse-drawn gun carriage at a stately pace down Sydney Road to Coburg Cemetery.

Will's father Colonel Wiebe Palstra had spoken at the funeral service, and at the graveside as well, thanking God that he had known Brigadier Holdaway, although he had not known him long. He also conducted a memorial service at Collingwood Citadel the following day, attended by the two families Palstra and Holdaway, and the families of numerous other officers.

The Palstras and the Holdaways had attended many of the same meetings since 1912, the year Will's parents and siblings had arrived in Melbourne. Will and May must often have attended the same Corps meetings yet before the war they were never so close as they became after the war, in 1919.

The Holdaway family during the early years in New Zealand, left to right: Gordon, Arthur, Agnes with Allan, Isabella ("Kuku"), Eva, Ernest, May. In front are the musical instruments played by the family. The children rang the bells, Ernest played the small glasses and Eva played the big glasses. Together they made an orchestra. Image from family archives.

The Holdaways in Maori traditional costume, gifted to them by the Maori people.
Back row: Agnes, Eva, Ernest, May. Front row: Isabella, Arthur.

The Holdaways in Australia, after the death of Ernest Holdaway.
Agnes and her eldest children are in Salvation Army uniform.

COURTING & BETROTHAL

If Will shared in the sense of anti-climax experienced by so many returned soldiers, there is no mention of it in his papers.

Life in the Salvation Army meant that he was at all times surrounded by crowds of supporters who showered him with nothing but love and admiration; this must have bolstered his spirits. Life, too, was a busy social whirl. Presumably there was little time to dwell on the horrors he had witnessed on the front line, and the sense of loss accompanying the disbanding of the AIF and the AFC.

Besides, Will was preoccupied with planning his future. He had experienced the sweet taste of success, and was keen to continue on his upward trajectory through life. While his ambition to be an airman was stymied by the fact that an Australian Air Force had not yet been formed, he determined to fulfil his other career ambition of obtaining a university degree. On a personal front, at the age of 27 he wanted to establish his own household, with a wife and children, a house to shelter them and income to support them.

The happy excitement of romance was in the air. Courtings and weddings were all the rage after the war, and it was no different in the Salvation Army.

The Palstras and the Holdaways frequently mingled socially at this time; fourteen vigorous, playful young people ranging from their teens to early twenties enjoyed each other's company under the kindly auspices of their parents. Will might have been impressed by May's looks, her gentleness, her singing voice, and her vivaciousness as a performer. He remembered his father's counsel (in one of his letters) saying that he hoped Will would find a wife as wonderful as Jacoba. In later life, Will would acknowledge the influence of his parents on his decision to remain chaste while on active service, and on his choice of a life-partner.

> "Much of this philosophy I learnt in a quiet kind of way from you and Dad long before I thought of getting married. I made up my mind that I would marry a girl who had been brought up in the same home atmosphere as myself, and that idea successfully kept me out of all entanglements whilst I was away at the war."[6]

Will and May shared a common world view, and their families—which were so important to them both—liked each other well. With all the stars aligned, love began to blossom and they commenced courting.

On 18th July, Peace Day processions to celebrate the signing of the armistice and the end of the Great War were held throughout Australia.

---

6   Letter from Will to his mother, 8 December 1926

This social and political turbulence provided the backdrop for the lives of the Palstras and Holdaways in Melbourne in 1919.

Will longed to ask for May's hand in marriage, but first he required a decent income. Married women were discouraged from working, because it put single-income families at a relative disadvantage. Society might consider them to be taking jobs away from men who were trying to earn their livelihoods, although there was no law against it. When May married, she would not have to quit her job with Reuters and depend on her husband's income, but Will did not want a wife who worked. He felt it would reflect badly on him. At that time it was generally accepted that the husband should be the sole breadwinner. A man of the early twentieth century would feel he wasn't doing his duty as a husband and father if he could not fully support his wife and family. Many people viewed men with working wives deprecatingly, as if they were incapable of looking after their families on their own. (That said, both Will's and May's mothers were, as active Salvation Army Officers, married working women.)

Will needed a job. His great love was flying, and he had applied to join the Australian Air Force, but it had not yet re-formed. On the 21st June 1919 his appointment with the Australian Flying Corps was officially terminated. The AFC, in fact, ceased to exist. It had remained part of the Australian Army until 1919, when it was disbanded, along with the Australian Imperial Forces (AIF). Although the Central Flying School continued to operate at Point Cook, military flying virtually ceased at this time.

It would not resume until 1920, when the Australian Air Corps would be born.

But that was in the future.

More immediately, Will needed financial stability before he could ask May to be his wife.

As an experienced clerk, Will had impressive office skills. He was proficient at shorthand and typing; he was efficient and a good communicator, adept at reading and writing, with excellent grammar and spelling and attention to detail. With his credentials, good references and outstanding military history, it proved easy for him to get a job.

Will was appointed in July 1919 to the staff of the Registrar's Office, Melbourne University, as assistant to the Registrar,[7] with an annual salary of £250.

As soon as he was assured of the job, he asked May Holdaway to marry him. Joyfully, she accepted. As tokens of his love he gave her his official AFC photo, his military cross medal, and the best engagement ring he could buy.

The betrothed couple at the beach, circa December 1919.

---
7   The Academic Registrar at a university is the official who administrates student records, student services and conduct, enrolments etc.

Portrait of May in 1920

It seemed like a dream come true. The happiness of the young lovers and their families knew no bounds.

Because there was only one university in Melbourne, people simply called it "The University". Will had applied for the job there because it would make it easier for him to integrate study and work. Back in the days before his enlistment, Will had wanted to obtain tertiary qualifications, but lacked the wherewithal to do so.

For Will, as a repatriated soldier, undertaking a course of tertiary education would be free of charge. If he enrolled at university, the government "repatriation authorities" would even pay him a small allowance of £2 per week to live on while he studied.

Studying for a degree would have to wait awhile, however. Will would later write, "It took me a year to become fully acquainted with my duties [as assistant to the Registrar], during which time study was out of the question."

To cap the joy of the Palstra family, on 1 November 1919, Will's brother Lieutenant Charles Palstra (an Anzac who had landed at Gallipoli) returned to Australia. What joyful celebrations ensued! The family was, once more, complete! Wiebe and Jacoba must have been persuaded that all their prayers had been answered. Both their soldier sons had returned from the Great War. By some miracle they were not among the thousands of grieving families who had lost sons, brothers, fathers, uncles, cousins in that bloody conflict.

The family could not know it, and he would never have dreamed of revealing it, but all was not well with Charles. Outwardly he would have presented himself as hale in all respects, for he was a proud man, and to admit that he was struggling would probably, to him, appear weak. It might also make him the target of disapproval and stern lectures from his family.

During the war Charles had suffered profound physical and mental hurts, with long-lasting consequences. At the end, after all he'd endured, he came home to find that his older brother not only outranked him and had beaten him home, but with his Military Cross and pilot's licence, he had almost become legendary. Charles must have wondered how he could ever hope to outshine, or even equal Will, in their father's eyes.

SETTING THE WEDDING DAY

"I think of you, and love you every minute of the day."
~ Will, in a letter to May, 1919.

Now that they were engaged, Will and May took to travelling by city tram to visit each other in the city, during their lunch hours. They had much to discuss, for they were planning their wedding day and discussing where they would go for their honeymoon.

They were excited, in love, deliriously happy. May would leave Reuters as soon as she was married, and they must then live on a single income. Will was working full-time as a clerk in the registrar's office at Melbourne University.

When December rolled around, summer officially commenced in Australia. The Salvation Army owned holiday accommodation at Parkdale, by the sea—this was available to families of officers. The Palstras and the Holdaways holidayed here and there still exist many photos of the two large families of young people mingling as one; on beach holidays as a happy group; sprawled on the sand together, picnicking under the tea-trees or splashing in the sea.

Meanwhile Will was saving every penny of his salary in the hope of buying a house for his bride and himself, preferably near his parents, who were living in the suburb of Surrey Hills. This suburb was only about 35 years old at that time, and still had plenty of house blocks that were not yet built on.

The following letter is included with apologies to Will and May for publishing their private and very personal correspondence. (The "liftman" would refer to the man in charge of operating the elevators in the city building where the Reuters offices were housed.)

Note to May from Will: 2.30 pm

4.12.19

Darling,

I believe I have just missed you, the liftman tells me you only left a minute ago. I will call to see you at 5.15 pm, but what I wanted to tell you now was that we can fix our wedding day for July 3rd. I saw the Registrar this morning, and it's fixed that I get a month from July 1st, so July 3rd will be the day, our day.

I think of you, and love you every minute of the day.

Ever yours,

Will.

The betrothed couple at the beach, circa December 1919.

PART II: 1920

"I thank God with all my heart for your splendid and beautiful heart and feel sure the qualities of mental and soul strength are going to carry you far in all the things that really matter."

Will put aside as much of his income as possible. He was used to being thrifty, and never expected luxury in any form, so this was not difficult. Before the wedding day, he had saved enough to obtain a bank loan and put a deposit on a recently-built weatherboard house at number 60, Guildford Road, Surrey Hills, the total cost of the house being £600.[8] It was fashionable to give names to houses. Will would call their new home "Aurunui", in honour of his bride. He was determined to have a fixed address—to own his own home and not be always renting and moving, as his parents were forced to do.

The young man's future happiness seemed assured.

---

[8] 600 Australian pounds in 1919 is roughly equivalent to $AUD 48,278.48 in 2019, or adjusted for inflation, AUD$1,200.00.

Throughout 1919 and 1920, the Australian government was planning the formation of the new Australian Air Force. This was a remarkably progressive step. The British RAF, formed on 1 April 1918, was the world's first and only independent air force at that time.

An article by Clark and Kainikara in the bulletin "Pathfinder" explains, "The event which prompted the rash of 'air forces' immediately after World War I was the offer by Britain in June 1919 to give 100 war surplus aircraft free to any of its Dominions that wished to set up their own air force."

In March 1920 the Australian Defence Department placed advertisements in national newspapers, inviting applications to fill vacancies existing in the "Australian Air Corps", Victoria. There is no record of Will re-applying at that time. Perhaps he assumed that his previous application would keep its place in the queue, or possibly he had decided that he ought not to abandon his studies, or maybe he'd heard that plans were moving slowly, and there was little chance that the new air corps would be formed until the following year.

WEDDING AND HOUSE

The date of the wedding drew nearer. Colonel Wiebe Palstra wrote to his son in May, 1920, a letter full of love and praise:

>The Salvation Army,
>
>National Headquarters,
>
>69 Bourke Street,
>
>Melbourne
>
>19.5.1920
>
>My dear Will,
>
>Just a line or so which is both to dear May and yourself.

We are well—Mother is enjoying the change and the rest will do her a lot of good. We both feel we want to make June month "yours". What about having a few of your friends and May's for an evening—what date? Then there are other things such as helping to make your home nice and comfortable with which we would like to have something to do.

I say—just for your ear alone—which means, of course May also—I thank God with all my heart for your splendid and beautiful heart and feel sure the qualities of mental and soul strength are going to carry you far in all the things that really matter. All I have felt about you in either the more remote or immediate past, I feel more strongly than ever. You know what I mean.

Heaps of love to you both.

God ever bless you,

Yours as ever,

Dad.

William Palstra married May Aurunui Holdaway at the Salvation Army Citadel in Hawthorn (a suburb of Melbourne) on the 3rd of July 1920. He wore his AFC uniform, while she was in her Salvation Army clothes. They could not afford fancy wedding outfits, but May wore a white sash across her body, with a spray of flowers pinned to it. Will's father was the marriage celebrant—what a proud moment it must have been for all concerned! On the marriage certificate, Will listed his occupation as "Administrative Officer in the Registrar's Office at Melbourne University."

The newlyweds travelled by steam-train to the Blue Mountains in New South Wales for their two week honeymoon.

The wedding of Will and May, 1920

Upon their return they moved in to their modest weatherboard house at 60 Guildford Road, in the suburb of Surrey Hills. This house still stands. More than a century later, it remains in the family and has never been sold.

[Photo: Will and May on their honeymoon.]

The House

As an adult, Jocelyn Goss (née Palstra) wrote about her parents,

"The young couple intended where possible to save money on food by producing their own, and this meant they first needed to construct a hen house, which included nest boxes for the hens to safely lay their eggs in, and to dig out the grass and weeds so that fruit and nut trees could be planted at the back of the house and vegetable beds could be created."

Will and May obtained a dog who they named "Digger" (probably in honour of the Anzacs) and a cat named Teddy (which would have been useful in keeping the rats and mice out of the chicken coop). They set about making their home and its surroundings as comfortable as possible.

May and Will at the front gate of their house at 60 Guildford Road

May seated at her treadle sewing machine in the back yard of No 60 Guildford Road.

Melbourne University

Every working day, Will would walk down Guildford Road to Chatham Railway Station, to catch the train to the city. From Flinders Street Station he made his way to Melbourne University where he performed his duties as secretary/assistant to the registrar.

Will and May, now settled at their new home, were very much in love. May treasured the little notes he wrote to her, putting them away in a drawer for safekeeping.

> Note to May from Will: 13.9.20
>
> My own Sweetheart,
>
> As I can't kiss you this morning, I thought I would just write a couple of lines to greet you on your return. Everything is O.K. although I have not been able to do much to the house. I carted 5 bags of fowls feed from the station this morning—up at 5.30 a.m.
>
> What a lovely day. I do hope you are feeling alright. Heaps and heaps of love and kisses
>
> (these will have to wait till this evening)
>
> Will
>
> 8.5 a.m.

Life continued joyously for Will. He and May were deeply in love, and he was, at last, living close to his parents. Wiebe and Jacoba had rented a house in the same suburb, within walking distance, and visits between the two households were frequent. The Holdaway generations and the Palstra generations mingled freely together at Army social occasions. The fact that there was no separation also meant that there was no need for letter-writing, so family archives hold few records from this period.

Their idyll was not to last, however.

The Salvation Army continued to hold the policy that missionary families must only spend a few years at one post before moving on. When ordered, they must pack their luggage and voyage to another new country. This was viewed as admirable self-sacrifice for the betterment of humankind.

```
The Argus (Melbourne, Vic.: 1848-1956) Monday 15 November
1920, Page 8 SALVATION ARMY
. . . Tributes were paid to their devotion to the cause
of Christianity in leaving their friends and their
home-land to extend the kingdom of Christ among the
heathen. . . "
```

PART III: 1921

Exciting news

On 1st January 1921, Army Headquarters announced that, after serving for seven years as Chief Secretary in Australia, Colonel Wiebe Palstra was to be posted to China, where the Salvation Army had been in existence for only five years. At this time Wiebe was aged fifty-four and Jacoba was sixty-three.

Will's parents were given extended leave as is usual in such circumstances so that they could return to their homeland, the Netherlands, if they wished to before taking up their new post.

However, as all their seven children now lived in Australia, that was where they spent their leave.

During the first few weeks of 1921, Will and May learned exciting news—they were expecting a baby! Their joy was tempered by their regret that Wiebe and Jacoba would not be on hand for the arrival of their first grandchild.

Around this time Will enrolled in the Bachelor of Arts course at Melbourne University. He was keen to have a higher education. Besides, the extra two pounds per week the government offered to to war veterans who wanted to pursue further education—£104 per year—would supplement his income of £250 per annum. The matriculation examination he had passed at the University of the Cape of Good Hope in South Africa was an acceptable entrance standard for the course.

While carrying out his office duties he began studying, in his own time. He was able to arrange with the Registrar's Office to get the necessary time off to attend lectures, and ensured that his office duties did not suffer by doing voluntary overtime when necessary.

Will took Philosophy, Psychology, Logic and Ethics, and Sociology, achieving excellent exam results at the end of the year. In 1925 he would write:

"I have been on the Varsity staff since my return from active service, taking a post at £250 p.a., with the object of fulfilling a long cherished ambition, namely the securing of a university education.

It took me a year to become fully acquainted with my duties, during which time study was out of the question. Since then I have completed in my spare time and in four years, what is normally a full three year's day course, and graduated B.A. in December last [1924].

My hours of duty have been from nine to five, and most of my lectures and all study have been done after office hours. I have never failed and have even managed to obtain honours, a record I feel quite satisfied about."

May and Will with Digger, on their front verandah, expecting their first child.

Mother and Father depart for China

May was eight months pregnant when she and Will, surrounded by a large throng of Salvationists in their black uniforms, sadly waved goodbye to Will's parents. Their steamship Aki Maru departed from Melbourne's Station Pier in September, 1921. Jacoba and Wiebe did not go alone; four of their seven children sailed with them.

The Palstras worked as missionaries in Peking, China, between 1921 and April 1924. (After 1979 "Peking" would become "Beijing".) Wiebe was Chief Secretary of China for the Salvation Army.

When my Baby Smiles at Me...

In Australia, towards the close of October, May began to experience labour pains. The new baby was on the way. The couple had decided that they would like their first child to be born at home, so they had arranged for a midwife to be present when the time came.

The midwife duly arrived, finding May lying in bed in the front room of the house, attended by her mother Agnes.

On October 31st, 1921, Will's and May's first child, a daughter, was born. The baby arrived crying lustily.

All was not well, however. Alarmingly, soon after the birth, May started haemorrhaging.

White-faced, she lay helpless in her bed as bright blood soaked into the sheets. It was clear that she was slipping closer and closer to death.

The family urgently sent for a doctor and with his help, May pulled through the ordeal.

In a few days both mother and child were doing well. One result of that close call was that Will and May agreed there would be no further home births. The new baby, fortunately, thrived, and her parents doted on her. They named her Maisie Margaret.

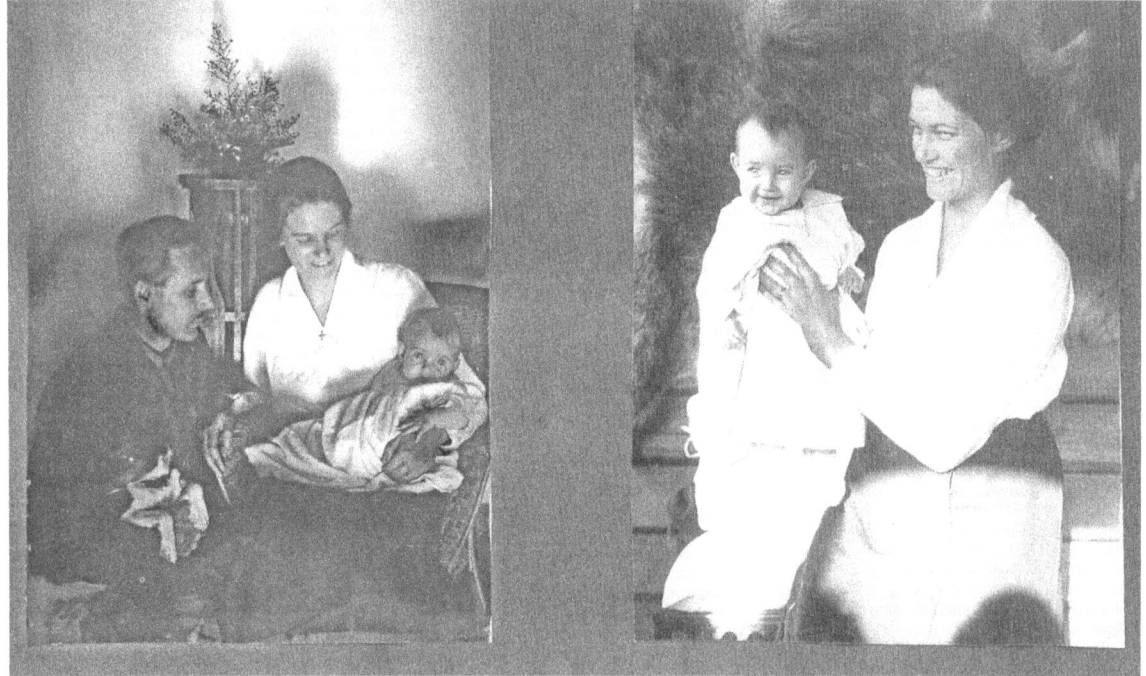

The proud parents with their daughter

Everyday Life

By this time May's 23-year-old brother Arthur had built a house for his mother, Agnes Holdaway (now aged 54), at number 58 Guildford Road, right next door to May and Will's house. Agnes moved in with three of her children, one of whom was Arthur. It was comforting for May, a new mother, to have her own mother so close at hand. A gate in the paling fence along the side boundary between the two properties allowed the two families to visit one another without having to walk out onto the street, and it was often used.

The Birth of the RAAF

After the British RAF formed in 1918, the RAAF became the world's next truly separate and autonomous air force when it was established on 31 March 1921. At the time of its founding the RAAF possessed more aircraft than personnel. There were 170 aircraft, and only 21 officers and 131 other ranks. They needed recruits.

```
[The Brisbane Courier (Qld.: 1864—1933) Tuesday
5 July 1921 Page 6]
One of the units of the recently established Royal
Australian Air Force, known officially as 'selection
boards,' which are at present combing the Commonwealth
for recruits, will commence interviewing prospective
candidates for enlistment in the force at Victoria
Barracks this morning.
The members of the Brisbane board, who arrived from
Melbourne last Friday, are Flight-lieutenant H N Wrigley,
DFC AFC, Flying officer C J Harman, MSM. and Warrant officer
W M. Murphy, DFC, A F.C. . . .
The Commonwealth Government . . . had received a
tremendous amount of materiel as a gift from the Imperial
Government, and there was at present in Victoria complete
equipment for four or five squadrons."
```

Officers H N Wrigley and Charles James Harman[9] would come to play significant roles in Will's story. So would Wing Commander Williams, who as the Director of Air Services was also involved in pilot recruitment at this time.

AIRSHIPS

The war had stimulated rapid technological advances. When it ended, the desire to pursue these new technologies blossomed all over the world. New aeronautical inventions were being unveiled at a fast pace, and aviation was hot news.

The RAAF was to use aeroplanes, seaplanes, and flying boats, which are all heavier-than-air craft. There is, however, another class of flying machines—the lighter-than-air craft; those that are lifted by a gas that is less dense than the surrounding air. In order to tell Will's story the background of these vehicles must be explained, so let us leave his little family enjoying the happiness and hope of their new life in Surrey Hills, and digress for a while.

Throughout history, long-distance air travel had remained an improbable dream. Hot-air balloons, even after a hundred years of evolution, could still not arrive at a planned destination unless the winds were favourable.

In the middle of the 19th century, another form of lighter-than-air craft began to arise. They employed both a system of propulsion and a method of steering. These gigantic, powered airships promised to triumph over the skies. They were also known as "dirigibles", which means "steerables" in French.

Even after the invention of the powered aeroplane, the only method of long-distance flight was by lighter-than-air aircraft. Large loads or long distances could not at that time be managed by heavier-than-air transport, because technology permitted only the building of small aeroplanes with short ranges and negligible payloads. Synthetic materials that combine strength with lightness had not yet been invented. Aeroplanes were mainly constructed of

---

9   Harman is sometimes spelled as "Harmon" in the newspapers of the time. The correct spelling is unknown.

lightweight but relatively weak materials such as wood and canvas, which limited their size, speed and capacity.[10]

Thus, by the beginning of the twentieth century, airships seemed the future of international travel.

From "The Story of Airships" by Rob McAuley Productions: "They were the largest and most romantic aircraft ever conceived, pioneering intercontinental air travel and exploration to uncharted corners of the globe. Behind every giant, a story of passion and political intrigue; none more so than those that became symbols of nations. In the quest for global supremacy they revolutionized warfare and their story remains today amongst the most controversial in the history of flight."[11]

The heyday of the airship lasted the first three decades of the twentieth century. During this time these eye-catching aircraft were widely used for both commercial and military purposes.

Types of Airships

Some airships, usually called "blimps" are non-rigid. They rely on internal gas pressure to retain their shape during flight. When not filled with gas, the whole envelope collapses. Other airships are semi-rigid.

Rigid airships have a stiff framework covered by an outer skin or envelope. The interior contains one or more gasbags, cells or balloons to provide lift. Most, but not all, of the German airships were of this type, and they came to be known by the name of their inventor: the zeppelins.

---

10   Stronger materials such as titanium, aluminium, and composites of polymers, carbon fibre etc., had not yet been fully developed. Such materials are rigid and strong, lightweight and resistant to corrosion.

11   McAuley, 2004

ZEPPELINS

Zeppelins were named after Count Ferdinand von Zeppelin, the wealthy, privileged German aristocrat who pioneered rigid airship development at the beginning of the 20th century. Von Zeppelin was driven by the desire to develop for Germany a weapon that would win any war. He envisioned great advantages for airships, in that they could not only spy on the enemy but also drop bombs. The construction of the first zeppelin began in Germany in 1899.

Von Zeppelin's airships were used in the world's first commercial air passenger service in 1909. During the Great War these aircraft were used to drop bombs on cities, causing destruction and panic. Germany built a total of eighty-four zeppelins during the Great War. More than sixty were lost—about half to accident and the other half to enemy action.

Count von Zeppelin died in 1917, before the end of the war. His former publicist and chief pilot Dr. Hugo Eckener, who had long envisioned dirigibles as vessels of peace rather than of war, eventually became chairman of the Zeppelin business, hoping to resume civilian flights.

In 1921, however, the Allied Powers demanded that all German zeppelins should be handed over as war reparations. Germany was not allowed to construct military aircraft and only airships of less than 28,000 m3 (1,000,000 cu ft) were permitted. This brought a halt to the Zeppelin Airship Construction Company's plans for airship development.

By the time Will and May's first child was born, German zeppelins had been crossing the skies of Europe for more than two decades. Their future, nonetheless, seemed uncertain.

AIRSHIPS R33 AND R34

After the Great War, in which the usefulness of aircraft had been clearly demonstrated, the British government and private companies became increasingly interested in aviation and all the new possibilities it offered. Aviation, though still in its infancy, was at the forefront of engineering innovation and experimentation. Interest in airships was very real.

During the war, British engineers had learned new design technology by studying zeppelins that had been shot down or made forced landings in Britain. Using this knowledge, they created two eye-catching airships. At more than 640 feet long, the R33 and the R34 were three times the length of a modern 747 aeroplane, and to that date, the largest ever built.

They were completed, but not until after the war was over. By then, the Royal Naval Air Service (RNAS) had merged with the British Army's Royal Flying Corps to form the Royal Air Force (RAF).

For a time, Britain was able to call itself the global leader in airship development, due to the terms of the Treaty of Versailles and the technology copied from the Germans. This situation, however, was soon to change.

In 1921 the R34 was damaged during a storm. She was subsequently decommissioned. After the expense of the war, funds were scarce. On 31 May 1921 the British government cancelled all airship development to save money. All military airships were to be sold (R38 was already sold to the USA) or broken up for scrap metal, but as a civilian airship, R33 was flown to Cardington, deactivated, and stored away in reserve for possible future use, next to the incomplete R37. Damaged R36 was left in the Pulham hangar and R80 was flown to Pulham and stored in the smaller hangar.

Despite appearances Britain's airship dream was not extinct—merely dormant.

The R34 airship. Image courtesy of the Airship Heritage Trust.

R34 landing at Mineola, New York in 1919. Image courtesy of the Airship Heritage Trust.

AIRSHIPS—THE HOPE OF THE EMPIRE

Not only did the world's airship dreams seem to be fading, but the great British Empire itself appeared to be on the wane.

The Empire once covered more of the earth's surface and included more of the world's population than any empire the world has ever known.

Historian Ashley Jackson explains that, "At its height the British Empire was the largest empire in history and, for over a century, was the foremost global power. By 1913, it held sway over 412 million people, 23% of the world population at the time, and by 1920, it covered 35.5 million km2 (13.7 million sq mi), 24% of the Earth's total land area… At the peak of its power, it was described as "the empire on which the sun never sets", as the sun was always shining on at least one of its territories…" [12]

In the early decades of the 20th century, however, other countries began to challenge Britain's global economic power; notably the United States and Germany.

The war had put immense strain on Britain's financial, military and manpower resources. It drained her coffers and slaughtered or disabled thousands of her people. When the conflict ended the Empire commanded its greatest expanse of territory in history, but it no longer held its place as the greatest industrial or military power in the world.

The Great War had activated a change in the world order.

As the decade of the 1920s opened, Great Britain felt her grip on her Dominions weakening. She would not, however, let them go so easily. The British government began to exert considerable efforts to save the Empire. Inevitably, ministers turned their attention to cementing the bonds between far-flung outposts of British territories, becoming increasingly concerned with Imperial communications, particularly for mail and trade.

At that time passengers, mail and freight travelled across the oceans by steamship, which was slow. For example, it took six weeks to make the voyage from England to Australia.

---
[12] Jackson, 2013

Faster travel would mean that government officials could transmit personnel and documents more swiftly, keeping their fingers on the pulse of current events.

Swifter, more capacious transcontinental passenger and freight services were needed to link the Dominions and keep the British Empire from fraying. Such a service could bind them together in a political and social union that was closer than ever before.

Many government ministers were attracted to airships because of their unique advantages over aeroplanes. Airships did not require runways. They had the potential to lift heavier loads than aeroplanes, and their buoyancy kept them safely in the air whether or not their engines failed. They could carry twenty to fifty people at a time over long distances, even during the hours of darkness. Their use would allow freer travel; news and ideas would spread swiftly,[13] and trade would improve immeasurably, as airships had great potential as cargo and mail carriers as well. A global airship network, it seemed, could save the Empire.

Airship travel, besides, was very comfortable and almost luxurious. It was envisaged that passengers would be able to travel in style, much as they travelled on the great ocean liners such as the **Titanic**. In addition to the passengers' cabins there could be a grand dining room, a writing room, smoking room, and rows of windows along the sides so that those on board could view the landscape below and the clouds through which they flew.

A correspondent for "Flight International", after a flight in the British airship R.36 on 14 June 1921 wrote,

> "During my short span of years I have journeyed fairly long distances by boat, train, motor- car, and aeroplane but have never experienced such travel-comfort as in an airship—no dust, no smoke, no sway, no draught, very little noise and practically no vibration. We could sit in our arm- chairs—or stroll about—and talk without the slightest difficulty."

---

13   People of the 21st century don't think of 60 miles per hour (around 100 km per hour) as being a high speed, but that was the speed airships could achieve, and in the early 20th century it was viewed as fast, in relation to their large carrying-capacity. It was true that small biplanes could dart through the skies pretty quickly. The fastest First World War fighter, the single-seater Sopwith Dragon, for example, could fly at speeds up to 149 mph (240 kph).

Despite a range of impediments, the prospect of an international airship service was viewed favourably by many people, especially Australians, to whom the "tyranny of distance" presented such an obstacle.

There were others, nonetheless, who saw insurmountable flaws in the dream of a global airship service.

Drawbacks of Airships: Hydrogen

Historically, the two primary lifting gases used by airships have been hydrogen and helium. One of the main disadvantages of British dirigibles was the fact that they were usually buoyed by hydrogen gas.

Invisible, odourless, undetectable by human senses, hydrogen is highly flammable when mixed with air. This makes it dangerous for use in airships, with their leaky gasbags, their hot and fiery internal combustion engines, the risks of static electricity, the flammable "dope" coating of the envelope's fabric, and their steel girders potentially rubbing together and generating sparks.

Helium is non-flammable, which makes it an ideal lifting gas for lighter-than-air craft. In practice, however, helium's lifting ability is about 88% of the lift of hydrogen. This can considerably reduce a rigid airship's payload. Helium is also scarce and expensive; nonetheless, it has every safety advantage over hydrogen, especially for manned flights.

Why, then, did airship manufacturers, such as the Zeppelin Company, use hydrogen?

Hydrogen is abundant, and it can be obtained relatively easily and cheaply. It can be produced using a number of different processes, including splitting water molecules (H^2O) into hydrogen and oxygen molecules.

The other lifting gas was rare and costly. There is no chemical way of manufacturing helium. It has to be painstakingly extracted from rocks, or the air, or from natural gas reserves trapped beneath the ground. Extracting it from the air is prohibitively expensive. Helium is lighter than the other gases in the atmosphere, so when it escapes from rocks or underground gas reserves it simply keeps floating up, and seeps out into space. That's why the atmosphere contains only a minuscule amount of helium.

Not all natural gas fields contain enough helium to make extraction worthwhile. In the 1920s the only known sources of helium-rich gas were located in the United States.

Since airships needed engines to drive them, those hot engines so close to large quantities of hydrogen could present a fire risk. Still, airship engineers viewed hydrogen as the most practical alternative. They thought they could minimise fire risk by taking elaborate precautions. The precautions included keeping the gas as pure as possible—because it only ignites in the presence of oxygen—and keeping it away from flames and sparks. Hydrogen had been used to lift blimps throughout the war.

Dr Giles Camplin[14] explains the prevailing attitude to hydrogen:

"On the use of hydrogen versus helium . . . long ago I met, in person, a pilot of WW1 blimps. One of the interesting things that he imparted was that at the time, hydrogen was treated simply as a 'consumable' along with petrol and oil. Standard practice was for a [blimp] pilot to tell his ground crew when he landed at the end of a mission to put in so many gallons of fuel and oil and so many 'tubes' of hydrogen. If the purity was low, (obviously far more serious with a combustible gas), then you simply put in more and more tubes and opened the gas valve and kept 'topping up' and 'blowing off' until a satisfactory purity was reached. . . . on occasion substantial amounts of lift had to be removed in order to effect a landing. {Therefore] such 'normal' operational practices would be prohibitively costly with helium."

Aside from the lifting gas, there were also other perceived problems with a proposed global airship network. Expensive "mooring masts" would need to be built at airship terminals across the world. Furthermore, depending on climate, weather amd terrain, airship flight could be hazardous.

The following newspaper article gives an idea of public sentiment towards airships in 1921:

---

14 Dr Camplin is Vice Chairman of the Airship Association and Editor of the Airship Heritage Trust Journal, 'Dirigible'.

The Sydney Morning Herald (NSW : 1842 - 1954)
Friday 10 June 1921, page 8
EMPIRE AIR MAIL.
THE AIRSHIP SCHEME. SOME OF ITS PROBLEMS.

. . . Probably such an air service from London to Australia will have to be performed in relays. Britain to Egypt has long been recognised as the first stage, whether for aeroplanes or airships. At Egypt there would be a double change, either for Cape-town or for the Far East, and on the latter journey there would in all probability be at least one more change for Australia at Singapore. One airship, it is considered, would make the trip from Singapore to Darwin, possibly on to Sydney, Melbourne, or Canberra; but it is easy in thus looking ahead to see another change station at Darwin, where Australian air routes would meet from Perth, Brisbane, and the south direct. The Sydney-New Zealand service would again be a separate link in the chain. Focussing the scheme down to our own interest in it, it may here be remarked that no airship has yet flown in Australia.

Experiments during recent years—especially the three years or so since the armistices—have convinced many air service pioneers and pioneering companies in Britain and Egypt that the airship, especially (so far) the small airship, possesses distinct advantages over the aeroplane. One is the primary advantage of buoyancy, which represents greater carrying-power, and, to some extent, greater safety. Another is more economical running cost.

> Engineers have overcome many of the early difficulties of mooring airships, which before the war perplexed the Germans with their Zeppelins. More often than not it happened that a gust of wind, rising as a Zeppelin was being pushed into or out of its shed on the landing-ground, would wreck the ship by carrying away its nose or tail. On one occasion a whole company of soldiers hanging on to mooring-ropes was not sufficient to hold down a Zeppelin, which rose and sailed away from its landing-ground with one unfortunate man clinging still to his charge, and drifted halfway across Germany before it came down and was destroyed.
> Commodore Maitland's idea of a modern airship anchorage is a high steel mast, to which the airship would be tied by the nose, in the open and off the ground, and, as he sees it, passengers would descend from and ascend into the ship by means of a lift inside the steel mast to the airship gangway. It is an attractive picture.

ASHBOLT'S IMPERIAL AIR COMPANY

The histories of Australia and New Zealand are closely tied to airships. They were the furthest-flung countries of the British Empire. They had spilled the blood of a generation for the sake of that Empire, and they wanted to strengthen their ties with Britain, just as passionately as the British government desired it. For the people of the state of Tasmania in particular—Australia's only island state, and the most isolated—a global airship network seemed the only way to conquer that "tyranny of distance".

In July 1921, only two months after the British airship programme had been put on hold, the annual Imperial Conference was held in London.

Present at this conference was Alfred H. Ashbolt, Tasmania's representative in London. His job was to seek investors in the industries of Tasmania.[15] Ashbolt proposed the creation of an Imperial Air Company to improve communication between Britain and the distant countries (dominions) of the British Empire by establishing international air routes for airships.

```
The West Australian (Perth, WA : 1879 - 1954)
Sat 9 Jul 1921 Page 10
IMPERIAL AIR COMPANY.
PROPOSED DOMINION SERVICE.
TASMANIAN AGENT-GENERAL'S SCHEME.

The following is a precis of a proposal submitted by Mr.
A. H. Ashbolt, the Agent-General for Tasmania, to the
British Government for further discussions with the rep-
resentatives of the overseas dominions at the Imperial
Council now being held in London. The proposition is for
utilising the airships, material, plant, etc., which
the British Government announce their willingness to
hand over. . .

1. An imperial air company to be formed, with a capital
of £1,500,000, or such other amount as may be arranged.

. . . "The proposal opens up immense commercial possi-
bilities and the advantages to be gained from an Empire
point of view bringing Great Britain within five days
of India and South Africa and within 10 to 12 days of
Australia and New Zealand are so obvious that detailed
```

---

15   As a result of his efforts, several British firms established branch factories in Tasmania. Notably, Cadbury® chose Tasmania as the site for its first chocolate factory outside the UK.

> reasons are unnecessary. The interests of the Overseas Dominions and Dependencies are so interlocked with those of Great Britain that an airship scheme must embody all interests in one common plan."

It was decided that Ashbolt's "Imperial Air Company" airship scheme would receive funding from three sources; the dominions of the British Empire, private companies and the British government.

After the Imperial Conference was over, the government established a sub-committee chaired by the Secretary of State for Air, to enquire into the feasibility of the idea. The committee approved it, with the proviso that additional consultation with the various governments of the countries within the Empire should be undertaken. This consultation was duly performed, but the only country prepared to invest in the necessary infrastructure to support a global airship network was Australia. Without the necessary financial backing, Ashbolt's scheme seemed doomed to fail.

> The Sydney Morning Herald (NSW : 1842 - 1954)
> Thu 26 Jan 1922 Page 7
> EMPIRE AIR SERVICE.
> ADVERSE DECISIONS.
> LONDON, Jan. 25.
>
> It is unofficially stated that New Zealand and South Africa have decided not to participate in the Imperial airship service. India, whose co-operation is vital to the establishment of an Anglo-Australian service, has not reached a decision.

THE R38 AIRSHIP

If civilians were half-hearted about developing airships, the armed forces were all in favour of them. They had seen what Germany's armed zeppelins could do. In particular, Britain's Royal Navy was keen on building an airship fleet.

During the final months of the First World War the Admiralty had commissioned a team, led by Constructor-Commander C. I. R. Campbell, of the Royal Corps of Navy Constructors, to design four rigid airships in what was to be known as the "R38 class". Intended for long-range patrol missions over the North Sea, they were to be named R38, R39, R40 and R41. The war ended, however, before manufacture had commenced.

These early British airships were based on the design of zeppelins—for example, when the zeppelin L33 was forced down over Essex and captured in 1916, British engineers had analysed its design and used it as a basis for future models. The British airships R33 and R34 had been "descendants" of L33.

R38, the lead ship of the class, was to be based on the zeppelin L70[16]. On 5 August 1918 British airmen Major Edgar Cadbury and Captain Robert Leckie had shot down L70 in flames, as it flew across England on an attack mission as part of a convoy of five zeppelins.

In February 1919 aircraft manufacturing company Short Brothers commenced construction of R38 at Cardington, near Bedford, in Bedfordshire, England. During the war, the company had bought land at Cardington to build two rigid airships, the R31 and R32, for the Admiralty.

In 1915 they had constructed a 700-foot-long (210 m) airship hangar (the No. 1 Shed). Opposite the airship construction site, Short Brothers also built a housing estate for workers, which they named Shortstown.

The British government remained short of funds after the expense of the war. Later in 1919 the Admiralty cancelled orders for R39, R40 and R41 as a peacetime economy measure. Funds were so scare that it began to look as if they would also have to cancel the

---

16   The Imperial German Navy Zeppelin LZ112, which bore the tactical number L70

unfinished R38. Work at Cardington was put on hold, but before the R38 project could be completely halted, the United States stepped in.

The Story of Airships explains, "The United States was also eager to exploit rigid airships, but not for commercial reasons. The Navy wanted to employ them like Germany had during the war, as aerial Scouts for its blue water fleets [oceangoing fleets able to operate on the high seas far from their nation's home-ports]. In 1919 the US Navy convinced Congress to fund the purchase of two huge airships."[17]

The United States Navy wanted to build the first airship themselves, in the United States. ZR1 was to be called *USS Shenandoah*. Construction of the first American-built rigid airship began in 1922 at Lakehurst Naval Air Station in New Jersey, USA.

The Story of Airships continues: "For its second airship, the US Navy went straight to the builders of the record-breaking R34. The order came as a godsend to the British government. Budget cuts were threatening to force the scrapping of the R38 airship being built at Cardington.

"Now it could be completed and sold for a profit. There was even hope that the sale would lead to further American orders and establish Britain as a premier builder and exporter of airships."[18]

The half-abandoned R38 was sitting, incomplete, in Shed No 1 at Cardington when in October 1919 the US Navy bought her for £300,000. She now bore the US designation ZR-2. Short Brothers recommenced construction.

```
The West Australian (Perth, WA : 1879 - 1954)
Tuesday 9 August 1921 P 7
AVIATION
New Type of Airship.
London, Aug. 7.
```

---

17   McAuley, 2004

18   ibid

```
A new type of aircraft, partly an aeroplane and partly a
ship, [the R38 airship] and which is capable of resting
on the ocean in the roughest weather, is expected to
fly from London to New York in forty hours, and is
undergoing trials.
In England gigantic flying ships are being designed
with the same principle. They are capable of carrying
one hundred passengers, in addition to crew, food and
stores, and can cross the Atlantic under 48 hours.
```

At the time of her first flight on 23–24 June 1921, R38 was the world's largest airship. Her modified design was in many ways experimental. The Royal Corps of Navy Constructors still had a great deal to learn about airship design and construction, for they had made no allowance for the structural stresses caused by manoeuvring at high speeds.

24 August brought R38's fourth test flight. She was passing quite low over the city of Hull in East Yorkshire, travelling at her maximum speed of 60 miles per hour (100 km per hour), when, driven by a keenness to hasten the flying trials and transfer R38 into the hands of the American crews, the helmsman manoeuvred the controls too sharply. R38 promptly broke up in mid-air and plummeted into the estuary of the Humber River. Of the forty-nine crew members, forty-four perished.

The crash of the R38 was the first of the great airship disasters.

Following the disaster, the British government suspended all work on airships.

```
The Argus (Melbourne, Vic. : 1848 - 1957)
Fri 26 Aug 1921, Page 7
GREAT AIRSHIP WRECKED
R38 FALLS IN FLAMES.
Forty-four Lives Lost.
Structural Defect Suspected.
(Australian Press Association.)
LONDON, Aug. 25.
```

The great British dirigible airship R38 which has been purchased by America and had been undergoing final trials preliminary to leaving for America today was destroyed yesterday near Hull when cruising over the city at twenty minutes to 6 yesterday afternoon.

The dirigible broke in two and fell ablaze into the Humber, belching a dense column of blue smoke and flame. The explosion which wrecked her smashed shop fronts in the centre of the city. Three parachutes were seen leaving the airship after her frame had collapsed. The R38 carried a crew of 49, of whom only five were saved. Those were the commander (Lieutenant A H Wann R N R), a member of the crew named Bateman, and three Americans. With her silver coat glistening in the sun the R38 was sailing above Hull apparently in perfect safety, at a height of 1,000 ft. The whole city was watching the flight and the spectators commented on the beautiful appearance of the airship.

Engineers observed that the engines were firing very evenly when the airship disappeared in a cloud. When she emerged the spectators were horrified to see the R38 break into two portions. Both descended slowly, the nose portion which was the larger coming down first. As it did so, a mass, believed to be the engine from one of the gondolas, fell from the airship. Two terrific reports followed. The foremost portion landed on a sandbank, and the rear portion half a mile away in the Humber.

Thousands of people rushed to a pier near the spot where the wreckage lay. Tugs and small boats hurried to give assistance, despite the fact that fragments of the airship were burning on the sandbank and floating in the water. They were able to pick up only two survivors—Flight Lieutenant Wann, who is reported to be seriously injured, and Bateman, a youth, who was able to walk to the ambulance after the tug brought him ashore.

Frame Made Stronger.
R38 developed certain structural weaknesses a few weeks ago, and her frame was strengthened. She went on an extended trial from Howden on Tuesday night and sent wireless messages stating that the trials were most successful It was intended to make a landing at Pulham in Norfolk.

For two hours a thunderstorm raged there and a wireless message was sent ordering the airship to wait owing to the heavy clouds. At 7 o'clock on Wednesday morning the dirigible was reported off Howden, and at 1.50 was east of The Wash proceeding to Pulham. The vessel had been in the air 35 hours when she approached Hull. Rudder tests were being made at the time of the disaster. Bateman was at the tail of the ship taking photographs of the rudder experiments.

An eye witness on the ground says that when it was apparent that the airship was cracking in the middle her engines were working at terrific speed. He believed that Lieutenant Wann, realising the danger, put on the utmost speed in order to travel clear of the city. The general opinion is that Lieutenant Wann's skilful navigation alone prevented the ship falling in the centre of the city. As it was, the force of the explosion wrecked windows in the main streets and shop fronts. Many people on the quays were thrown to the ground.

Apart from Lieutenant Wann and Bateman, three Americans who took to parachutes were rescued from the Humber.

Their names are I. Davies, W. Porter, and O. Walker. Davies was taken to a hospital. His two companions were not injured.

Lieutenant Little was taken from the debris alive, but succumbed while being taken to the hospital. It is possible that some bodies are inside the envelope, or are floating in the river, but there is no chance of there being further survivors.

Green Vapour and Fire.

The "Daily Telegraph's" correspondent, describing the scene said—"I watched the giant airship and thought that its sylph-like appearance suggested a visitor from some fairy world. I said to a friend, 'It makes one want to cheer.' A few moments later the airship's nose pointed down, clouds of green vapour poured from her side, and as the vapour increased the airship appeared to bend or break in the middle. The rear portion detached itself, and began to fall and bright red flames appeared. I realised", said the correspondent, "that the airship which rode so proudly a moment earlier was afire, and in two. Four reports in quick succession told the amazed spectators that R38 had come to her doom. The stricken monster crumpled up. Some of the crew were seen descending in parachutes. All was over in less than a minute.

The effect on the spectators was stupefying. Many women burst into tears. When I reached the pier the vessel which had been the aerial pride of the world lay in the water, a twisted mass of fabric and framework, with portions of its length burning for hundreds of feet along the top of the water. The only part bearing any resemblance to an airship was the stern, which ballooned at a considerable height.

Brave Man Saves City.
The correspondent of the Daily Chronicle recounts that he was watching the airship as its long, graceful shape came out of a light summer cloud and it suddenly buckled and broke in two. Flames shot from her aide with a loud explosion and the mass fell headlong to the river. Many spectators were panic stricken but it seemed that the navigating officer had a few seconds warning and with supreme effort he took the airship clear of the city.
This was the last thought of a man facing death to avert an even more terrible disaster. Sergeant Busby, of the American Air Force, who was a spectator, told the correspondent who is of the same view that there was some fire amidships. The airship collapsed in the centre and was turning when the disaster occurred. It was God's mercy that the disaster did not occur over the city.
In his description the "Daily Express" correspondent says that there were explosions like intense rockets. When the material touched the water a huge wall of flames and smoke went up and it seemed that nothing could live in this inferno.
Pilots who were first to reach the sinking airship saw that the fore end broke away 40 seconds before the after part. They saw beds and blankets dropping from the air

ship but they fell into other portions of the wreck, which was a mass of flames.

These rescuers had to cut sections of the envelope open with jack knives to reach the survivors, but they were unable to extricate the dead bodies. The first man brought ashore was unconscious but the second survivor was smoking a cigarette and was none the worse except for a ducking. He said 'I saved myself by climbing with an officer on to the rudder of the airship. This man was Davies the American, who was picked up swimming in the river. When he landed he walked through a crowd of 1,000 people who cheered his pluck to the echo. Interviewed later Davies said—"We had a terrible time. It was all over in a minute. Many of the poor fellows hadn't a cat's chance. Some jumped overboard. I was one of the lucky ones."

Air Worthiness Questioned.
The official communique states —"The time of the accident was 5,45 p.p. The cause is unknown owing to difficulty in obtaining information as to the members of the Air Force personnel near the scene." The loss falls on Great Britain.
The newspapers point out that the loss of life is greater than in any previous airship disaster. There had been rumours last week regarding the airworthiness of the airship, serious enough to warrant a denial by the American authorities.

The Argus (Melbourne, Vic. : 1848 - 1957)
Sat 27 Aug 1921, Page 19
AIRSHIP DISASTER.
SURVIVORS' STORIES.
Thrilling Experiences.
(Australian Press Association.)
LONDON, Aug. 26

The search for the bodies of those killed in the disaster to the dirigible airship R38 was continued at Hull throughout Thursday. Tugs and launches made huge sweeps but no further bodies were discovered. The task of the searchers was hampered by high tides.

Pathetic figures among the crowd which watched the search were two English widows of American airmen, one carrying a baby girl aged six weeks, who refused to believe that her husband was dead. It is officially stated that the crew of the R38 numbered 51, and that the death toll was 46.

Lieutenant Wicks, the wireless man on the airship, gallantly remained on duty till he was burned to death. He actually sent a wireless message to Howden that the airship's back was broken and that she was on fire and was falling.

His Majesty the King has sent a wireless message to Air Marshal Sir Hugh Trenchard, chief of the Air Staff, stating:—"I was shocked and grieved to hear of the terrible disaster which has resulted in the loss of so many valuable lives of American and British subjects with whose relatives I deeply sympathise."

Interviewed in hospital Lieutenant A H Wann, commander

of the R38 who is suffering from injuries to the head and eyes, and severe burns and bruises on the body said that he was in sole control of the vessel in the forecar. The R38 had just passed over Hull when a violent crack was felt, and the forecar fell. It then rose at a high angle. He pulled over the water ballast to level the keel, and then there was a terrific explosion, which must have killed many of the crew. He did not notice any fire preceding the explosion.

The R38 had done a full trial, and slowed down from 60 to 50 knots an hour before the explosion. The snapping of the vessel was apparently due to some structural weakness. The whole thing happened in five seconds.

Lieutenant Wann denied that he had turned the ship over the river in order to avoid the city. She was running perfectly over the city, he said. The accident happened over the river. He went down with the ship until it was close to the water, when he jumped. He was caught in the wreckage and pinned down there for 15 minutes.

He did not know how he was rescued, as he was unconscious. He awoke to find himself in hospital.

Bateman, another survivor, in an interview, said—A quarter of an hour before the accident the airship was tested at full speed, and everything seemed all right. I was then told to take observations in connection with a special control test. Major Pritchard said, "The controls are going to be moved fairly rapidly to demonstrate the airworthiness of the ship to cross the Atlantic."

When the disaster occurred, my feelings were that the airship was shaken three or four times laterally and a few times longitudinally. When explosions followed I knew we were doomed. I was thrown into the cockpit but a parachute was handy, there being one for each man. I jumped out over the airship's side, but the parachute rope caught in the wires and I hung in mid-air from the parachute while the airship dropped. In that position I fell with the tail of the vessel into the water. I was dazed by the fall, and when I recovered consciousness I found myself on a sand bank with Potter who was with me in the cockpit, and Walker, who was in one of the fins."

Barrier Miner (Broken Hill, NSW : 1888 - 1954)
Fri 2 Sep 1921, Page 1
LOSS OF THE R38
COMMANDER'S BODY FOUND

A cable message from London states that the body of Air Commodore Edward Maitland; C.M.G., D.S.O., F.K.G.S., who commanded the great airship R38 when it collapsed and fell into the River Humber, has been found. His hand was still on the control rope, and it was evident that he had died like a hero, trying to save his ship. He was shockingly injured, and his clothing had been blown off by the explosion.
The forepart of the airship, which portion was under water, has been raised.
The body of Lieutenant-Colonel Coil, who was to have been second in command of the R38 on the projected Atlantic flight, has also been recovered.

By 1921, worldwide interest in dirigibles for commercial and military purposes had ebbed, but still it simmered. It had not gone away.

Some events in Australia in 1921[19]:

April
- 11 Bert Hinkler flies from Sydney to Bundaberg, Queensland, non-stop in 81/2 hours, breaking his own long-distance flying record.
- 4 Estimated population of Australia: 5,510,944.

July
- 12 Harry Hawker dies in a test-flight accident in England.

August
- 11 Essendon airport opens in Melbourne.
- 23 Bubonic plague breaks out in Brisbane (to April, 1922; 64 deaths)

December
- 5 Australia's first official airmail service begins, between Geraldton and Derby, Western Australia. (Service disrupted by the crash of one of the three planes on the inaugural flight, killing the crew of two.)

Also in 1921
- Ginger Meggs comic strip character created by Jimmy Bancks.
- Roy Cazaly, after 12 years with St. Kilda Australian Rules football team, begins playing for South Melbourne and gives rise to the cry, "Up there, Cazaly".

---

19 Barker, 1992

PART IV: 1922 AND 1923

THE BURNEY SCHEME

Following the R38 disaster, but prompted by other reasons too, the British government decided to abandon any plans for an international fleet of Imperial airships, and dismantle their existing dirigibles. The Imperial Airship Service plan was scrapped.

Another major airship disaster took place early in 1922. Roma was an Italian-built semi-rigid airship that served in the US Army from March 1920 until 21st February 1922, when she crashed in Norfolk, Virginia, killing 34 people. She was the last hydrogen filled airship flown by the US military. All subsequent ships were inflated with helium.

By March 1922, it seemed the idea of a global imperial airship network had fallen flat. It was at this time, however, that a visionary airship enthusiast with political clout and connections in high places stepped in. Sir Charles Dennistoun Burney, 2nd Baronet, was an English aeronautical engineer, private inventor and Conservative Party politician.

Vickers Limited was a British armaments firm and industrial conglomerate that had been involved in British airship construction since the company had designed and built His Majesty's Airship No. 1 in 1911. The company proposed a scheme for the development of large commercial airships to provide a passenger service to link the countries of the British Empire. It involved the construction of six airships at an estimated cost of £4 million, to be constructed and operated by Vickers.

In May 1922, helped by the keenness of Commander Burney, a modified version of the project was officially approved by the British Air Ministry and the British Admiralty. It attracted the nickname "The Burney Scheme." In spite of this approval, Treasury's doubts about the financial details delayed the scheme's implementation.

```
Queensland Times (Ipswich, Qld. : 1909 - 1954)
Mon 3 Apr 1922 Page 6
AIR CONQUESTS.
NEW IMPERIAL SCHEME.
Restaurants on Airships.
LONDON, March 31


Commander Burney R.N. of Vickers Limited, who is largely
responsible for the proposed Imperial airship scheme,
states that the company proposes to build six new airships
at a lower cost than ever before. They will contain
restaurant and sleeping cabins, smoking, and bathrooms,
and will be capable of carrying 100 passengers, at rates
below first-class steamer fares, in addition to 10 tons
of mails and goods.
Mr H. A. Ashbolt, Agent-General for Tasmania; in an
interview, said: "Though my scheme did not succeed, it
prevented the destruction of the Government airships, six
months ago. The position has now wonderfully improved,
```

```
and money is available for the new project which, I
believe, Australia will consider favourably."
```

AIRSHIP ENTHUSIASM WANES

In England, Sir Dennistoun Burney continued to push for an imperial airship service, whose international air routes would connect the outposts of the British Empire. To further this aim, he helped set up the Airship Guarantee Company, a subsidiary of British engineering conglomerate Vickers Limited, whose purpose was the construction of dirigibles. The AGC was based at the Cardington site founded by Short Brothers; the precinct that had been nationalised in April 1919, becoming known as the Royal Airship Works.[20]

A modified version of Burney's airship service scheme was proposed by Sir Samuel Hoare when he was Secretary of State for Air. He planned a transcontinental fleet of airships built and operated by a government-subsidised private company.

Britain and Germany, however, were not the only countries with the capacity to build airships. France, Italy, the USA and Japan were also in the game. Another airship disaster occurred at the close of 1923.

In *The R101 Story*, Peter Davison states:

> The French airship, the war reparation Zeppelin (L-72) rechristened 'Dixmude', was lost over the Mediterranean in December 1923, probably due to severe weather breaking its lightweight structure. A journalist specialising in aeronautical correspondence declared: 'It is acknowledged that airship navigation has received another serious set-back, illustrating the great difficulties and dangers involved, but, this must not lead to the abandonment of such pioneer work as is represented by Commander Burney's scheme[21].'

---

20   134.org.uk 2012.

21   Davison, 2015

Advocate (Burnie, Tas. : 1890 - 1954)
Mon 31 Dec 1923 Page 1

DIXMUDE MYSTERY.
COMMANDER'S BODY FOUND.
NO TRACE OF SHIP.
Sympathy with France.
SET-BACK TO AVIATION. (Reuter.)

PARIS, Saturday. —The Italian authorities state that the body of the commander of the Dixmude (Lieutenant de Plessis de Grenadan) has been picked up by a fisherman near Girgenti, Sicily.

France has accepted Italy's offer to convey the Lieutenant's body to Toulon aboard an Italian warship.

It has now been officially announced at Paris that the Dixmude has been lost at sea.

It seems now to be generally regretfully assumed that the Dixmude has been lost at sea and that the report that the airship was seen by natives over the Sahara is erroneous.

French warships have been ordered to search the neighborhood where the body of the commander of the Dixmude was found.

"The Morning Post's" aeronautical correspondent declares: "We deeply sympathise with France. It is acknowledged that air ship navigation has received another serious set-back illustrating the great

difficulties and dangers involved, but "This must not lead to the abandonment of such pioneer work as is represented by Commander Burney's scheme."

The mystery of the Dixmude has not yet been cleared up.

> The Paris telegram declaring that the loss at sea of
> the Dixmude had been officially announced, now appears
> at least to have been premature. Reuter's correspond-
> ent has transmitted the text of the French Ministry for
> Marine's communique, which does not mention the loss of
> the airship though confirming the news of the finding of
> the body of Lieutenant de Plessis do Grenadan, commander
> of the Dixmude, by fishermen six miles from tho shore
> near Girgenti, Sicily.
> Reuter's Rome correspondent reports that a thorough
> search of the coast has been made without result. No
> trace of any other body or aeronautical material has
> been found.

The catastrophic crash of the R38 in 1921 (44 dead), followed by the Italian-built US semi-rigid airship Roma in 1922 (34 dead), and the French Dixmude in 1923 (52 dead) aided the stagnation of British interest in a world-wide airship service by the mid 1920s.

Plans for Burney's Airship Scheme had been sunk by a Labour Government wishing to sponsor a state enterprise, unwilling to grant a monopoly to an 'armaments firm and an oil company'. Ashbolt the Tasmanian, however, still optimistically held hopes for the future of an Imperial Airship Network.

THE FAMILY IN SURREY HILLS

By 1922 Wiebe and Jacoba Palstra, with four of their children, were living and working in China, as Salvation Army missionaries. Meanwhile May was busy raising little Maisie Margaret at 60 Guildford Road. She was aided by her mother Agnes, who was installed in the house next door, and her younger siblings Arthur, Allan and Winnie, who lived with Agnes. Will pressed on with his work at Melbourne University and studied for his degree in his own time.

1923: The Wonderful in Everything

Far off in China, Will's sister Blanche contracted typhoid fever. Bed-ridden, she was desperately ill, and her family feared she might not survive. Blanche fought on, her blonde hair falling out of her scalp in clumps until she was bald.

Eventually she began to get better, but her baldness was a source of anguish and she despaired of ever having hair again. To her joy, as she regained her strength her tresses began to grow back, but surprisingly, instead of being straight, as before the illness, it reappeared in curls.

Probably it was this brush with death that prompted Wiebe and Jacoba Palstra to send Blanche back to Australia where, at the age of 25, she moved in with Will and May at number 60 Guildford Road.

Next door, at No. 58, lived 25-year-old Arthur Holdaway, a six foot two, broad-shouldered, handsome war veteran, capable of fashioning almost anything with his own hands. His twinkling eyes were full of laughter, and he playfully nicknamed Blanche "Girl". With their Salvation Army backgrounds in common, their siblings married to each other, their mutual interest in music and their frequent contact at social gatherings, Arthur and Blanche began to fall in love.

Will and May's daughter turned two in October 1923. She was a dark-haired, earnest, intelligent child, already demonstrating an innate grasp of language. Although Maisie was her first name, as she grew older she asked to be called Margaret.

Will's October letter to his father overflows with his love and pride for his little girl.

Letter from Will:

> The University Melbourne 31.10.23
>
> Dear Dad,
>
> Yesterday brought us your letter dated 24th Sept and a week earlier I received Mother's letter written from the Hills and enclosing a piece of old Chinese embroidery to match what I previously had. I am delighted with it.

This must be just a very small note—all my spare time is taken up with study and I am just snatching a few moments from my work to let this catch the mail.

Today is Margaret's birthday. Her birthday presents this morning included a bucket and spade from Mother & Daddy, a dolls pram from Auntie "Barf"* and Uncle Arthur, and a doll from grandma Holdaway. The pram and doll are the great attractions. Her eyes just shone. I had to kiss the dolly goodbye when I went to work. Two years old today and such a grown little daughter, the day of her arrival seems very far distant. I am so glad Mother will be over next year and will see her whilst she is yet in her baby days. She is extraordinarily well developed for her age, both physically and mentally. Her memory is remarkably good, and she understands just about all that is said to her. If she has left something somewhere it may be hours ago or even days, a moments reflection enables her to recollect where it is to be found.

She is a particular little miss and takes after her Daddy in that respect. Doors must be properly closed, her blankets must be tucked in, in the approved manner and things must be in their place, slippers in the cupboard etc. Excellent habits don't you think.

Of course she must do everything we do. It's a bit of a nuisance sometimes but she will be a great little helper later on and it's good to foster the spirit of service. She has got to the stage where she thinks she ought to be able to dress herself. She has a pretty good idea of how it is done, but buttons etc. cause her considerable annoyance.

My tentative offers of assistance are rejected until she is quite convinced that she hasn't mastered the trick of the thing and then it is "Daddy haku (help you) please".

What a lot we would miss as we grow older if it wasn't for the children. They seem to keep the wonderful in everything for you. I've got as much pleasure in seeing Margaret play with her toys almost as she has.

If you don't come over to see her soon I shall have to send her to China to see you.

More after the exams.

I am hopeful,

Love

Will.

* "Aunty "Barf" was the childish pronunciation of "Blanche" Holdaway, Will's sister..

Young Margaret with her uncle Arthur Holdaway and some puppies

Will with his beloved daughter Margaret and their dog Digger, at their home.

PART V: 1924

Scarlet Fever

May started to feel unwell towards the end of March 1924. She developed a fever, a sore throat, chills and a headache, in addition to other alarming symptoms including red creases in the armpits, elbows, and knees, a flushed face and swollen tonsils. The doctor was summoned. After examining her, he announced that she had contracted scarlet fever. This was a serious, highly transmissible disease, and May was rushed straight to Fairfield Infectious Diseases Hospital for treatment and quarantine. Visitors were not permitted.

Thus began a wonderful spate of correspondence between Will and May. Through their letters to each other we glimpse the profundity of their love.

From Will to May, 8 April 1924:

> "I've thought of you, dearest mine, ever so often today. What a darling you are, and how happy I am to have you as my sweet little wife, and to be able to kiss you and hold you in my arms, and when I can't do these things, to be able to write love letters to you."

From May to Will, 10 April 1924:

> "Last night I had such a longing to see my Billy, and I felt I just couldn't wait, but I don't allow myself to feel like that too much. Sometimes I just lie and luxuriate in thinking of you and Margaret, and our happiness together."

... and 13 April 1924:

> "I went to sleep with my lips on my wedding ring. It was the nearest thing to you... It is like losing part of myself to be separated from you. I would give anything to feel your arms round me."

Far across the sea, Will's parents were on the move again. Following their stint in China, the Salvation Army appointed Wiebe Palstra as Territorial Commander of Korea. He and Jacoba departed for Seoul on 7 April 1924. Hettie and John accompanied them.

The Palstra family were splitting up. Victor remained in China, in the employ of the China Indent Company Pty. Ltd. Will, Charles, Frank and Blanche were all back in Australia, which was where the senior Palstras longed to be. Duty, however, came first.

In November, 1924, Will became the organising secretary in charge of establishing the new Faculty of Commerce at Melbourne University. And on 23 December 1924 he took out the Degree of Bachelor of Arts.

Thus closed the happy year of 1924. It was summertime, and in the suburban gardens of Melbourne the lavender bushes were in full bloom, humming with bees. The Great War was over and the Spanish Flu had receded. Will had a good job and a university degree, and his career was on track. May had recovered from scarlet fever. The two of them, very much in love, were living with their little daughter in their Surrey Hills home with its fruitful garden and May's mother Agnes in easy reach next door. Will's sister Blanche and May's brother Arthur were married and living in nearby Canterbury. Will's mother Jacoba was holidaying back in Australia and dividing her time between her son's house and Blanche's.

All seemed blissfully well.

THE GOLDEN AGE OF AIRSHIPS

By 1924 the United States Navy owned two airships; USS *Shenandoah*, which they built themselves, and USS *Los Angeles* constructed by Hugo Eckener's Zeppelin Airship Construction Company. Both were lifted by helium gas.

Why were *Shenandoah* and *Los Angeles* filled with helium, when German and British dirigibles continued to use highly flammable hydrogen gas? Look back to February 1922 when the US airship *Roma* was destroyed by fire in an accident near Norfolk, Virginia. This tragedy led Congress to decree that all US airship operations would in the future use helium instead of hydrogen as the lifting gas.

"The only known sources of helium in the world," as explained in "The Story of Airships", "were naturally occurring vents in Texas and Kansas. If it hadn't been for helium's scarcity and America's reluctance to share it, the fate of many airships may have been completely different."[22]

Following successful flights by USS *Los Angeles*, 1924 ushered in a spectacular new era in aviation history and ignited keen rivalry between nations for airship superiority. During the late 1920s hundreds of people would cross and re-cross the Atlantic Ocean by rigid airship, in both directions.

Now began the Golden Age of Airships.

---

22   McAuley, 2004

Lord Thomson

In Britain, it was a change of government that helped to revive the dream.

In January 1924 Britain's conservative government was ousted by a Labour administration. Christopher Birdwood Thomson, a forty-nine-year-old bachelor, had stood as Labour candidate in the general election, but was not returned. He happened to be a comrade of the new Prime Minister, Ramsay MacDonald.

Wanting Thomson to be part of the government, MacDonald created a baronetcy for his friend, which entitled him to sit in the House of Lords. Once elevated to this position, Thomson became Secretary of State for Air.

Thomson, now "Lord Thomson of Cardington", was an airship enthusiast. He had romantic, flamboyant visions of dirigibles, and once wrote, "In fancy one can see them floating like monstrous insects over a hostile land while from their flanks, winged offspring would emerge like angry wasps, to fight defending aeroplanes or to rain death and destruction from the skies. An air encounter between two fleets of these aerial mammoths can be more easily imagined than described. No conflict on land or sea could approach it in terror or sublimity."[23]

---

23   Hansard, 1928

Under Lord Thomson, the Imperial Airship Scheme came into being in October 1924. As ever, the plan was to shorten journey times for passengers and cargo requiring safe passage to the Dominions, in particular, India, Canada, Australia and South Africa.

This time, though, the proposal for a global British airship service had the full might, power and financial resources of the British government supporting it. It was expected that the new Scheme would cost £1,350,000. It would begin with the construction of two giant, state-of-the-art airships.

The R100 and R101

For the Imperial Airship Scheme the British Air Ministry decided to commence design, production and flight testing of two prototype airships of competing designs—the R100 and R101.

The R100 was to be designed and built as a private enterprise, by a specially established subsidiary company of Vickers Limited[24], the Airship Guarantee Company (AGC). The company's sole purpose was the construction of the airship, which would be built on conventional lines, on a fixed price contract.

Apparently to prevent this firm's getting a monopoly in the air as it had with submarine development, the British government decided to build the other ship, the R101, under its own authority and set up a "rival" concern at Cardington; the Royal Airship Works. The R101 would be designed with maximum innovation.

The two airships came to be known as the "Capitalist Airship"(R100) and the "Socialist Airship" (R101).

Both ships were contracted to similar specifications. It was bruited about that while R100 would be designed using existing technology and structure, R101 would employ new structural concepts and modern materials. It was also said that future airships would include the best features of both R100 and R101.

---

24   A major British engineering conglomerate.

By 8 May 1924, the common specifications for both airships must have seemed quite achievable, even targets to be bettered. Some parameters included: Hydrogen capacity 5,000,000 cubic feet empty weight not more than 90 tons, useful lift 60 tons, full speed 70 miles per hour (mph) cruising speed 63 mph, fuel capacity 57 hours at 63 mph to dry tanks, commercial capacity: comfortable living, sleeping, dining, and sanitary facilities for "at least 100 passengers" plus 8 tons of mail and freight. The specifications for airworthiness were to be determined.[25]

Following the investigations into the accidental destruction of the R38, the Air Ministry formed an Airship Stressing Panel. The panel's report, published in August 1922, offered criticisms and suggestions regarding future airships. By June 1923 the Conservative Government, which held office at that time, favoured these recommendations.

In January 1924, the Labour Party succeeded the conservatives. The new government created an "Airworthiness of Airships Panel" consisting of seven members, including the three members of the old Airship Stressing Panel. The old Stressing Panel's 'criticisms and suggestions' were incorporated and a table of strength requirements added. Collectively, this doomed both ships to be overweight and commercially unviable.

Both ship's designers added new passenger accommodation within the body of the airship. This was a real innovation. On all previous commercial passenger airships, passenger accommodation had been located outside the envelope, behind the main cabin in the command gondola The command gondola always hung down below the belly of the airship. In the R100 and R101 the gondola was considerably shorter, consisting only of the control cabin.[26]

Both R101 and R100 would be buoyed by hydrogen gas, because there was no better choice available. The designers felt, however, that their precautions against accidental ignition were sufficient, and they had solved the problems that had brought disaster on the hydrogen-lifted airships of former days. In their keen desire to create a global fleet of airships they focused on all the advantages of hydrogen over helium.

---

25 Masefield, Peter G., Sir. To Ride the Storm: The Story of the Airship R.101. William Morrow & Company, 1982.

26 Airship Heritage Trust 'Interiors R101'

PART VI: 1925

The Helium Conservation Act

On 3 March 1925, the US Congress authorised the Helium Conservation Act of 1925. This law banned the export of helium, thus forcing foreign airships to use flammable hydrogen as their lift gas.

While US airship crews on the airships USS *Shenandoah* and USS *Los Angeles* were borne aloft in the embrace of helium, the airship crews of other countries—such as Britain, France, Japan and Italy—had to risk the dangers of hydrogen. So did the German zeppelins (including the airship Hindenburg, which was yet to be built, and which would not be launched until 1936).

There was no way the British could obtain helium for the Imperial Airship Scheme. After the USA's Helium Act of 1925, if R100 and R101 were to fly at all, they would have to be lifted with hydrogen.

In 1925, after being inactive for nearly four years, the reconditioned R33 airship emerged from her shed at the Royal Airship Works (R.A.W.), Cardington. Will's old colleague Dicky Williams went to England in March of that year. He paid a visit to the R.A.W., where he was able to inspect the airship.

One of the 'Pulham Pigs' (as they were nicknamed), she was older and smaller than the two giant airships that were about to be constructed for the Imperial Airship Scheme. The Royal Airship Works planned to use R34 to test design innovations that could be used in the building of the great R101.

Dicky Williams felt optimistic about the future of airship travel.

```
The Advertiser (Adelaide, SA : 1889 - 1931)
Tuesday 17 March 1925, Page 16
AUSTRALIA'S AIR FORCE.
A PROGRESSIVE PROGRAMME.


Just before leaving England Commander Williams visited
the airship works at Cardington and Pulham, which
were reconditioning some of the airships which were
in commission just before the termination of the war.
One of these was the R34[sic], which flew across the
Atlantic. It was intended to experiment with the recon-
ditioned craft and then build an immense airship which
would fly from England to Egypt, and thence to India
and Australia. It would hold 100 passengers, and flying
between 70 and 80 miles an hour would make a trip to
India in five or six days. There was a party in India[27]
selecting sites for mooring masts and air-ship sheds.
He did not see any reason why people should not be
travelling by airship between here and England within
the next few years.
```

---

27 The 'party in India (who was) selecting sites for mooring masts and air-ship sheds' was Sir Sefton Brancker.

AUSTRALIA'S AIR FORCE

The RAAF is integral to Will's life story. The following newspaper article sheds light on its evolution in 1925, when Dicky Williams was pushing for 'landing grounds' to be built across the country. At that time the RAAF owned 150 aeroplanes, most of which were similar in type to those used in the war, since the Air Board of Australia considered it 'unwise to spend the limited funds at their disposal in the purchase of more modern machines before the ground organisation was completed'.

```
The Advertiser (Adelaide, SA : 1889 - 1931)
Tuesday 17 March 1925, Page 16
AUSTRALIA'S AIR FORCE.
A PROGRESSIVE PROGRAMME.


The air forces of Australia will be considerably
strengthened in the near future by the establishment of
squadrons at Sydney and Melbourne. Arrangements are in
hand for the erection of extensive work shops.
In an interview yesterday Wing-Commander R. Williams,
chief of the Australian Air Forces, said the air force
for purposes of defence was of little use to Australia
unless it could be concentrated quickly in any part of
the country. With conditions such as existed to-day it
was necessary to have an efficient ground organisation.
The Air Board of Australia, of which Commander Williams
was the first member, was endeavoring to build up that
organisation by establishing landing grounds throughout
the country. It was then intended to build hangars
```

```
and erect workshops. There was already in existence a
training school at Point Cook. During the next two or
three months the board hoped to establish squadrons
at Sydney and Melbourne. They would be operated by a
staff, one-third permanent and the remaining two-thirds
recruited from the citizen forces.
```

EVERYDAY LIFE

In March 1925, after many tears and sad embraces on the wharf, Will's mother Jacoba came to the end of her working holiday with her children who lived in Australia. Once again she departed, sailing to Korea where Wiebe was waiting for her.

Will's responsibilities were increasing. He was playing an integral role in setting up the new Faculty of Commerce at Melbourne University. His work involved dictating letters, attending meetings, planning and organising. His salary was increasing too, so he was well able to provide for his beloved family, but he was becoming somewhat dissatisfied. In the army and the air force he had been a man of action and adventure, risking his life almost every day, hurtling through the air in a flimsy flying machine while dodging bullets. The life of a secretary was quite the opposite of all that had thrilled him during the war years. He was beginning to wonder whether he should change course.

Letter from Will to his father:

"Aurunui" 30:3:25

Dear Dad,

It's Sunday evening, May is off to the [Salvation Army] Congress meeting in the [Royal] Exhibition [Building] and I am staying home to look after Margaret, and have a quiet evening.

I have had a busy week, Monday, Tuesday, Wednesday and Thursday nights I did not get home from the University till 11pm, so today I have just taken things quietly, as I expect another busy time in the coming week. My responsibilities are increasing, and I find there is much to do at this time. I am to all intents and purposes entirely responsible for the new school of Commerce in the University which has started off well this year with 250 students. There has been a great deal of organising to do, and I have found it very pleasant and stimulating to have to run the job on my own.

Tonight I have been listening in on the wireless to a very fine sermon at one of the city churches. For the moment I can't lay my hands on the newspaper cutting which would say what church it was. Anyhow it was a good sermon, the text being "What doth the Lord require of thee—to do justly, to love mercy and to walk humbly with thy God" the speaker held that these three requirements epitomised a creed of practical Christianity and his elaboration of each of the three requirements was forceful, convincing and eloquent.

This Radio is a great and wonderful thing. As far as I am concerned it is one of the blessings I have to thank Mother for, for she provided the money.

Naturally my thoughts have been much with mother tonight. She is, as I write, still in Australian waters, probably at Brisbane, and my heart is still very sore at parting with her. It was a terrible business seeing her go, and to know that years must elapse before I shall see her again. It has been wonderful to have had her here. She is a wonderful personality and time only adds to the force of her character. She has been and always will be an inspiration to me. I think I can say without a doubt that I have been spiritually strengthened and blessed through having her near me for this short time.

Frankly, it is hateful for me to reflect that we are living our lives so far removed from that personal contact with each other which means so much when there is deep sympathy, love and understanding. It is just one of the crosses of life. I try to make a habit of regularly concentrating my mind on you both so that at any rate in my own mind the closeness of association should not become in any way disintegrated. I thank God for you both, and for your lives spent in His service.

Mother has done wonderfully well here as a speaker. I have heard her and am thus able to judge. She has the gift of moving the hearts of the people. The night she spoke at Malvern I felt the emotion gripping my own throat, and there were wet eyes and sobs in various parts of the building. I was amazed at her eloquence and natural aptitude on the platform when I recollected that her opportunities in the past for this kind of work have been very scarce. Surely she will be a great help to you now that the cares of family are gone and you are both in charge.

She will have much to tell you. I am sure it has been a great trip for her and that she has stored up many very happy memories. I feel that having her here has brought us all much more together again.

May is back now—she was too far away in the Exhibition to hear anything at all so is somewhat disappointed. I feel that Radio has served me infinitely better.

Goodnight till next week,

Your eldest,

Will

A chance encounter with an old comrade

Now came another turning point in Will's life.

One day he caught the train to work as usual. On this day, however, while in the city, perhaps at some meeting, or maybe at a railway station—we may never know—he bumped into his old AFC acquaintance, Richard "Dicky" Williams.

Williams, now thirty-five years old, was the first military pilot to have been trained in Australia. He had commanded both Australian and British fighter units during the Great War. By June 1925, when Will chanced to meet him again, he was involved in the newly formed Royal Australian Air Force (RAAF). Williams would come to be remembered as the "father" of the RAAF.

On seeing Williams dressed in his RAAF uniform, memories of flying experiences must have come flooding back to Will. He had thrived on a life of action, of using his practical skills, working with his hands and facing challenges. More than that, this once shy and self-effacing man had tasted the euphoria of adulation and public recognition. He had been celebrated as a military hero, a magnificent man in a flying machine. To top it off, his father was truly proud of him.

It's likely that the experience was like a drug that once tried, could never be forgotten, and the craving for it would forever course through his blood, driving him on. In the letter below, his brief allusion to "improving my status in the community" conveys all this. How he must have longed for that life in uniform—a life of daring deeds and recognition, instead of the endless paperwork and committee meetings of his life as a secretary.

In the drab single-breasted three-piece suit of a 1920s clerk he blended in with all the other white-collar workers of Melbourne. His humdrum life contrasted starkly with his triumphant 1919 homecoming! Back then, he had sported his pilot's uniform emblazoned with the acclaimed "crowned wings" insignia of the AFC, and heads would turn as he walked down any street.

As his mother-in-law Agnes Holdaway observed, Will was filled with "nervous energy" and was "… never still, and always planning for the future…"

He knew he was capable of more. He had proved it to himself repeatedly. Life as a secretary was becoming stultifying. It was time to reach, again, for the stars.

Letter from Will:

"Aurunui" Surrey Hills Melbourne

29th June, 1925

Wing Commander R. Williams Headquarters R.A.A.F. Melbourne.

Dear Wing Commander,

Seeing you in the City the other day after your absence in England started a train of thought of which this letter is the outcome. Let me first bring myself to your recollection. I am an officer on the administrative staff of the University, and made your acquaintance whilst you were attending lectures before your recent trip. Also, I am an ex-pilot of No. 3 Squadron A.F.C. I have been on the Varsity staff since my return from active service, taking a post at £250 p.a. with the object of fulfilling a long cherished ambition, namely the securing of a university education. It took me a year to become fully acquainted with my duties, during which time study was out of the question. Since then I have completed in my spare time and in four years, what is normally a full three year's day course, and graduated B.A. in December last. My hours of duty have been from nine to five, and most of my lectures and all study have been done after office hours. I have never failed and have even managed to obtain honours, a record I feel quite satisfied about.

I have achieved my first objective and during the past few months have been taking stock of my position. My salary is at present £360, rising with two further annual increments to £400.

My present designation is Correspondence Clerk, that is I am responsible for dictating replies to the bulk of our correspondence. Further, I am a kind of understudy to the Registrar and Assistant Registrar. I act as Secretary at Faculty and Committee meetings whenever my chief is unable to do so. The recently constituted Faculty of Commerce has been entirely my charge since its inception, and I have had a good share in its organisation.

In short I have been spared a good deal of the usual routine work of the office and employed more on matters of organisation.

When I ask myself however, what my prospects are, I do not feel altogether satisfied, and I have come to feel that my abilities and energies could perhaps be used elsewhere to greater advantage and with more satisfaction to myself. Can you help me? Let me state briefly what my qualifications are:

Business experience before the War:

1. As Private Secretary (I write shorthand)

2. Assistant Accountant to a leading Collins Street firm.

During the War:

Enlisted as Private with 39th Battalion A.I.F. with no previous military knowledge. Promoted Acting Corporal after 14 days in Camp. This rank was confirmed some weeks later. Promoted Sergeant about three months later.

Three months later again sent to Officers' School at Oxford, and rejoined Battalion with Commissioned rank.

Awarded M.C. after the battle of Messines.

Transferred to Australian Flying Corps towards the end of 1917. I am well known to the following to whom I would refer you for further information regarding myself: Squadron Leaders Anderson and Wrigley, Captain Jones (of Civil Aviation), and Captain Hodgson of the Intelligence staff. I think I can say that I proved capable and useful as a pilot and in connection with other duties that came my way.

Educational qualifications: BA, University of Melbourne. I have also made a specialty of languages and am expert in Dutch. French is included in my Varsity course and I have a working knowledge of German. I have in recent years had much practice in expressing myself both in public, and on paper.

I am concerned not so much with adding to my immediate income as with the prospect of improving my status in the community. My age is 32, and I am married. I am a keen student and would be only too happy to pursue any course of study which would increase my usefulness in a new post. My trouble at present is that I seem to have come to a dead end.

If there is any possibility of my services being utilised either in your own Department or that of Civil Aviation, I should feel indebted to you for any assistance or information you may be able to give me.

I am enclosing for your information copies of a number of references which I used some time back in connection with an application which I was afterwards induced to withdraw. To these I could add if required one from the Registrar and one from the Professor of Commerce, both of which I have every reason to believe would be satisfactory.

Yours sincerely,

William Palstra

Flying Instructor's Course at RAAF Point Cook

"Dicky" Williams responded to Will's letter of 29 June with enthusiasm and asked him to join the RAAF. He was officially appointed to the rank of Flying Officer on 10 August 1925 and proceeded to undertake a Flying Instructor's course at RAAF Base Point Cook (the birthplace of the Royal Australian Air Force).

Will's wife and parents were probably not as pleased with his change of career as he was. Flying remained a dangerous profession. When their eldest son returned from the war, Wiebe and Jacoba had been relieved from their constant anxiety over his safety. Now they would start worrying all over again.

These days, the distance between the Point Cook Air Base and the Melbourne suburb of Surrey Hills would not seem too great to prevent daily commuting, but in 1925 cars did not travel fast enough to easily permit this. Nor were the roads—some still unmacadamised—as direct as they are now. The journey took several hours. This made it impractical to drive to and from work every day.

Will and one or two other officers used to share a motor vehicle and make a weekly trip. They would travel together to the air base on Sunday nights or Monday mornings and board there until Friday afternoons, coming home at the weekends.

Now May was not only faced with long separations from the one she loved most in the world, the man whose support she relied on, but she would also have to endure the same anxiety for his safety as his parents.

Will's return to his flying career meant more separations for this extremely close and loving couple and it was hard to bear, particularly for May and little Margaret, left at home. May's brother Allan came to stay in the "spare room" during the week so that there would still be a man about the house, if needed, but May was so desolate when her husband departed each week, that she wept. Her misery communicated itself to her eldest daughter.

Margaret missed her beloved father, and whenever an aeroplane chanced to pass over the house (a rare occurrence) she ran outside and waved to it.

One day, while accompanying some other officers on a car trip to Point Cook, Will was involved in a minor accident—the car hit a horse that had strayed onto the road. His foot was injured; his head also.

Hotham was one of Will's fellow aviators; presumably he used to accompany him to and from Point Cook. It was he who drove to Surrey Hills to inform May about Will's accident.

Letter from May to Will. Envelope addressed to:

Flying Officer W. Palstra, No. 1. Training Squadron,

R.A.A.F. Point Cook, Vic.

60 Guildford Road,

Surrey Hills,

11.8.25

My darling boy,

Now Hotham is gone, and everything is quiet, and I have settled down a bit, I can write you a decent letter. Kuku [May's youngest sister] was out today at Mother's so I stayed over there till they left, about eight o'clock and had just got back to my lonely house and got Margaret tucked off to bed when your messenger arrived.

Naturally I was a bit upset about your accident, but am so very very thankful for your escape from serious harm. Oh, Boy, please look after yourself, for you are just everything to me you know.

You were quite right about the "good cry" on Monday, only (fortunately) I couldn't do much of it as Margaret wept too, and had to be comforted. Try as I would, I could not sleep last night, but I suppose I will get used to the big bed all to myself. Allan [Holdaway] occupied the spare room.

Gordon [Holdaway] informed me with many gurgles that Allan habitually slept with his head well under the clothes, so he will be a mighty defender. However, it's nice to feel I'm not quite alone in the house.

Margaret forgot when she woke this morning, and seeing me alone said, "Have you had your cup of tea?", but alas, there was no cup of tea. Still things are not so bad considering, and I am not worrying or letting myself get morbid. After all, our separation is very short in comparison with what many husbands and wives have to undergo, and perhaps after all, as you say, it will show us more than ever, our love and dependence on one another.

I told Margaret that you would write us a letter, and explained all the processes of its reaching us—how you would put it in the letter box etc., "but", she said, "how can Daddy put it in the letter box when he is in an aeroplane?" So I had to explain that you wouldn't live in an aeroplane.

There was a terrific south wind today, and the wire door was snatched out of my hand, crashed into the [food] safe and bang went a hinge, so that is something for my handy-man. The chicks are doing well. Were all out today pecking away.

I've found out where the moaning noise (which we attributed to the parrot) comes from. It worried me so today, that I determined to discover its source, and traced it to the meter, when the gas is alight. I will speak about it to the collector when he comes. [The "collector" of money for gas; the meter-reader.] Margaret suggested that it was "Bye Bye" who was shut up in it.[28]

I am looking forward to Friday. That will be my happy day. Love and a big hug from

Your wife

P.S. I find I only gave one puttee to Hotham. Will post the other tomorrow.

Maisie

---
28 Bye Bye" was Margaret's imaginary friend.

(Enclosed with the above letter:)

Dear Daddy,

I am sorry for you and I am sorry for the poor horse, I will give you a big love when you come home.

Love from your little girl, Margaret.

xxx xxx xxx xxx

* * *

Note From Will to May:

31st August 1925 Point Cook

Dearest & best,

Just a short note to let you know I have arrived here safely this time and am in the best of spirits. I went up [in an aeroplane] with Hotham this afternoon and took control as soon as we were up. Did some turns of varying steepness, two landings and a take off. The only part that seemed strange and where I want practice is judging distance in coming in to land. In the air I feel quite at home at once, and the actual landings went without trouble. Love to all and a kiss for you and our little pet,

Will.

* * *

31.8.25

Point Cook.

Dear Margaret,

Daddy went up in a big aeroplane today, high up in the air. He saw the sea, and in the distance Surrey Hills, and he thought of you and our darling mother. Please look after mother whilst Daddy is away won't you. I'm coming back soon and I shall want a big hug from my little girl.

Lots of love and kisses,

from

Daddy.

Another airship disaster was reported in the newspapers around this time. On 3 September 1925, after fifty-seven flights, the U.S. Navy airship U.S.S. *Shenandoah* (ZR-1), was destroyed in a squall-line over Ohio, USA. Fourteen members of the crew lost their lives. Will and May would have read about it in the newspapers, but with no more than normal interest. Airships seemed to be remote phenomena that never touched their lives.

Will's mother wrote to him in advance of his October birthday:

The Salvation Army,

TERRITORIAL HEADQUARTERS

INSIDE WEST GATE SEOUL, KOREA

PHONE KOKAMON 830

Seoul, Sept 12th, 1925

My dear Will,

It seems to me ages since I have written you, and still there has not been a day that I have forgotten you, or that my thoughts have not been occupied with you—my dear loving eldest son. It is sometimes so wonderful to me, that this feeling of nearness to you and union with you never has left me or weakens. And now soon the day of your birth will come round again, and it never passes without the memory of all these years since God has given you to us, comes up in my thoughts again. What a joy to me to dwell on them, there has never been a flaw in the love to your mother my dear Will, thank the Lord for that, it has made me richer than money could make me. May this love spring up and flourish in the heart of your dear little daughter like a seed that never shall die in our family.

And now you begin life again on this your new years day under such different conditions as on the same day a year ago. From Oct [19]24 until Oct [19]25 has been indeed a very eventful year for the family. What ever the future may bring, I pray that the Lord will bless you abundantly in soul and body, family life and surroundings, may your happiness be secure…

In Korea, the senior Palstras were busy overseeing the building of a home for abandoned girls.

"The other day," Jacoba wrote in October 1925, "a Chinese was caught in the act here in Seoul of transporting four little girls between the age of 8 and 10 to China. There are plenty of these poor little things about, if only we could get hold of them in time. They are dreadful on the money and don't see any wrong in getting it in exchange for a girl, bride, concubine or worse they are not very particular about, I mean the common people, we have to watch even girls in the home, as long as there is a relation who can claim them."

The RAAF at Victoria Barracks

After his refresher course at Point Cook, Will became a head office man. As the Air Force needed its numbers to be strengthened, his first duties were as Deputy Director of Personnel Services, beginning on 19 October 1925.

By that year, the Commonwealth Department of Defence (first formed at the turn of the century), housed its headquarters in Victoria Barracks, an impressive blue-stone edifice completed in 1872. It still stands at the main southern entrance to the city of Melbourne, fronting the tree-lined boulevard of St. Kilda Road. Will would have been able to catch public transport from Surrey Hills to the Barracks each work day. What a relief it must have been for May and Margaret, to have him coming home each evening. (For us, however, it means their letters cease for a while.)

Meanwhile, on the other side of the world, the groundwork for the Imperial Airship Scheme continued. British airship design was evolving. The engineers at the Cardington Airship Works were continually experimenting, even as the R101 was being built. It was thought that airships could be used as aircraft carriers. The little R33, one of the 'Pulham Pigs'[29] was frequently also used for testing new ideas.

```
The Daily News (Perth, WA : 1882 - 1950)
Wed 14 Oct 1925 Page 2
"VERITABLE HORNETS' NESTS."
IMPORTANT AERIAL EXPERIMENTS.
AIRSHIP AS 'PLANE CARRIER.
LONDON. October 13.


When the airship R33 was taken from its shed and attached
to a mooring mast to-night, a monoplane of the D.H.53
type was observed to be attached to the bottom of the
hull by means of a special fitting resembling a trapeze.
It was explained that is a prelude to a naval experiment
for launching the 'plane in mid-air while the R33 is in
flight, which is now awaiting favorable weather.
The Air Ministry is attaching considerable importance to
the experiment, as preparing the way to convert airships
into veritable hornets' nests, from which a large number
of 'planes may be launched. The experiments will consist
of the monoplane detaching and re-attaching itself to
```

---

29   Other "Pulham Pigs", built at RNAS Pulham, included the airships R9, R23, R24, R26, and R34.

the airship. It will be necessary to regulate the speed of the 'plane to that of the R33. The experiments will help to test the possibility of the airship as a carrier. Trials will be carried out at a height of 6,000 feet.

PART VII: 1926

Jocelyn Helen

It had been more than four years since Will and May's first child was born, and there had been no sign of another pregnancy. May began to worry that she might never conceive another child. She wondered whether the trouble she'd had with Margaret's birth had rendered her barren. Early in 1926, however, she and Will were relieved and ecstatic to discover that she was "with child" again.

In October Will was gazetted to a permanent commission in the Air Force. "I continue to be very happy in my work," he wrote to his mother, "much more so than I ever was at the University."

That same month brought the new addition to the family.

```
The Argus (Melbourne, Vic.: 1848 - 1956)
Page 13
BIRTHS
PALSTRA—On the 29th October, at Mosgiel private hospital,
to Flying Officer and Mrs. W. Palstra, 60 Guildford road,
Surrey Hills—a daughter (Jocelyn Helen).
```

Shortly after the birth of his second daughter Will went away again, this time for a month. He piloted an aeroplane around Queensland and New South Wales, on a flying "recruitment drive" for the RAAF.

Their many letters to each other during this period survive.

Letter from Will to May:

COMMONWEALTH OF AUSTRALIA.
AIR BOARD ROYAL AUSTRALIAN AIR FORCE
HEAD-QUARTERS,
Sydney, 28:11:26

Dearest sweetest and darlingest love,

What a dear darling little wife you are. I have just finished reading through once again the two letters I have had from you and my heart is just glowing with love for you sweetheart. Isn't it a shame that just at the time when you want your husband so badly he should be far away from you. How I long to cuddle you up kiss you and tell you all that you are to me. Never mind, the days won't be long now when I shall be able to love you as much as ever I can. Won't it be great, the coming home…

Will and May with their daughters Margaret and Jocelyn, circa 1927

As the year came to a close, the Golden Age of Airships was in full swing. The British Air Ministry was making preparations for the launch of the Imperial Airship Scheme right across the globe, with the newspapers calling it "The Dawn of the Air Age".

THE PROGRESS OF THE IMPERIAL AIRSHIP SCHEME

The Imperial Airship Scheme had commenced in October 1924 with high expectations for the speedy completion of airships R100 and R101. For two years, the British government poured funds into the Scheme, yet eighteen months after the Australian newspapers reported that the huge airships at Cardington were "nearing completion" neither of the two airships was, as yet, anywhere near ready for testing.

The Air Ministry's optimism remained undaunted, nonetheless.[30]

The Royal Airship Works was slowly putting together the R101 in No 1 Shed at Cardington. A second airship shed was proposed, to house the R100.

```
The Sydney Morning Herald (NSW : 1842 - 1954)
Tue 30 Nov 1926 Page 11
HUGE AIRSHIP SHED.
(British Official Wireless.)
LONDON. Nov. 28.

The Air Ministry contemplates the construction of a
second huge airship shed at Cardington. On building
will accommodate R100, and the other a second State
airship, which is being built for the Government by a
private firm. Both airships will be completed by the end
```

---

[30] In February 1926, English scientist, engineer and inventor Sir Barnes Neville Wallis, designer of the R100, said, "The advantages of speedy intercommunication are obvious to all who have studied the political economy of a scattered Empire such as ours; and the airship is now admitted to be the ideal vehicle for this purpose even by those who have devoted their interests to the development of its only rival—the aeroplane." [Wallis, 1926]

```
of next year. The only shed in the Empire comparable in
size to those at Cardington is now nearing completion
at Karachi, in India.
In view of the Imperial Conference discussions, it
is expected that Canada's lead in erecting suitable
mooring masts for new airships will be followed by other
dominions.
```

Readers will recall that the R100 and the R101 were being built by two separate organisations, the private Airship Guarantee Company (a subsidiary of Vickers), and the British Air Ministry's government-backed Royal Airship Works. Unfortunately, instead of cooperating (as had been expected), the two design teams almost immediately developed a rivalry.

In *Catastrophe and Crisis*, J. Kingston and D. Lambert offer the opinion that "undertakings were often duplicated and a great deal of money was wasted, mainly by the Air Ministry team". This, they said, was due to the teams working independently for five years, neither team conferring with the other on problems confronting both.

Dr Giles Camplin and Peter Davison, who have meticulously researched the history of airships, explain that this was not, in fact, the case. We know from records that there was some contact between the two groups, and it is certain that both were competent.

Nevil Shute Norway (1899 – 1960) was an English novelist and aeronautical engineer. While working as a design engineer for Vickers Ltd., he was involved with the development of airships, working as Chief Calculator (stress engineer) on the R100 airship project. In 1929 he was promoted to Deputy Chief Engineer of the R100 project and later Chief Engineer.

Shute gives a detailed account of the development of the R100 and R101 in his 1954 autobiographical work, *Slide Rule: The Autobiography of an Engineer*.

"It was no fault of the Cardington party that they had the Air Ministry press department always nagging at their elbow for a story to put out in order that the expenditure of public money might be justified, but the effect was a stream of optimistic forecasts in the newspapers from the men who were building the R101 which in the end built a fine fence around them from which there was no escape. It was our good fortune on the Vickers staff that we had no press department, and therefore few published statements to prevent us from changing our plans quickly when we found it necessary to do so, and in that design we were venturing so far into the unknown that we perforce made many changes of plan. In the end, and largely through the press department, I think, the Cardington designers found themselves hemmed in behind a palisade of their own published statements which could not be broken through without some personal and public discredit, till one course only was left open to them, a course which they would never have taken had they been free men, a course which was to lead to tragedy and death."

PART VIII: 1927

The Argus (Melbourne, Vic. : 1848 - 1957)
Sat 22 Jan 1927 Page 12
DAWN OF THE AIR AGE.
AVIATION IN THE EMPIRE.
BY AIRSHIP TO AUSTRALIA.
(FROM OUR CORRESPONDENT.)

. . . AIRSHIPS FOR LONG DISTANCES

Sir Samuel Hoare has some interesting remarks upon the special work in Empire aviation to be done by airships as opposed to aeroplanes. He says that here, too, demonstration flights are required in Australia and New Zealand, in which the co-operation of Dominion Governments is necessary. In particular, the Australian Royal Air Force is asked to co-operate with the Royal Air Force at Singapore in flights between Australia and Singapore.

There must also be mooring masts, and there must be a collection of meteorological data. The provision of masts and the collection of meteorological data will alone take two years, by which time the Empire airships will be ready.

Not the least interesting pages of the report are concerned with the description of R101 and a comparison of the vessel with earlier airships. The pictorial suggestion of passenger accommodation on the upper deck of R101 is a romance of engineering.

Preliminary surveys suggest the following saving of time by the use of airships—

	Total Times		
	Steamship Days	**Airship Days**	**Saving Days**
England-Egypt	6	2 ½	3 ½
On to Bombay	15	5	10
On to Perth	28	11	17
England-South Africa			
Via W. Africa	20	6 ½	13 ½
Via E. Africa	20	6	14
On to Australia		10 ½	

Australia-New Zealand	6	1 ½	4 ½
England-Canada	6	2 ½	3 ½
India-Australia	22	6 ½	15 ½
India-Canada, via England	24	9	15
Australia-Canada via South Africa and England	48	15 ¾	32 ¼

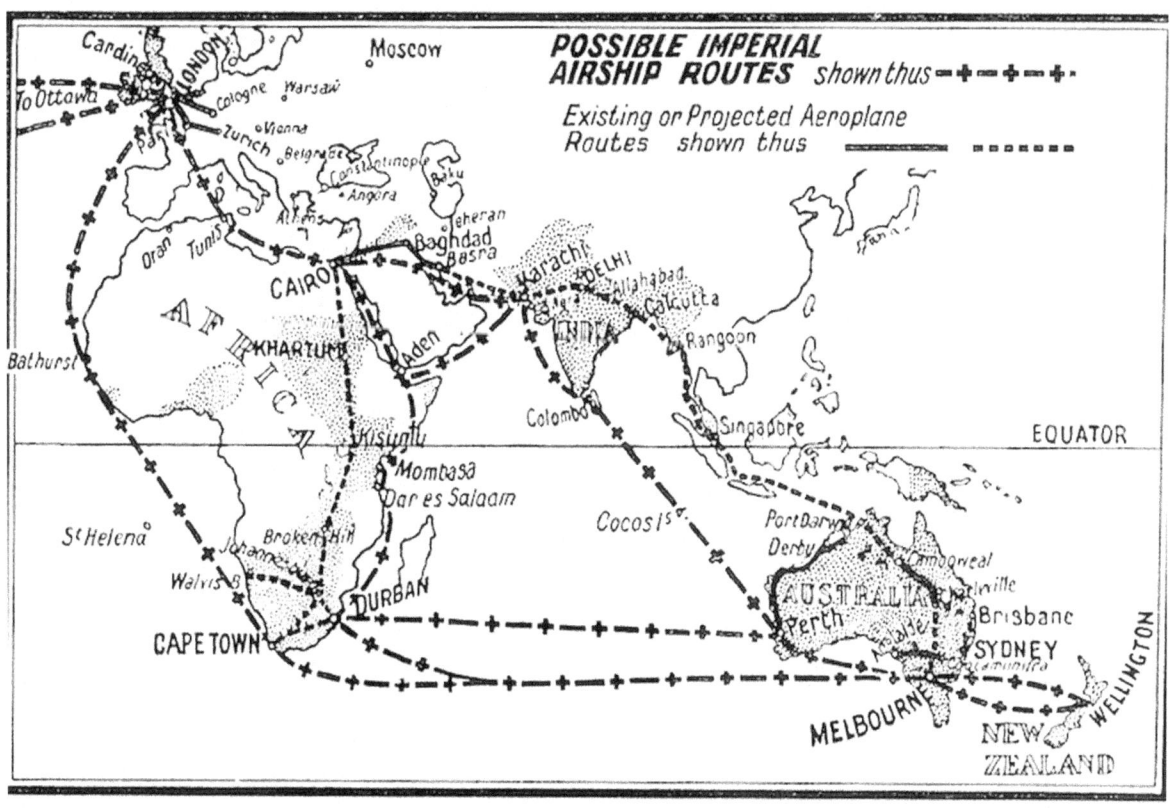

World map circa 1927 showing "possible Imperial Airship Routes" Image source: *The Argus*.

May suffered a bout of ill-health after Jocelyn was born. By the time Will returned she had recovered sufficiently for the family to go on a much-needed holiday in Seaford, a seaside suburb about 40 km from Surrey Hills.

Imagine Will in his bathing suit, kneeling on the fine, pale sand to help young Margaret build sandcastles with her bucket and spade, while May—sitting with infant Jocelyn and a large picnic basket beneath the shade of a beach umbrella—looks on indulgently, or takes turns with Will to go for a swim. The shouts of happy children mingle with the squawking of seagulls, and the lapping wavelets of sheltered Port Philip Bay.

Meanwhile Charles Palstra, who had not been in long-term employment since the war, applied for a job as a travelling salesman selling insurance. His prospective employers, The Ocean and Accident Guarantee Corporation, wrote to the A.I.F. Records Branch asking for references, because for whatever reason, Charles could not show them a military discharge. With no fixed address, Charles seemed like a lost soul. Whether they gave him the job is unknown.

Will, by contrast, was literally soaring to new heights. On 1 March 1927 he was promoted to the rank of Flight Lieutenant in the RAAF. He was also upgraded to Staff Officer to C.A.S. and Director of Manning (sustaining the Australian Air Force's manpower). He continued as Deputy Director of Personnel Services, as he had done since 19 October 1925.

Letter from Will's father Wiebe, who was working for the Salvation Army in Indonesia:

> 19.III.1927
>
> …Can you wonder when I say that I am becoming impatient to see and be introduced to the two grandchildren? That's just how I feel and I want the holiday period to come quick, for it's getting on for six years since I saw you all in Melbourne.
>
> We enjoy getting the snaps—Margaret appears to be so big a girl already, I am going to write her for her very nice letter, but in the meantime please tell the wee lassie that I have received it [her letter] and am very pleased to have it.…

The opening of Parliament House, Canberra

Melbourne had served as Australia's original federal capital until 1913, when the city of Canberra was established. It was a momentous occasion, the opening of the new Parliament House in Canberra on 9 May, 1927. Now known as Old Parliament House, it was Australia's first purpose-built federal parliament building.

The Duke and Duchess of York sailed from England for the opening ceremony, joining many other notable guests including the Prime Minister and Dame Nellie Melba.

At this time Will was A.D.C. (aide-de-camp) to Dicky Williams, Chief of the Air Staff (CAS) for the Royal Australian Air Force. The Armed Forces also each had their official party at the ceremony, and Will was part of the contingent representing the RAAF. He flew from Point Cook to Canberra in a deHavilland 9 biplane, and stayed in Canberra from 2 to 11 May. The family archives hold photographic records of his visit.

The Duke of York (Queen Elizabeth II's father, later to become King George VI) used a golden key to unlock the doors of the new building. The spectacular ceremony was broadcast over radio stations in Queensland, New South Wales, Victoria and South Australia, and reached more than a million people.

The opening of Parliament House, Canberra, 9 May 1927. Images from family archives.

The Duke of York inspects the troops at the opening of Parliament House.

Airship news

All the while, newspapers continued to publish progress reports on that fascinating subject—the Imperial Airship Scheme. The Australian Government, like other governments around the world, had already approved the construction of mooring masts in major capital cities.

```
The Sydney Morning Herald (NSW: 1842-1954)
Thu 29 Dec 1927 Page 9
AIRSHIP READY IN APRIL.


Will Fly to Australia.


(FROM OUR SPECIAL REPRESENTATIVE.) LONDON, Nov. 24.
It is now expected that the R100—the 5,000,000 cubic foot
airship under construction for the British Government—
will be completed in April next, and it is confidently
expected that she will visit Australia during the year.
The framework of the vast structure is well advanced...


100 PASSENGERS.
The R100 has a length of 709 feet and a maximum diameter
of 130 feet. She has a designed speed of 82 miles per
hour. The actual displacement of the vessel is 156 tons,
nearly double that of the "Santa Maria," the vessel in
which Columbus sailed to discover America. Accommoda-
tion is provided for 100 passengers and a crew of 35...
```

MOORING MASTS.[31]

In contemplation of this programme the British Government at the Imperial Conference held in London in October, 1926, suggested to the dominion Premiers that the necessary mooring mast bases should be provided by the dominions, and since then the Governments of South Africa, Canada, and Australia have approved the erection of the necessary masts. Sites have been selected with the assistance of advice from the Air Ministry officials, and bases in Egypt and India are already complete.

---

[31] You can view "How to Moor a British Rigid Airship" on the Airship Heritage Trust's YouTube channel @airshipheritagetrust1419.

PART IX: 1928

An Extraordinary Opportunity

Early in 1928 May and Will were overjoyed to discover that May had conceived their third child. Would it be the longed-for son?

That year it was expected that the airship R100 would make its first international "demonstration" flight to Canada late in 1929, while the R101 would fly first to the Cape of Good Hope in South Africa, and subsequently to Australia, in 1930. Newspapers eagerly followed developments as they happened.

As the year progressed, however, delay after delay impeded the programme. Many people in Britain were becoming increasingly impatient with the slow progress of the Imperial Airship Scheme, and the amount of money being poured into it.

The British Parliament's Hansard, 12 March 1928, recorded the honourable member for North Aberdeen (Mr. Rose) as saying, "In three years the [air]ships were to be in service. It is now four years since . . . Parliament has sanctioned this scheme. What are we to say to such a state of things? How can the right honourable gentleman have the temerity to come to this House and ask for more money to carry on this fantastic folly?"

In August, another momentous event occurred in the lives of Will and May Palstra. The RAAF offered an extraordinary opportunity to Will and his colleague, airman George Jones. It was announced in the newspapers.

```
The Argus (Melbourne, Vic.: 1848-1956)
Thursday 9 August 1928
Page 10
Squadron-Leader G. Jones and Flight Lieutenant W.
Palstra have been selected to go to England to attend
the next course at the Royal Air Force staff college at
Andover, Hampshire, which will begin in January. The
course will last for a year, after which the two officers
will be attached to the Royal Air Force before returning
to Australia. Flight-Lieutenant Palstra is at present
secretary of the air accidents committee and Director
of Personnel Services.
```

A select handful of other Australians was selected to do the course, in addition to airmen from other British Commonwealth countries and England itself.

"The RAF Staff College at RAF Andover was the first Royal Air Force staff college to be established. Its role was the training of officers in the administrative, staff and policy aspects of air force matters. From its foundation and through the 1920s and 1930s, the Staff College provided training to selected officers (usually promising flight lieutenants or squadron leaders) to prepare them for staff duties at the Air Ministry or at Command or Group headquarters."[32]

---

32 "RAF Staff College, Andover". Wikipedia, retrieved 9 February 2021.

Will's family was to accompany him during the two year sojourn in England. Allan Holdaway would write in 1967,

> "Will was selected to do the Staff College Course in England against quite a deal of competition... My sister May had not been outside Australia and New Zealand so that this was a great opportunity for her."

Will had risen swiftly through the RAAF ranks, from Deputy Director of Personnel Services (October 1925-March 1928) to Director of Manning (March 1928-July 1928) to Director of Personnel Services, a position he would hold until 27 November 1928, the date set for his departure to England.

He was concurrently secretary of the Air Accidents Investigations Committee, and RAAF Staff Officer to the Chief of the Air Staff from 31 March 1927 to 14 June 1928.

He had been promoted from Flying Officer to Flight Lieutenant on 1 March 1927. This was the highest rank for a junior officer. The rank above Flight Lieutenant was Squadron Leader; above that was Wing Commander, then Group Captain. The four ranks above that were Air Commodore, Air Vice-Marshal, Air Marshal and ultimately, Air Chief Marshal.

This life course must have felt familiar to Will. He was ascending the ranks of his third "military force". Once, he had been a captain in the Salvation Army. Next, he'd achieved the rank of lieutenant in the AIF. Now he was soaring up through the hierarchy of the RAAF. He felt sure that if he continued to be so successful, there was a fair chance he would one day achieve the rank of air marshal.

> "I am not certain yet whether the authorities have woken up to the fact that there is an Air Marshal's baton sticking out of my hip pocket," Will jovially wrote to his brother-in-law Allan in May 1929, "but I flatter myself that I am somehow keeping my end up, and that the RAAF are not likely to give me the sack for a few years to come..."

Squadron Leader William Palstra with some RAAF colleagues in the later 1920s. He is second from the left. Dicky Williams is third from the left.

A son is born

To top off the excitement of 1928, on 3rd September a much longed-for event occurred—a boy was born to May and Will. Their happiness knew no bounds!

```
The Argus (Melbourne, Vic.: 1848–1956) Tuesday 4
September 1928 page 1
FAMILY NOTICES.
BIRTHS.
PALSTRA.-On the 3rd September, at Mosgiel private
hospital, to Flight-lieutenant and Mrs. W. Palstra, of
60 Guildford road, Surrey Hills a son (William Ernest).
```

Airship R100 and Graf Zeppelin

In 1928 the journal Flight International[33] reported on the two giant British airships. R100, they said, would "carry out the first Canadian Demonstration Flight while R101 would perform the first flight to India, and later to South Africa.

The airship R100 had not yet reached completion, but newspaper journalists were permitted to go aboard to report on the work in progress. A vivid description of the R100 was published in *The Spectator* in September 1928, and it found its way into Australian newspapers.

```
The Brisbane Courier (Qld. : 1864 - 1933)
Thu 27 Sep 1928 Page 21
HUGE AIRSHIP.
A "MAURITANIA" OF THE AIR.
INTERESTING DESCRIPTION.
By F. YEATS-BROWN, in "The Spectator."
```

---

[33] "Flight International" was published in the United Kingdom and founded in 1909.

I lay on a little duralumin bed in a buff-distempered, fire-proof cabin, with a mica porthole, imagining myself flying to Canada or Cairo.

It was a dream, but one that may come true this autumn, for Commander Burney's great airship has been clothed with half its skin and all its passenger accommodation. At present it fills the huge hangar at Howden from top to bottom and from end to end. In a few months it will be ready to fly. It is like some mammoth in a museum, but bigger than any mammoth, and instinct[sic[34]] with the present instead of the past. The engine gondolas have not yet been fitted, nor the fins and rudder, but three hundred men are working on it day and night, and before the year ends we shall see the largest airship in the world come gleaming over London.

To the top deck cabin, where I lay thinking, came the sound of many voices and the tramp of feet from the people who were inspecting the ship.

Vibrations of both voice and movement will always be apparent to the air traveller I should imagine, for the partitions between the cabins are thin and the whole framework resilient. But the engines will be almost inaudible, for they are far astern. Sea-breezes and seasickness will be unknown, for the motion is expected to be very gentle and the passengers will be completely enclosed by the envelope, and, although able to look out through windows in it, will not come in contact with the outer air save through ventilators. All the fittings are extremely light and neat.

---

34 "Instinct" in the sense of "imbued or filled with (a quality, especially a desirable one)." [Google Dictionary]

The companion-way leading from the top deck cabin to the dining-room is of aluminium veneered with mahogany. A buffet and electric grill opens on to the saloon on one side. Opposite is another companion leading to the crew's quarters, while further cabins open out from the saloon to port and starboard. Beyond the cabins, there is a small promenade deck (still inside the envelope, however) where a small dance could be held.

What are the dangers and difficulties confronting the makers of "R.100"?
To begin with, her handling. She is as big as the Mauritania, and would nearly fill Northumberland avenue if she were laid in it. To manhandle such a monster without tugs and winches will be very difficult.
The mooring mast as it exists to-day is suitable for demonstration flights, but it hardly sufficient for a regular service. A complete equipment similar to that available for sea-going ships has, however, been invented, and patented by the Airship Guarantee Company, and as soon as the necessary money is forthcoming they will be applied to the "R.100" and her prospective sisters and heiresses-apparent.

PERIL OF PETROL.
ANOTHER danger is that the ship will break up owing to structural weakness, as did the "R38" and the "Shenandoah." Commander Burney claims that his ship can withstand conditions five times as severe as that which broke the "Shenandoah." He would admit, I think, that there are conditions which would be dangerous to the

"R.100," but with the advance of meteorological knowledge a very reasonable margin of safety can be assumed. Danger from fire is more serious. "R.100" carries 30 tons of petrol, contained in a confined air-space throughout the envelope of the ship. Oozing and weeping at some of the many joints in the system is inevitable in temperate climates, petrol is not sufficiently volatile to render this a great source of danger, but under tropical conditions it might easily become inflammable, and Commander Burney does not intend to fly to India until he can eliminate the petrol engine altogether. His company has already developed a new engine (the hydrogen-kerosene) and Diesel engines of the necessary lightness are being experimented with: it is only a question of time before the power for airships will be derived from engines of far greater efficiency than those now in use, burning a heavy non-volatile oil.

Soon the "R.100" will make her maiden trip across the Atlantic. Here is no grandiose dream of the far future, but a child of this dangerous and delightful year of grace, with all earth's sky for nursery. Bigger children of the air age will follow (the next airship will be half as big again) and England may well become carrier of the world by air as well as by sea if she will listen to those of us who see a new world to win, richer than was the Spanish Main. All civilisation will be affected by what we do, or fail to dare. Steamship rates will fall, school teachers from the Middle West will fly to Europe for their fortnight's vacation, the world will emancipate itself from tariff walls, currencies, armies. The mutterings and rumblings of this change are upon

```
us. Time and space are being altered before our eyes,
if we will but open them. It is an adventure greater
than any in history. Let us not lose our sense of wonder
nor stifle our admiration for the men who have made this
possible.
Commander Burney has prepared a thunderbolt that shall
shake the world.
```

In 1926 the post-war restrictions on airship construction in Germany had been lifted. The Zeppelin Company started work on the construction of a new airship, LZ127 (Deutsches Luftschiff Zeppelin 127), at Friedrichshafen in Germany.

The new dirigible's name was Graf Zeppelin ("Graf" means "Count" in German). She flew for the first time on 18 September 1928. With a total length of 236.6 metres (776 ft) and a volume of 105,000 cubic metres, she was the largest dirigible ever to have been built, at that time (the R101 would later be lengthened). She was also, of course, filled with hydrogen.

To begin with, Hugo Eckener intended to use the spectacular Graf Zeppelin for experimental and demonstration purposes. She would carry fare-paying passengers and mail back and forth across the Atlantic Ocean, showing the world how airships were the key to the future of regular air travel.

Eckener captained Graf Zeppelin on most of her record setting flights, commencing with the world's first commercial passenger flight across the Atlantic. On 11th October 1928 the zeppelin completed her first long-range voyage—from Friedrichshafen to Lakehurst, USA. The intercontinental voyage took 112 hours and set a new endurance record for airships. She carried 20 passengers.

Eckener and his crew of forty men were once again welcomed to America with great enthusiasm. There were confetti parades in New York, and as before, they were invited to the White House.

```
The Argus (Melbourne, Vic.: 1848—1957)
Sat 13 Oct 1928 Page 19
GRAF ZEPPELIN. ATLANTIC CROSSING. LONDON, Oct. 11.
. . .Three Americans paid £600 each to travel in the
Zeppelin, upon which 20 passengers will live sumptuously
on veal and chicken sausages, vegetables, sweets, and
fruit.
The Munich Brewery presented 2,000 bottles of beer, and
another admirer sent 200 bottles of champagne. For the
beer and champagne the passengers will be charged the
same prices as on luxury sea liners. . .
```

After leaving the USA, Graf Zeppelin toured Germany and visited Italy, Palestine, and Spain. During 1928 Eckener commanded the zeppelin on six successful proving flights, covering thousands of kilometres. The success of the German airships added impetus to the British plans for an international commercial passenger service.

Graf Zeppelin LZ127 circa 1928. www.schockwellenreiter.de

As Graf Zeppelin was being prepared to make its trans-Atlantic crossing, Jacoba and Wiebe Palstra were departing from Indonesia aboard the steamship Nieuw Holland. At last they were able to make their longed-for visit to Australia. Their arrival, on 8th October 1928, was not a moment too soon. They were able to spend six happy weeks with Will and his family, before their departure for England.

OVER THE SEA

Wiebe and Jacoba spent several happy weeks with their children and grandchildren before it was time for Will and May to leave for England.

The following photograph was probably taken in late October or early November 1928. The family group is posing in the front garden of No. 60 Guildford Road, squinting into the sun on a bright day.

Will is on the left in the back row. May and Margaret are in the front row.

In November, May Palstra and the wife of George Jones were guests of honour at a special farewell afternoon tea with music.

```
The Argus (Melbourne, Vic. : 1848 - 1956)
Tuesday 20 November 1928 P 12
AIR FORCE WIVES AND MOTHERS.

The Air Force Officers' Wives and Mothers' Association
will hold its monthly meeting tomorrow at half-past
2 o'clock. . . Mrs. George Jones and Mrs. W. Palstra,
who will leave shortly for England, will be given a
farewell. A musical programme will be given.
```

On 27 November, 1928, Will and May Palstra and their three children, accompanied by Will's father Wiebe, embarked on the Royal Mailship Ormonde for the United Kingdom.

In the company of three other high-ranking Salvation Army officers, Will's father was bound for the Salvation Army's world headquarters in London. A special meeting of the High Council had been called, due to an unprecedented crisis in that organisation[35]. Will had managed to book his family's passage on the same ship as his father, so that the two of them could enjoy an extended time together.

Nobody could know that this was to be Will's last farewell to Australia, and that Jacoba would never see her beloved eldest son again.

A crowd of familiar people lined Melbourne's Station Pier to wave goodbye as the ship moved slowly away. Holdaways, Palstras, and Salvation Army friends called out their farewells. Young Margaret, leaning on the deck railing and looking out through the metal bars as the strip of water widened between ship and land, must have sensed the bittersweet poignancy of the parting and been struck by the momentousness of the occasion. She was only just seven years old, and discovering the world to be a wide and fascinating place.

---

35   General Bramwell Booth, the Army's leader, was in his seventies and suffering from ill-health, but he refused to retire.

A postcard of the SS Ormonde in May's photo album. She has written, "The ship that took us to London. Left Melbourne 27/11/28. Arrived London 3/1/29.

May's caption: "Seeing us off at Port Melbourne".

May's caption: "Lifeboat drill at sea".
Right to left: Margaret, Will, Jocelyn, May and two friends,
probably George Jones and his wife.

Christmas aboard the SS Ormonde

PART X: 1929

LIFE IN ENGLAND

The RMS Ormonde docked at London on 3rd January, 1929. What an eye-opener this busy, modern, ancient city was for May and Margaret!

After about a week in the metropolis, the family moved to their new home in Andover, Hampshire. Here they were to remain for twelve months, while Will and George Jones attended their year-long course at the Royal Air Force Staff College.

The young Palstra family's new, rented home was a two storey house at "The Beeches", 60 Junction Road, Andover, Hampshire. In the early 20th century most Australian houses were single- storey, so right up until the 1960s most Australians viewed multi-storied houses as belonging to the wealthy. To May and Margaret, this house must have seemed quite luxurious. It seems to have come complete with a couple of pet cats.

Will was on a good salary, so he and May hired a live-in maidservant. In England, many families of their status had servants, but domestic help was almost unheard-of in Australia.

May had never been in charge of a servant, nor had anyone in her social circle. Such a luxury must have seemed like a dream come true!

To top off these comforts, Will decided to buy motor-car; a four door, six cylinder Essex sedan. Privately-owned motor cars were comparatively rare in 1929.

Wiebe's stay in England was not long. In February 1929 he said goodbye to Will, May and the children, and headed for Australia, via France, to rejoin his wife. He and Jacoba would return together to their post in Java.

Jocelyn and Bill were too young even for kindergarten but Margaret, being of school age, attended school in England. What a daunting prospect it must have been for this sensitive seven-year-old, starting a new school where she knew nobody, and had an antipodean accent that sounded so different from everyone else's.

Will's drive and ambition was unflagging. He was loving life, loving his success, and keen to achieve even more by ascending through the ranks of the RAAF.

Now began, perhaps, the happiest time any of them would ever know.

A blurry photo of the Palstra family setting off for an afternoon walk from their home, "The Beeches" in Andover, UK.

May's caption for this blurred photo: "Off for a walk, Andover."
The maid/nanny Lizzie is in charge of the three children.

Will in the driver's seat of the family's Essex sedan. May is about to step in, holding baby Bill.
The two girls might already be in the car.

"The river at Andover - town mill in the background."
Margaret and Jocelyn admiring the ducks.

"In the garden at Andover."
Will is holding the two youngest, while Margaret stands beside the swing.

A picnic at Pangbourne with Air Force personnel

Newspapers reported that the British government's plans for an airship service to Australia were progressing.

```
The Queenslander (Brisbane, Qld.: 1866—1939)
Thu 21 Feb 1929 Page 23
AIR SERVICE.
Important Proposal. CANBERRA, February 12.
An assurance was given by the Prime Minister (Mr. S.M.
Bruce) to Sir Eric Geddes (Chairman of Imperial Airways)
that Australia would certainly be prepared to co-operate
in the establishment of an airship service from Great
```

```
Britain to Australia, via Karachi, Calcutta, Burma, the
Malay States, and Singapore, if a thorough examination
of relevant subjects revealed that Australia would
derive an advantage from the service.
```

AN ENGLISH SPRING

They were glorious, those two years in England. Will was doing the job he loved, and earning a good income. May was living in relative luxury, and the children were growing up in a stimulating environment, supported by loving parents who frequently took them on sight-seeing road trips. There were plenty of interesting things to see and do, including beach holidays at a rented house in Teignmouth during the summer. Everyone was happy.

In the northern hemisphere, winter gave way to spring. For all except Will, it was their first British spring, and it made a lasting impression on them.

Letter from Will:

Andover

15th May 1929

Dear Dad and Mother,

This must be the briefest of notes. It is now getting on for 11 o'clock. I have been working like mad all day. Indeed this week has been by far the busiest we have had. . .

The family are all hale and hearty. . . The country side at present is really beautiful. Wild flowers everywhere, blue bells, violets, primroses and a host of others. Margaret in particular is thrilled. A pair of thrushes have made a nest in our back yard—more excitement. The season is rather late, but the rains have now come and the countryside is responding rapidly.

It is really wonderful how well we have all kept through the change. I think it has done me a lot of good. . .

Next week I shall be away from Andover with the Staff College crowd for a few days. We are doing an exercise in the neighbourhood of Bristol.

The family send their love,

Your loving eldest,

Will

"How do I like this country?" Will recorded in another letter. "At present it is lovely and no mistake. Words can't describe the beauty of an English countryside in spring, at any rate my words can't, and I'm leaving that to May..."

And in another missive to his parents Will wrote:

> "How I wish I would take you round the sunny countryside here in England for a few months. Things are just lovely at present. May and Margaret are in continuous raptures over the beauties of the trees, the wild flowers, and the animal life. What a difference to the winter. We spent last Sunday afternoon in a wood close to Andover. There was a large tract of bluebells in one part, and we picnicked under a wonderful old beech tree..."

The glories of the English spring made an indelible impresssion. The native flora of the family's home in southern Australia is not as seasonally showy as the flora of the northern hemisphere. For example, there are very few native deciduous trees to provide autumn colour. Native acacia trees burst into clouds of golden blossoms in late winter, and suburban parks and gardens are filled with colourful imported species, but springtime across the rural Australian landscape is relatively bland and muted.

May's caption: "Picking blackberries in Devon. Note Jocelyn's method—eating them."

Seven-year-old Margaret's encounter with the lush beauty of an English spring profoundly affected her. It engraved itself indelibly on her young mind as a heaven-like experience, filled with colour, blossom, bird-song and the love of her happy parents, who took her and her siblings on picnics and rambles in the countryside.

At their home "The Beeches", Margaret even had had own little flower-garden.

Often, the maidservant and May would pack a wicker picnic hamper with a portable feast. Will heaved the hamper into the car's boot, while May settled the children in their seats. After leaping in behind the wheel Will started the engine. Off they would go, bowling along the narrow streets and lanes and by-ways, past hedged fields sprinkled with daisies, and bluebell-carpeted woods in a mist of new green foliage.

60 Junction Road, Andover.

1/5/29

Dear Daddy,

I think I see one of my climing nasturtuns [sic] up, and my primroses are doing well. This is not a very long letter course I have got to go to school. goodbye.

with love from

Margaret

x x x x x x x x x x x x x x x x x x x x x x x x x x x x x x x x x x xx x x

x xx x x x x x x x x x x x x x x x x x x x x x x x x x x x x x xx x x x x x

x x xx x x x x x x x x x x x x x x x x x x x x x x x x x xxxxxxxxxxxxxxxx

The following letter was written by almost-eight-year-old Margaret Palstra to her grandmother, Jacoba. It is written neatly in ink, using a nibbed pen, and is reproduced faithfully here.

Teignmouth Devon 10.9.29

Dear grandmother,

Thank you very much for your letter. I had been wondering where all the letters had gone before, but at last I got one. I have not got much to tell you about school, only that I won a second prize at the school sports. Why I can't tell you much about school is that I am on my holidays. We are down at Teignmouth where there is a lovely beach. We have had some lovely weather, and I have been in bathing quite a lot. Billy [Margaret's younger brother, aged one year] has been in too, and he loved it. There are some ponys [sic] on the beach and Jocelyn and I have had rides on them. One day Daddy mother and I went on the rocks the other side of the harbour. We had great fun leaping over the rocks. We had to go over on a ferry, and all the sprays that the ferry made kept coming up on us. On the other side of the rocks was a dear little beach.

I have been for some rides in the car too. One day we went to dartmoor [sic] and saw some wild ponies. We took a photo of a mother and her foal. Some time ago, daddy and me went up a very big hill we can see from our house. When we got to the top of the hill we found that there were a lot of blackberries there, and we got a lot this afternoon. They were lovely, I wish you could have had some.

I must go to bed now so good night. heaps of kisses from

your loving granddaughter

Margaret

May's caption: "A Teignmouth joy"

May's caption: "Durance vile"

May's caption: "The journey home from Devon. Stonehenge in background."

Charles Palstra and the Prickly Pears

Around this time Will's 36-year-old Anzac brother Charles, who had been traumatised during the war, was enduring a hard life. He'd obtained a job poisoning prickly pear in outback Australia. This was a job nobody wanted, so he must have been desperate for work.

Since 1788, people had been importing cochineal insect-infested prickly pear plants (Opuntia) to Australia, with the view of starting a dye industry. Cochineal insects, from which a red dye is extracted, thrive only on Opuntia species.

Being an extremely vigorous, invasive species with no natural predators in Australia, the cacti flourished, virtually exploding across the landscape. Thousands of acres of land became choked with masses of impenetrable, thorny vegetation.

Removing the plants frequently cost more than the land was worth, so many farmers simply abandoned their infested properties. Eventually 40,000 square km (15,000 square miles) of farming land became unproductive and impassable. Photographs from that era show dense tangles of vicious thorns stretching to the horizon.

At that time, poison was the only effective method of control. Charles Palstra became part of a team operating a wheeled poison-spraying machine.

Throughout the Australian outback the wildlife, the stock, the people, the soil, the rivers and creeks, the native flora and the crops all suffered severely from mass poisonings. The government continued to claim the poison was "safe", and "the soil bacteria is [sic] not affected," despite the fact that arsenic is toxic to all living things. Short term exposure can lead to symptoms such as vomiting, abdominal pain, brain damage, skin lesions and bloody diarrhoea. Prolonged exposure can be fatal. Gallipoli veteran Charles Palstra, wounded twice during the war, now had arsenic poisoning.

". . . he was just a skeleton by what he was when I saw him last;" wrote his mother in June 1929. "He had good clothes on, but they hung on him. He says that he got severely poisoned by fumes supervising the destroying of prickly pear, and had been for seven months in the hospital . . ."

The countryside was infested with a dense tangle of prickly pears. Photo taken in Chinchilla, Queensland, during the 1920s. Source : qcl.farmonline.com.au

Will's parents Jacoba and Wiebe were so intent on retiring in Australia that they bought a house in Surrey Hills. With three of their married children living in that suburb, it seemed the perfect place to settle down when their wandering days were over.

1929: The Imperial Airship Scheme

Lord Thompson returns

1929 saw a new Labour government take office, with Lord Thomson re-appointed Secretary of State for Air. However, his arrival coincided with mounting concerns about the R100 and R101 airship projects, already facing delays and budget overruns. Driven by a personal passion for airships and a fervent ambition to become Viceroy of India, Thomson exerted immense pressure on both teams, particularly favouring the R101. His vision? A triumphant voyage to India in 1930 aboard this luxurious behemoth, a spectacle guaranteed to solidify his claim to the coveted position of Viceroy.

Ambition, however, often clashes with reality. Ignoring warnings from airship experts, Thomson fixated on this grand launch, refusing to acknowledge the R101's true capabilities. Engineers scrambled to meet his demands, proposing impractical solutions like gas cell extensions and new bays, all requiring months to complete. Ignoring logistical constraints and potential safety concerns, Thomson fixated on a September 1930 flight, setting the stage for a series of decisions that would ultimately contribute to the R101's doom.

Peter Davison argues that ironically, it was Thomson's support that kept the project afloat, attracting funds through his charisma and his close relationship with Prime Minister Ramsay MacDonald. However, this pressure to meet his personal goals may have contributed to the overlooking of safety concerns and ultimately, the R101's tragic fate.

"Without Thomson's backing the scheme might never have started and would certainly have faced cutbacks in the face of an approaching recession."[36]

In later years, many airship experts would blame Thomson for putting pressure on the R101 team.

The pressure grows

Graf Zeppelin continued her successful flights. In August 1929, she created a worldwide sensation. Captained by Hugo Eckener, she became the first airship to circumnavigate

---

36   Davison, 2015

the globe. This dramatic feat gripped the imagination of millions. It also stirred up the rivalry of other airship-developing nations, who were impatient to challenge and outdo the daring exploits of their erstwhile enemy, Germany.

Rivalry also existed between the builders of the R100 and the R101—the privately-owned Airship Guarantee Company, and the state-owned Royal Airship Works at Cardington.

```
The Advertiser (Adelaide, SA: 1889-1931)
Sat 26 Oct 1929 Page 15
Empire Airship Rivalry London, September 18, 1929.
By T. STANHOPE SPRIGG, Editor of "Airways"


As the time draws near for the two Empire airships R100
and R101 to emerge from their seclusion and embark on
their trials it becomes plain that there is a rivalry
in the airship camps which may prove to be even bitterer
than that between German Zeppelin and British rigid.
It is the rivalry between the builders of R.100 and
R101. . .
```

It is believed that one unfortunate consequence of this rivalry was that the two teams working on these experimental aircraft were reluctant to share information with each other.

Inspection of the R101

On 3 October 1929 a party of journalists was invited to board the R101 at Cardington for an inspection tour. Here's a report from one of them:

The Sydney Morning Herald (NSW: 1842—1954)
Sat 2 Nov 1929 Page 16
AIRSHIP R101.
The Completed Giant. INSPECTION IN HANGAR.
(FROM OUR SPECIAL CORRESPONDENT.)
(By Air Mail from Perth.) LONDON, Oct. 3.

Australia has a keen interest in the Government airship R101. If its trials are successful, it will make the voyage to the Commonwealth as soon as facilities are ready there to receive it.. . .

. . . Just before construction was completed and the trials began, a crop of adverse rumours arose concerning R101, and it was partly to allay these suspicions and partly to provide the public of the Empire with eye-witnesses' accounts of the great ship that the Air Ministry yesterday provided an opportunity for representatives of the Press to inspect her.

. . . STAGGERING IMMENSITY.

When looking at the R101 in its hangar at the Royal Aircraft Works at Cardington, near Bedford, one is staggered by the immensity of the elongated egg-shaped bag which envelopes everything in the airship except the navigating cabin and the five engine units.
These are suspended by strong steel girders from the steel frame inside the envelope, which is painted silver grey. Of its bulk, figures give the best impression. From end to end it is 732 feet. At its thickest part the envelope has a diameter of 132 feet. If it were moored in Martin-place, it would reach almost from George-street

to Castlereagh street. With its control car resting on the ground, the top of the envelope would be only a few feet below the highest building in that street. Given this comparison, it must be left to the reader's imagination to understand the impression of immensity which a first glimpse into the Cardington hangar brought. Much of the immensity is waste space, for there are 16 huge circular gasbags inside the envelope, strung to the miles of steel girders, crosspieces and longitudinals which form the tremendously strong framework of the airship.

Likening the whole to the human body, this framework might be called the skeleton; the gasbags, the flesh; the miles of wiring, and other connections, the arteries; the navigating and control room, the nerve centre. As the human frame is no stronger than its weakest bone, so R101's health and strength depends on the staunchness of its steelwork. In this there is no weak part. The smallest section has been tested for stress and strain, both before and after its installation. Nor is there any doubt concerning the gasbags. The fabric of these and the goldbeater's skin covering it have been subjected to the most severe tests. The same can be said for the engines.

These are of the most experimental order, burning crude oil instead of petrol.

Installed in the R101, they have satisfied the designers

and constructors that their faith has been justified. They may be heavier than originally proposed; they may not be powerful enough to drive the giant as rapidly as was planned. But security has been the first and last thought in the minds of the builders. R101 is an experiment.

Better performance has been sacrificed to security and safety. If R101 is a success, modifications have already been proved practicable to make succeeding airships faster and more powerful without sacrificing security.

PASSENGER ACCOMMODATION.

To inspect the airship, we first had to don rubber-soled shoes to prevent possible damage by ordinary footwear. We climbed up a ladder through a hatchway in the bottom of the envelope, and found ourselves in a corridor on the lower deck. A guide conducted us to the passenger deck, where we saw a dining-room to seat 50, and served by a lift from the electric kitchen on the lower deck; a smoking-room with fireproof walls and duralinium [sic] floor; a row of small cabins, each containing two narrow berths, the latter being placed one above the other, as in a ship's cabin; and the spacious lounge-room.

The latter is the best room on the ship. It extends from one side of the envelope to the other. Windows of safety- glass placed in the fabric of the envelope enable a passenger to survey the country over which the airship is travelling. It was easy to imagine that the raised platform for deck chairs at each side of the lounge will be the most popular part of R101 when it is carrying passengers, for the rest of the passenger accommodation is cramped.

Corridors are narrow, the sleeping cabins are small, the rooms where the washing basins are installed are not large enough to be comfortable. It was impossible to understand how 50 passengers could ever live for a fortnight in these quarters, to say nothing at the discomforts which the crew must suffer in their even more cramped quarters. A voyage could be undertaken for novelty, but it was difficult to envisage travellers patronising the airship on long voyages for any other reason.

A TUNNEL-LIKE CORRIDOR.

There were other interesting parts of the airship to inspect. From near the dining room, we stood in a corridor, less than three feet wide, that ran for 100 yards towards the nose of the ship. It was like a long, narrow tunnel, sloping upwards as if following the oval shape of the ship. The corridor was lined with coarse fabric, which hid the series of gasbags and steel framework on either side. We walked along the "tunnel" and came out on a level platform, which is raised into the shape of the fabric while the ship is in flight, but on arrival at a mooring tower is let down as a landing stage, leading to the lift in the tower.

Standing on the extreme edge of this, the floor of the shed was 100 feet below; the tip of the airship's nose about 10 feet above.

In a small cabin at the tip of the nose is machinery for use when the airship is being moored. This cabin is reached by a long, gradually-sloping ladder from a bay off the main corridor. The machinery in it consists mainly of three powerful winches, around each of which is wound 300 yards of threeinch steel ropes. In explanation of the mooring, it may be said that the ropes are played out as the ship approaches the tower, and allowed to trail on the ground.

The end of each is attached by a ground staff to corresponding ropes trailing from the top of the tower. The ship's winches then wind the rope and the ship is drawn gradually and evenly to the tower. When the ship's nose touches the tower, a projecting cone is lowered from the nose into a groove on the tower, and there secured by a locking device with a swivel arrangement, which permits the airship to swing according to the prevailing wind. In this cabin in the nose are also connections to the main supply of electric current, water, gas, air, and fuel when the ship is riding at the mooring tower.

THE NERVE CENTRE.

In a bay towards the end of this corridor is the airship's nerve centre—the navigating, control, and wireless rooms. The former carries a chart table, and an arrangement of controls for manipulation of gasbags, water ballast, engines, and electric current. One man, standing in front of this board, has all these controls within an arm's length of him.

There is an indicator board, like the telegraph of a steamer's engine-room, to tell him the effect of his movements. A perpendicular flight of 20 steps leads down to the control cabin, which, as previously described, projects below the envelope. This will be the place of the officer on duty, and he has before him instruments similar to those on a ship's bridge, with several extras necessary for aerial navigation and manoeuvring.

```
He is assisted in this work by two coxswains, who have
in their charges, wheels like a small helm of a ship
to steer and raise or lower the airship. Adjoining
the chartroom is the wireless-room, where instruments,
ingenious in their compactness, will enable messages to
be transmitted over a range of 3000 miles, and received
for 300 miles. There is also apparatus for telephonic
reception.


TREADING NEW PATHS.


There are many other wonders in this greatest of all
aeronautical experiments, but enough has been written to
prove what new paths have been trod by British airship
experts.
. . . it was, and is, the hope that if the airships
prove technically satisfactory, steps will be taken
which will lead to the establishment of regular airship
lines. . .
```

Modifications to R101 in 1929

After the airship's trial flights in 1929, even with 138,490 cubic metres of hydrogen in her bags, R101 didn't have enough lift to maintain her ideal flying height of 457m. She then spent six months in Cardington Shed No. 1 while the wire nets holding the bags were lengthened, increasing the volume of gas to 141,460 cubic metres. The many holes that had appeared in all but one of the bags were repaired and the metal joints padded to prevent further chafing.

THE DESIGN OF THE R101

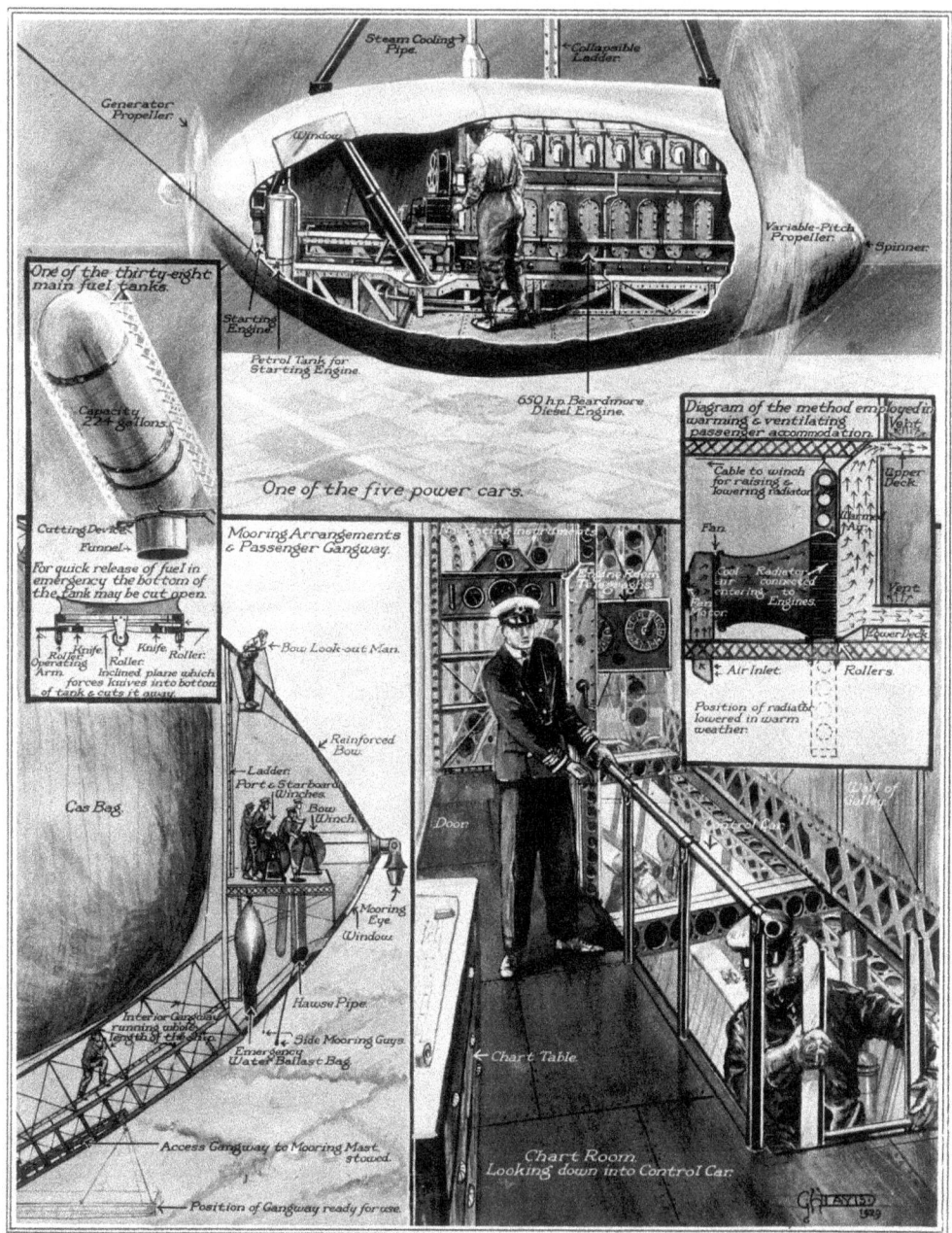

Source: Chronicle. Alamy ID: 2M3NJ7R

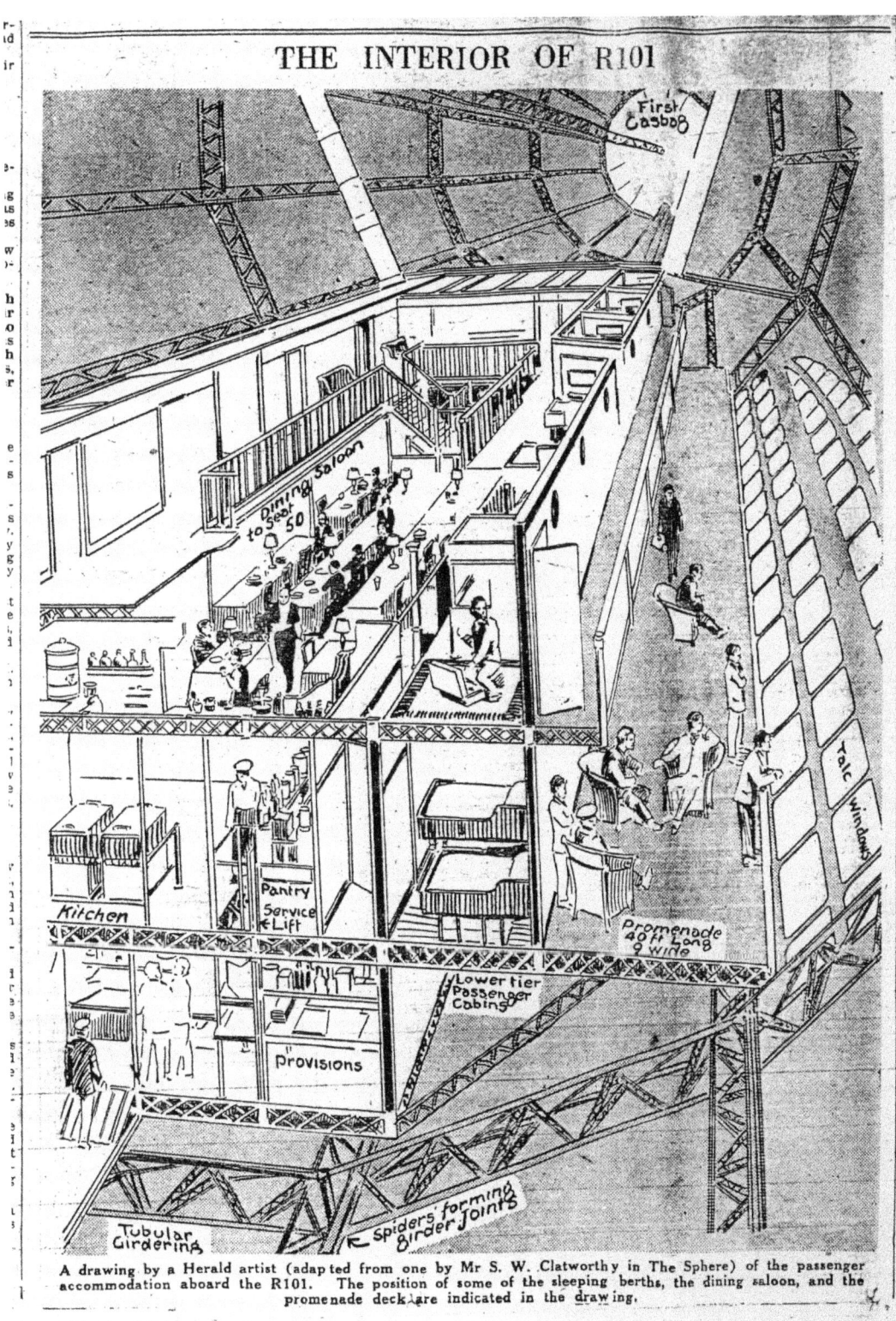

Source: The Herald, 1929. C.P. Hall corrects the headline: this is in fact R100's passenger compartment, very similar to that of R101.

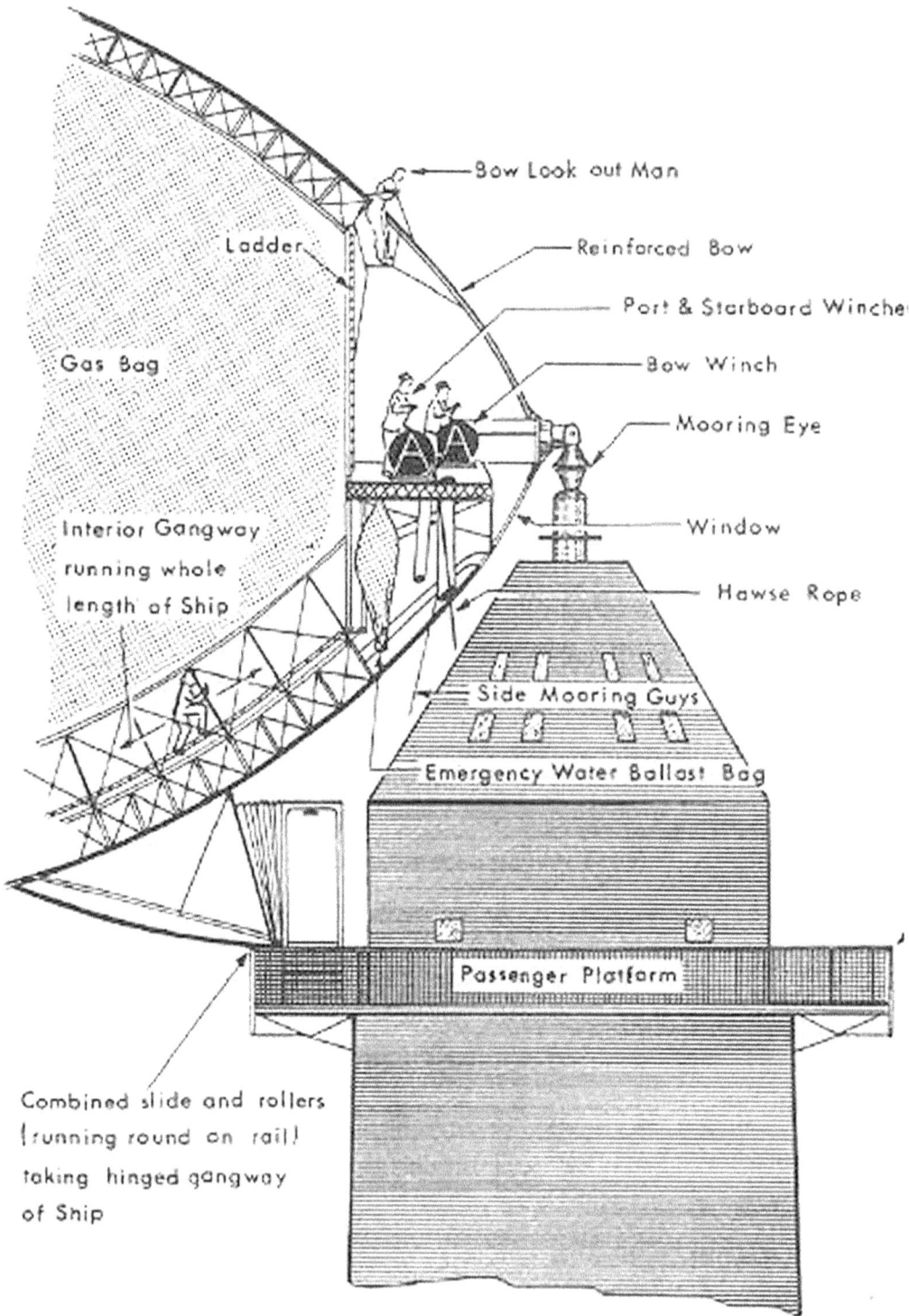

"A plan of the masthead and entry to the airship"
From: Mooring Mast Technical Information, Testing, Construction and Designs
Image (C) The Airship Heritage Trust

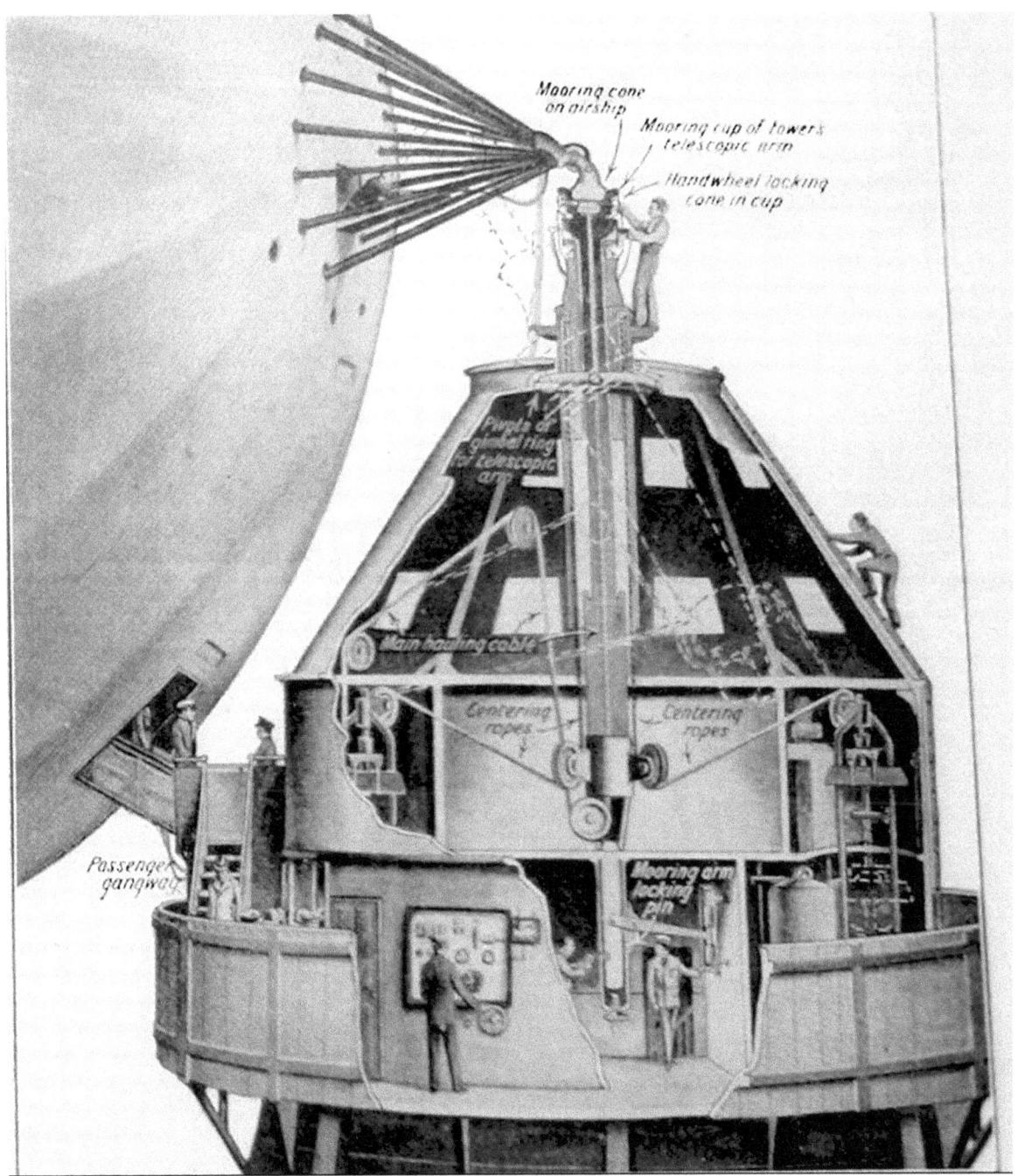
The head of a mooring mast. Image (C) The Airship Heritage Trust.

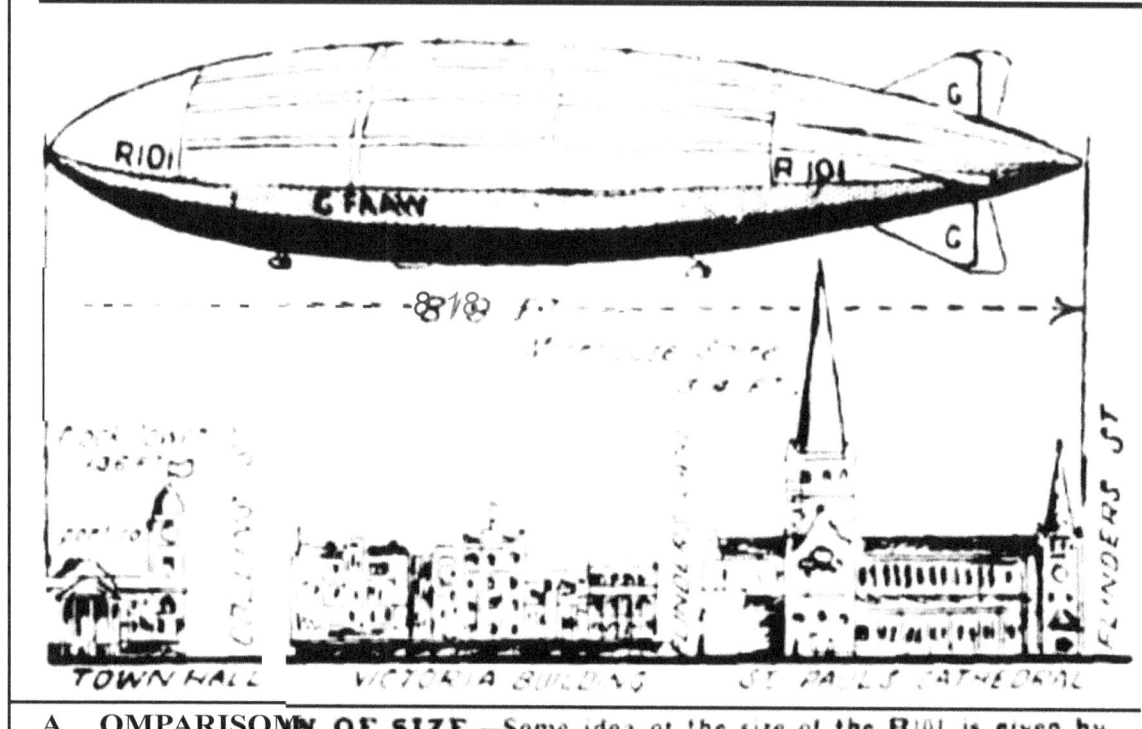

"A comparison of size—some idea of the size of the R101 is given by this drawing to scale of the airship compared with the buildings on the eastern side of Melbourne. "
Image from The Argus, circa 1929.

AIRSHIP CONSTRUCTION MATERIALS

References to "goldbeater's skin", a component of early twentieth century airships, deserve some explanation. Aviation fabrics in the early 20th century were primitive compared to modern materials. They were largely derived from plants and animals.

The R101's internal gas bags were lined with goldbeater's skin, which is the processed outer membrane of the intestine of an animal, usually an ox. The name stems from its traditional use by the makers of gold leaf. Goldbeaters used to interleave layers of this material between sheets of gold stock while beating the gold to a thinness 120 times less than the width of a human hair, thus producing many "leaves" simultaneously. Goldbeater's skin was used in airships because it is gas-impermeable and has a high strength-to-weight ratio. The skins were imported from the Chicago cattle market. Tissue from approximately a million animals was used to make the gasbags of one airship.

The gas bags unfortunately absorbed moisture quite readily, which weakened them and made them susceptible to rip if exposed to the wind by a break in the cover.[37]

The airship's outer covering, on the other hand, was made from linen, a textile made from the fibres of the flax plant. Airship builders would pre-paint the linen panels with aircraft "dope", a liquid lacquer that is applied to fabric stretched over airframes. "Dope" shrinks and stiffens the fabric, supposedly making the aircraft airtight and weatherproof. By the early 20th century, a wide variety of doping agents was being used. Many of them were manufactured from wood pulp, which is rich in cellulose. Typical doping agents included nitrocellulose (also known as gun cotton), cellulose acetate and cellulose acetate butyrate, all of which are highly flammable.

On airships, the pre-doped fabric turned out to be unsatisfactory. Many of the linen panels split due to fluctuations in atmospheric humidity. Airship captain George Meager commented that,

> "The outer cover [of R100] leaked badly. This meant that the gasbags became soaked if the airship flew or was moored in rain. This was a potential danger as the gasbags were not designed to withstand wetting."[38]

Moreover, over time and with weather exposure, the doped fabric outer coverings were prone to deterioration and splitting.

---

37   Long Branch Mike, 2016
38   Meager, 1961

THE R101 TAKES TO THE SKIES

Finally, well behind schedule, the R101 was ready for her first trial flight. On 14 October, 1929 she carried a group of RAW officials over central London. Lunch was served during the flight.

```
Mirror (Perth, WA: 1921—1956)
Sat 13 Dec 1952 Page 9
October 14, 1929, dawned a perfect day, and the workmen
at Cardington, Bedfordshire, sang at their work as they
hauled the airship R.101 from her hangar for the first
of her air trials.. .
```

Imagine dawn spreading a pale light across the airship base at Cardington. Somewhere far off, faint, a rooster crows. Dew glitters on the grass bordering the tarmac, and shimmers on the gable roofs of the two enormous airship hangars. The sun's rays first touch the corrugated steel sheets that clad the walls of the new Shed Number Two, in which R100 will soon be housed, before illuminating Shed Number One, standing close by, to the west. In that shed, the R101 sleeps.

Shadows gather in the narrow alley between between the hangars.

Side by side the huge edifices loom in the growing daylight. Both airship hangars are 812 feet long, 180 feet high and 275 feet wide. They contain bays of steel portal framing, with double side aisles used as workshop annexes, and huge central nave. Enormous doors at both ends soar to the full height and width of their naves.

As the sun rises, Cardington Airship Base comes alive with movement. A bevy of motor trucks appears, snorting exhaust fumes, and men climb briskly out. Some disappear into a side door of Shed Number One. A party of about thirty groundsmen wearing flat caps—some in shirtsleeves and vests, others wearing coats because the air was chilly—man the four arms of two large capstans, four men to each arm, and others help on the outer rim, winding back the doors of Shed Number One.

The R101 in her hangar, Shed No 1. www.carnetdevol.org

The mighty portals swing wide to reveal a huge, rounded silver nose rearing above the ant-like human beings who scurry across the ground. Men crawl over gantries and climb up ladders. The R101 floats several feet above the floor, straining at her tethers.

The refuelling crew swarms around the docked craft. Pumps drone as hydrogen gas is piped from the on-site hydrogen plant into the gasbags, topping up the airship's fuel in readiness for the journey ahead.

Riggers and engineers are already aboard, inspecting the gasbags and the engines. The captain, along with the steering and altitude coxswains, climbs down the ladder from the chart room into the control car that depends from the airships' belly. They check and test the control mechanisms.

At length, a groundsman blows a whistle. In the shed, all talk ceases. Attention turns to a man standing on the concrete apron in front of the giant doors. Raising a megaphone to his lips he commands, "Release the ship".

The taut docking wires against which the airship tugs are released, while a team of around two hundred men grabs hold of the cables that trail from her underside from bow to stern. Some take hold of a metal lattice affixed to the control car, while others grasp handles on each of the five exterior engine cars.

"Walk her forward," comes the order, and the team begins to pull. The R101 begins to move.

Slowly they tow the floating giant out of the airship shed.

Inside the control car the captain and the coxswains kept their eyes on the white guide-lines painted on the ground outside the shed. With only 7.6 metres (25 feet) between the sides of the airship and the shed door frames on each side, there's little room for error. The steering coxswain works the rudders gently, almost imperceptibly, to help keep the airship moving in a straight line.

A white bag hangs from the airship's nose. It's filled with balls of shot to weigh it down, and serves as a guide to help the ground crew line up the airship as they draw her forth. She emerges, poking her head out into the pale light of the October morning.

It takes more than three minutes for the full 731 ft (223 m) length of her body to get clear of the shed. Last to appear is her towering tail fin. As this passes under the doorway a groundsman at the rear gives the "all clear".

R101 is outside in the world at last, shimmering and hovering overhead in the morning light, quivering, alive and eager to fly.

In their relief and joy, four hundred men let out a mighty, spontaneous cheer.

A queen attended by her minions, R101 floats majestically, away from the sheds, across tarmac and concrete paving to the Cardington mooring-mast. Inside her control car the coxswains manoeuvre levers and switches. The groundsmen let the cables slip gradually through their hand, giving the airship some slack, allowing her to ascend gracefully, until the coupling on the tip of her nose makes contact with the matching socket at the very apex of the mast's roof, where it is locked into place.

R101 emerging from her hangar, towed by ground crew. [en.wikipedia.org]

Onlookers watch as the R101 is hauled to her mooring mast in 1929. airshipsonline.com

Strong sideguys hold her down. They are attached to twenty-four snatch-block anchor points embedded in concrete, sunk securely into the surface of the airfield, flush with the ground. These are spaced in a circle around the mast at a radius of 750 feet from it, and are capable of taking a maximum pull of 25 tons in any direction.

With her long body floating horizontally, the airship is now held captive. There she waits to cast off, gently bobbing, as the sun continues to rise and cast a silver sheen across her mighty hull; His Majesty's airship R101.

You can watch part of this 21 Oct 1929 trial flight on YouTube:

- "R101 Airship" on the British Movietone channel
- "R101, Britain's Million-Pound Monster, Comes to London (1929)" on the BFI channel (British Film Institute)
- "R101's Triumph (1929)" on the British Pathé channel

```
The Argus (Melbourne, Vic.: 1848—1957)
Wed 16 Oct 1929 Page 7
R.101 OVER LONDON. FIRST TRIAL FLIGHT.
World's Largest Airship. Fifty-two Persons on Board.
(British Official Wireless) LONDON. Oct. 14.


The new British airship, the R.101, made a successful
trial flight to-day. At 20 minutes past 11 o'clock, the
R.101 was released from the mooring mast at Cardington
(Bedfordshire). The water ballast was let out, and the
airship drifted in the wind to gain height. Then the
engines amidships were started, and the leviathan air
liner moved majestically southward. After travelling
for 12 minutes, the commander (Major Scott) sent out the
wireless message:
```

"Everything is going well. The ship is behaving splendidly." At a height of about 1.200 feet the airship circled over Bedford, affording a magnificent view to thousands of watchers. No attempt was made to attain great speed, and only the three back engines were running. The airship made for London, passing over Hitchin, Luton, Leighton Buzzard and Saint Albans. At half-past 1 o'clock the R.101 was over Hampstead, a northern suburb of London, and five minutes later it was flying low over the city."

The great airship passed over the Palace of Westminster and St Paul's Cathedral.

"As it was lunch hour, there was the maximum number of people in the streets, and the traffic was delayed by the spectators gazing at the airship. From the windows and roofs of offices and shops people watched the R.101 manoeuvre over the city. Three aeroplanes acted as escort.

The R.101 was moving at only 40 miles an hour, and the aeroplanes, appearing like midgets against her, had to dive and climb, twist and turn, in order not to outstrip her.

General admiration was expressed by the spectators at the graceful lines of the air monster. It had the appearance of a huge silver fish gliding through the sky. Having circled over London for half an hour, the R.101, rising higher, turned northward, and in an hour it was back at Cardington. . .

```
Return to Mooring-mast.
Cheers greeted the return of the R.101 over the mooring-
tower. Many of the spectators, having become stiff-necked
through looking upward, relieved the strain by lying on
their backs. The airship began a slow descent from a
height of three quarters of a mile, contending with a
15 miles an hour breeze. The mooring was completed in
about 40 minutes.
```

This first trial flight had lasted only five hours and 40 minutes. There would, however, be others.

The R101 flying over the town of Bedford on her first trial flight, October 1929
Alamy ID: 2AW44NW

THE R100 COMES TO CARDINGTON

The R101's sister airship R100 made her first flight from Howden on 16 December 1929, to join the R101 at the Royal Airship Works at Cardington, Bedfordshire, where the recently- assembled Shed No. 2 was waiting for her.

Far away from all this excitement, Australian newspapers continued to report on plans for the much hoped-for air transport service that would diminish the distance between the northern and southern hemispheres.

```
The Argus (Melbourne, Vic.: 1848-1957)
Sat 30 Nov 1929 Page 19
AIRSHIP R.101 May Visit Australia. LONDON, Nov. 28.
It is understood that the Air Ministry hopes that the
airship R.101 will voyage to Australia in the spring.
This will mean that Australia will have to make an early
beginning with the erection of mooring masts which are
already available for the other connections between
Cairo and Karachi.
The arrangements for the Australian mooring mast rest
entirely with Australia. It is also hoped that the An-
glo-Australian aeroplane service will operate in 1930.
It is explained that the ground work in India is a little
slower than was expected but, nevertheless progress is
satisfactory.
```

PRIDE AND JOY

By the close of 1929 Will had successfully completed the course at the Royal Airforce Staff College.

<u>Confidential.</u>

<u>R.A.F. Staff College.</u>

<u>7th Course.</u>

<u>Commandant's report on Students at the end of the Course.</u>

Flight Lieut. W. Palstra.   Royal Australian Air Force.

A thoughtful, self-confident and strong personality who has taken the greatest interest in his work here, and has maintained a consistently high standard.

He has a well developed, keen and receptive mind, and is capable of sound reasoning and logical argument. He speaks exceptionally clearly and well, and writes in a good style.

An officer of outstanding ability who has proved himself to be one of the best students of the year. He will undoubtedly make a first class officer.

Recommended for p.s.a. (Passed Staff Air)

(Signed) E.R. Ludlow Hewitt.

Air Commodore. Commandant,

R.A.F. Staff College. Andover, (Hampshire, England)

29/11/29.

Will sent a copy of the commandant's report to his parents. Brimming with pride, his father wrote back, saying,

> ". . .I must say that which has been bottled up these weeks and have wanted to shout out all the time. I refer to your Report—what a splendid encomium it is and as both Mother and I are included with the wife, as having the right to glory and swell out a bit, I will make no apology for saying that I believe pride and satisfaction must have shown themselves very powerfully for all kinds of thoughts kept on thrilling me inside, as I read it. The sheet of paper will be kept as one of our treasures. You have my most hearty congratulations—we, Mother and I say to each other, why, of course we knew he'd get there and you will see what is still to happen, for this is not the end. Well, old Boy, its just splendid. Congratulations to you both. I'm glad for your sake and ours but also very specially for dear May's sake and for those of the boy and the girls, who will presently feel there's no one quite like their father. . .
>
> . . . I can imagine what must have occurred to you as you once more found yourself walking from the London terminus station to your office—shades of 1913—what a difference between then and now and so there should be for you have set yourself to it as a Greatheart. Shall I tell you where you, as has often been the case, entwined yourself round my heart? That you should succeed, and to it so gloriously seems to me to be sure almost without saying. . ."

How Wiebe's loving, glowing words must have pleased his eldest son! Like all those who knew Will, his father could not help but believe that he was destined for even greater things in the future. ". . . you will see what is still to happen, for this is not the end. . ."

Now that Will was no longer studying at Andover, the family moved to a new home in Thames Ditton, a suburban village on the River Thames, in Surrey. Like their homes in Surrey Hills and Andover, this one too had a name—"Melita".

PART XI: 1930

THE EMPIRE'S AIRSHIP

By January 1930, the R101 was still undergoing modifications at Cardington. An inspection on 20 January 1930 by officials of the Fabric Section had revealed serious deterioration of the fabric on the top of the airship in places where rainwater had pooled, and the officials ruled that it was necessary to add reinforcement bands along the whole length of the outer envelope.

For Will, life continued to be full of excitement and achievement. On 24 March 1930 he was appointed Liaison Officer for the Royal Australian Air Force with the British Air Ministry at Adastral House.

May's mother, 62-year-old Agnes Holdaway, accompanied by her friend Mrs. Harlow, travelled to England to stay with Will, May and the children. By the time they arrived, Will and May had hired a new maidservant, Doris, who doubled as a kind of nanny.

"Will has just come home," wrote Agnes Holdaway in a letter dated 15 April 1930, "and is saying he might get a chance to go in this new airship to Canada next month. He would like it and if I am with May, it would not be so bad for her."

"This new airship" going to Canada was the R100, sister to the R101.

You tan take a virtual tour of the R100 on YouTube: "Welcome Aboard the R-100" on the Airship Heritage Trust's channel. For more details of her flight, watch YouTube: "R. 100 and a Voyage Across the Atlantic" on the Airship Heritage Trust's channel, and "Airship Dreams: R100—Cardington to Canada and Back with Roger Allton" on the Bedford Creative Arts channel.

The R100 departed from Cardington on 29 July 1930, without Will aboard. She reached her mooring mast at the St-Hubert, Quebec Airport (outside Montreal) in 78 hours. The Canadians were fascinated with the enormous dirigible—more than 100,000 people visited her daily during the twelve days she remained in Montreal.

While in Canada, the airship also made a 24-hour passenger-carrying flight to Ottawa, Toronto, and Niagara Falls. She departed on her return flight on 13 August, reaching Cardington after a 57½ hour flight.

DESIGN OF THE R100

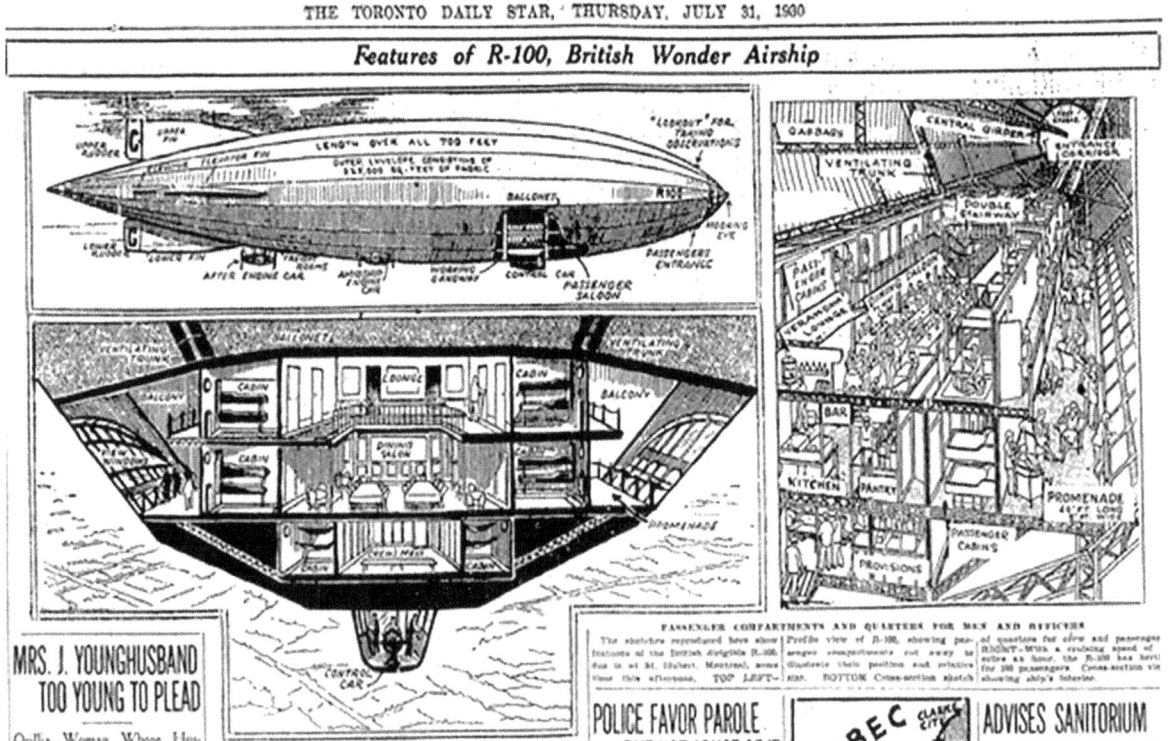

Toronto Daily Star, Thursday July 31, 1930. "Features of R100, British wonder airship."

Before the R100's transatlantic endurance flight, the Cardington team was in a position to suggest that neither of the two airships was ready for such a long haul. Nevil Shute Norway later suggested in his book "Slide Rule: Autobiography of an Engineer" that when R100 returned from Canada in triumph, the Royal Airship Works had to either make the flight to India or admit defeat. This would have harmed their reputations, possibly leading to the loss of their jobs.

ROAD TRIP TO WALES

Meanwhile in Thames Ditton, having two extra pairs of trusted hands available to look after the children allowed May and Will to go away on some sightseeing holidays together.

"I am finding it rather hard to write this letter today," wrote Agnes, "for May & Will went off this morning for a four days [self-driving] tour in Wales & altho' Doris (the maid) is here yet the children are always in my mind. I have just been having a "tea-party" with Margaret & Jocelyn & am expecting Doris in with Billy any minute…Will & May are still lovers & went off this morning as if they were going on their honeymoon."

Will's ill-health

While in Wales, Will suffered an attack of acute pain. Agnes wrote of their return from Wales,

"…May was half dead with anxiety, for Will had had one of those terrible turns which he had last year; terrible pains in his back and in the two days' drive home she had been terrified that he would faint at the wheel. He just put the car in the garage when he got home and went right into bed, and May sent for a doctor…"

Will rallied, but was admitted to the RAF Officers Hospital in Uxbridge for tests. From his hospital bed he wrote, on 5 May, 1930,

> Looking through the window it seems as if the day has been quite a fair one. The sunshine this morning was beautiful. I thought of our little brood playing in the garden at 'Melita' and the picture was a very pleasing and cheering one. Tell them Daddy sends them each his love and a kiss.
>
> Of course you my dearest are also very much in my thoughts. I am as much as ever in love with you as you know. I do want to make you happy. Remember me also to Mother.
>
> Your loving husband,
>
> Will.

The surgeons ended up removing Will's appendix. By Friday 30 May, he had recovered, been discharged from hospital and was attending the Anzac Day service in London. Because he was representing the RAAF, his presence at the service was reported far away in the Australian newspapers, accompanied by a group photograph.

```
The Argus (Melbourne, Vic.: 1848–1956)
Friday 30 May 1930 page 7

ANZAC DAY SERVICE AT LONDON.

Many well-known Australians and New Zealanders attended
the Anzac Day service at St. Clement Dane's Church,
London. In the group (left to right) are the naval rep-
resentative at Australia House (Capt. H. P. Cayley),
the Commonwealth military representative in London (Ma-
jor-General J. H. Bruche), the Minister for Trade and
Customs (Mr. Fenton), the liaison officer of the Royal
```

```
Australian Air Force (Flight Lieutenant W. Palstra),
the Australian High Commissioner in London (Major-Gen-
eral Sir Granville Ryrie), Sir George Fuller, General
Sir Ian Hamilton, General Sir W. Braithwaite, and the
High Commissioner for New Zealand (Mr. T. M. Wilford).
```

Will's sister in Australia cut out the article and photograph, and posted them to her parents in Indonesia. Jacoba would later write to Will,

"Blanche sent us a newspaper cutting, a group taken on Anzac day on which you stood amongst so many "big guns". I can tell you Dad was as proud as Punch, off it went to H.Q..."

ROAD TRIP TO SCOTLAND

Making the most of Will's returned health and the presence of the trusted babysitters, at 7.15 am on 6 June, 1930, Will and May set out from Thames Ditton in their aged but still useful Essex motor-car. An eight-page typed document by May, entitled "The Log of the 'Flying' Palstras," details their eleven-day camping road-trip through England and Scotland.

"May and Will have had a most wonderful time," wrote Agnes, "and have seen all sorts of things and places, been married again at Gretna Green by the blacksmith over the anvil."

Family photo albums illustrate the happy story. The tent they stayed in was rudimentary, as tents were in those days. It was no more than a couple of poles upholding a sheet of canvas, stretched taut by guy ropes whose pegs were—as seen in the photos—hammered into the ground by May. Their camp sites had no facilities. They were often on private farmland, surrounded by inquisitive cattle. They washed their clothes in streams or lakes.

The holiday was far from luxurious, but this couple were no strangers to a spartan life.

The Palstra family at "Melita", Thames Ditton, Surrey, with May's mother Agnes and her friend Mrs Harlow.

"Under the laburnum tree at Melita"

Road Trip to Scotland: Will and May camped at Bowness on Lake Windermere, 1930

May's caption: "The first house in Scotland just over the Sark bridge".

In Scotland on the road to Glasgow.

"Camp at Loch Fyne 9th June 1930"

Camp near Oban 10 June 1930

May's caption: "'Midge' Camp at the Trossachs 11th June 1930

May's caption: "Camp in Ochil Hills Scotland"

May's caption: "Camped in old quarry near Galashiels"

May's caption: "Camp in a field near Catterick (Yorkshire)"

May's caption: "Carter's Bar (The Border)"

May's caption: "Cow camp near Grantham - Lincolnshire 15th June, 1930"

Extract from "The Log of the 'Flying' Palstras" by May Palstra.

... We camped near Catterick Bridge, in a very pretty field which we christened "Cow Camp", as there were a lot of young heifers there. They were intensely curious and every now and then would come around and take great sniffs at our belongings. Mileage that day—145.

Before we left "Cow Camp" Will discovered that one of the wheel nuts was loose, so we crawled very slowly into Catterick where we had it adjusted.

We lunched in the beautiful city of York. The walls are in a good state of preservation, and we walked around them a little way and also had a good look at the "Mickle Gate", on which the heads of some very famous people have been exposed after execution. York Minster is just beautiful, both inside and out. The stained glass is glorious, and the spaciousness and lighting of the interior impressed us very much. The city abounds with quaint old houses, and we were sorry not to be able to explore it further. However, we had now to turn our faces homewards, and made for the Great North Road again. That night we camped at Grantham at 6.30 pm., having covered 153 miles.

The following day was the eleventh and last day of our trip. We left camp at 9.15 am. with 100 miles between us and Barnet on the outskirts of London. The road was perfect, traffic was light and we covered the distance in 2 1/2 hours, thus averaging 40 miles per hour for 100 miles.

We lunched near the Stag Lane and Hendon Aerodromes,[39] and were regaled by the Royal Air Force, who were very busy practicing for the Big Display.[40]

We reached home at about 4 pm. having covered 121 miles that day. Total mileage for the trip—1464 miles.

---

39   Hendon Aerodrome, in North London, played a key role in aviation from 1908 to 1968. It was from there that ground-breaking experiments took place. [Unit history, RAF Hendon. https://www.forces-war-records.co.uk/units/599/raf-hendon]

40   After the First World War, the first RAF "Pageant" was held at Hendon in 1920 [https://www.rafmuseum.org.uk/about-us/our-history/Hendon-cradle-of-aviation.aspx], and it soon became a regular event, known from 1925 as the Royal Air Force Display.

THE HENDON AIR DISPLAY

In Shed No.2 at Cardington, the airship R100 was being prepared to make the long flight to Montreal. She was to depart at the end of July.

Meanwhile the famous Hendon Air Display was to take place in June, and the R101 was selected to make a major public showing there. The team at the Royal Airship Works was keen to prove that the R101 was as good as the R100, if not superior.

On 23rd June 1930, the ground crew towed her out of No.1 Shed, and once again she was moored to the mast. The humid weather caused two splits to appear in her outer cover, which were repaired *in situ*. R101 made three flights in June 1930—a brief test flight to test her cover and her *in situ* repairs; the Hendon rehearsal, and the Hendon event.

On 28 June, R101 appeared over Hendon Aerodrome during the Royal Air Force Display. The great airship flew low over the heads of the excited crowds at about 500 feet. The watchers greeted the airship with exuberant acclaim.

She dipped her nose in salute to the King, who was present among the audience. Some of the crew and watchers thought that this change in pitch was, in fact, caused by serious instability.

According to Kingston and Lambert, the R101 had in fact gone into a steep dive, only pulled out by swift, skilful handling by the coxswain. Sweat was pouring down the height coxswain's face. "'It's as much as I can do to hold her up,' he gasped."

In *The R.101 Story*, Peter Davison comments that, "R.100's First Officer, George Meager, who was on his only flight in R101, then had to release ballast to assist the height coxswain during the return to Cardington who was 'fighting' to keep her level. Although Captain Irwin considered this unnecessary, the experienced Meager described it as 'the only time he ever got the wind up in a rigid' and requested not to fly in her again."

"Meager comments in *Leaves from my Logbook* page 55 (Meager, 1961): 'This should have warned them at Cardington that something was radically wrong somewhere. I am afraid, however, that the ship was so much the "apple of their eye," that they thought nothing could be wrong with her in spite of this heaviness at the end of each flight being a regular experience, judging by the amount of ballast that was dropped on each occasion.'"[41]

It is pretty certain that Will attended the RAF Display at Hendon in June 1930, and May might have accompanied him, because there's a photo of the event in the family archives. Newspaper photographs of the time show R101 flying above London on her way from Cardington to Hendon, her enormous cigar-shaped hull dwarfing the dome of St Paul's Cathedral.

R101 emerging from Shed #1, Cardington, at dawn. www.dailymail.co.uk

---

[41] Davison, 2015

W & K London. R101 THE WORLD'S LARGEST AIRSHIP No 199. OVER LONDON.

R101 over Hendon. eBay russtysilver (28805)

May's caption: "Air Force display at Hendon, England, 1930"

The R101 over Cardington 1929/1930

Cows graze as the R101 floats at her mooring mast in Cardington. [en.wikipedia.org]

The Argus (Melbourne, Vic.: 1848–1957)

Mon 30 June 1930 Page 9

AIR FORCE DISPLAY.

Scenes at Hendon.

New Types of Speed Craft.

(British Official Wireless) LONDON, June 28

Airship R.101 left her mooring mast at Cardington, and flew over London on her way to take part in the Royal Air Force display at Hendon. The King, the Prince of Wales and Duke of York, Cabinet Ministers, and diplomats were among those who watched the air pageant.

The pageant not only provided spectacular items illustrating British flying skill at its best, but gave evidence of technical progress far in advance of any achieved in the history of this notable service exhibition of flying.

. . . There were scores of aeroplanes, thousands of motor-cars, and 100,000 spectators, and the programme was gone through without a hitch.

A TICKET TO RIDE THE R101

Will was promoted to the rank of Squadron Leader on 1 July 1930. It was belatedly reported in the newspapers:

```
The Register News-Pictorial (Adelaide, SA: 1929—1931)
Tue 29 Jul 1930, Page 7
About People


The following promotions have been made in the Royal
Australian Air Force:- Flight-Lieuts. A. W. Murphy, W.
Palstra, and L. J. Balderson have been promoted squadron
leaders.
```

The first reference to the R101 in Will's archived letters occurs during this month. As the representative of Australia's Air Force, he was chosen to make the long-awaited trip to India aboard the R101. His job was to prepare a report for the British Cabinet on the prospects of inaugurating an airship service to Australia.

Originally Will's Australian colleague, Flight-Lieutenant Charles J. Harman was designated to undertake the journey, but in view of Harman's impending retirement, the arrangement was cancelled. The RAAF boss, Dicky Williams, asked Will to take Harman's place.

"The next few months promise a variety of interest," Will wrote to his brother- in-law Allan on 14th July. "The good old Aussie Govt. have appointed me a delegate to an Aeronautical Congress at the Hague in September. They have also agreed that I may travel in R101 to India and back in the autumn... If all goes well, I aim at leaving for Melbourne in December [1930] or January [1931]..."

"Will has not been too well," wrote Agnes in a letter with the same date as Will's. "He has worn off the good the rest and 'stuffing' he had to do in hospital and neither takes enough rest or food to keep up his nervous energy. He is never still and always planning for the future..."

On July 28 Agnes wrote,

"May and Will are going to France next Friday for a week so I'll have the children again..."

THE TRIP TO FRANCE

Will wanted to take his wife with him or a return journey to the battlefields of France, twelve years after the end of the war. They set out on Friday 1 August. On this trip, the couple travelled by public transport and stayed at Salvation Army hostels, which were cheap and far from luxurious, but an improvement on the tent that had accommodated them on their Scottish tour. Will wrote a jocose description of the holiday, which May later typed, calling it "Log of our trip to Belgium and France."

Having secured two capable nursemaids—Mother and Mrs Harlow—at a cheap rate, namely a little food and lots of responsibility, May and I started off from Victoria Station, London, on the morning of Friday August 1st, 1930, to see the "Continong".

We had booked through the S.A. Immigration office, and I had written to the Army Hostels at Ostende, Ypres, and Arras a few days before. There had been no time for replies, but we did not mind. Once again we were a carefree honeymoon couple.

Getting a seat on the train at Victoria was a case of scramble for your life. However, we came off very well, securing corners opposite each other...

The journey to Dover was uneventful. We had some beef tea, surveyed the landscape— beautiful Kent—and felt that we had at last solved the age-old riddle: "What shall we do with Grandmas?"

At Ostende, they—

". . . peeped at the outside of the Casino, but my newborn Highland caution got the better of me. In case the allusion seems strange be it known that after our Scotch trip I claim to be descended from the Highlands, having accomplished the feat in the amazing space of one day. . ."

In Antwerp the next day they visited the International Belgian Exhibition, where they proudly "Blew out our chests at the British pavilion—a good show and a credit to the Empire." Like so many Australians at that time, Will draws no distinction between being British and being Australian.

Ticket to the International Belgian Exhibition, purchased and saved by Will and May.

On the Sunday they arrived in Brussels, Belgium, where, ". . . we gazed at the outside of the house in the Rue de l'Évêque where we lived and where Dad was so ill."

In some ways, in the August of 1930 Will was coming full circle. He and May were taking photos of each other outside a house in which he'd lived in 1896, when he was about five years old. Later he would revisit landmarks and battlefields that had seared themselves vividly on his memory.

"Next morning off again early for Ypres, where we stayed at the fine S.A. [Salvation Army] Hostel ... During the morning viewed the magnificent Menin Gate Memorial. Over the gate is the British Lion looking ever towards the old front, and underneath the following stirring inscription: 'To the armies of the British Empire who served here from 1914 to 1918, and to those of their dead who have no known grave.' Inside the Arch there is another inscription which reads:

'Here are recorded the names of officers and men who fell in the Ypres salient, but to whom the fortune of war denied the known and honoured burial given to their comrades in death'.

"There are tens of thousands of names written all over the walls of the huge structure. I stood besides those of my own battalion, the 39th AIF. Poor Southby, Grant and Nichols—how their names brought back memories."

"In the afternoon we had a drive round the battlefields of the salient. Gone was the former bog of shell torn country, gone was the barb [sic] wire, the wreckage of war, derelict tanks and guns, and the dead who used to lie unburied for months. All is now a smiling countryside of which every inch is cultivated. No unevenness of the ground remains where once were trenches and craters. The only relics of the titanic struggle are an occasional concrete redoubt [fortified concrete "pill-box"] not yet blown up, and the cemeteries where the dead lie in their thousands and thousands. In the salient I found it impossible to realise I was on the same ground where I had taken part in the struggle for Zonnebeke and Passchendaele."

May standing beside a ruined concrete "pillbox" on a old battlefield

"We visited Tyne Cot British Cemetery... The British cemeteries are lovely gardens where amongst roses and lavender stand rows upon rows of tombstones headed with the regimental crest and inscribed with the name of the dead lying below. We saw many Rising Suns, the badge of the A.I.F. We passed 'Hell Fire Corner,' marked by a cairn whereon are inscribed the words 'Ici fut arrete L'envahisseur 1918' [Here the invader was stopped in 1918]. Evidently the highwater mark of the German onslaught in the spring of that year."

May at Tyne Cot cemetery

"After supper that night we returned to the Menin Gate to witness the ceremony of the sounding of the Last Post. This is done every night. The night was that of August 4th, anniversary of the Empire's entry into the War, and a large number of members of the British Legion was present. Four Belgian soldiers sounded that haunting melody from silver bugles. Then a moment's silence, followed by a Padre's voice saying 'They shall not grow old as we grow old. Age shall not wither nor time decay, and at the rising and the going down of the sun we shall remember them.'

"Then the voices of the Legion in unison, 'We shall remember them,' followed again by the Padre's benediction, 'Let your light so shine before men, that they may see your good works and glorify your Father which is in Heaven'. A ceremony grand in its simplicity and worthy of the best British traditions of quiet homage and reverence.

"What of Ypres itself? When I saw it last it was a heap of rubble. With the exception of a portion of the Cloth Hall, there was not one stone left standing on another. Gone is the wreckage and in its place a city of attractive houses, many of them built with the pleasing gables of the old Flemish style. It takes a good twenty- five minutes to walk the diameter of the town. A beautiful new Cathedral, a huge affair, is nearing completion. Not much work has yet been done on the Cloth Hall, indeed this is the only part of the town where ruins remain. Everywhere along the old battlefront we found the same amazing restoration. It is almost unbelievable to one who had seen it all during the years of war...

"On the morning of August 5th we set out by steam tram for Messines... Messines, which had crumbled before my eyes early in 1917, was almost completely rebuilt.

"We took our bearings to the south of the town, and with the aid of an old war map made for where Grey Farm ought to be, scene of the exploit which won me the Military Cross in the Battle of Messines, 7th June 1917. Although the view presented the usual smiling countryside with its fields of wheat-stocks and beet crops, the lay of the ground could not fail to bring back old memories. Here was where I had seen the tanks go into action, there the site of a German strong point.

"We found Grey Farm without difficulty. We lunched in a field of flax over which I had advanced on the day of the battle. Then we sought out the actual place where my gallant platoon had carried the strong point by assault. The River Douve made it impossible to go wrong, and in a few minutes we stood amid the ruins of the concrete redoubt which we took in the first charge.

"A little exploration along the hedge disclosed another concrete dugout forming part of the system. This one was still intact though more than half buried and filled with water. We found pieces of equipment and other signs of war including a Mills bomb, which we were careful not to touch.

"In front of Grey Farm where I had dug in after taking the position, there was a field of waving corn. We took some photos and then went to the farm, which had been rebuilt. Madame received us graciously, and seemed most interested to hear of my associations with the place. The name "Grey Farm" is of course a war map name. The actual name is La Petite Potterie, and the name of the farmer is Paul Coppin. After several cups of coffee we were allowed to go."

May at Grey Farm or La Petite Potterie.
The French farming couple can be glimpsed in the doorway.

Will at Grey Farm redoubt, Messines, August 1930

May in some deserted trenches. possibly at Vimy Ridge, August 1930

May among overgrown trenches on the Somme, August 1930.

"We tramped back to Messines village and had a look at the New Zealand War Memorial. Some more tramping towards Wytschaete, but being threatened with a divorce by my wife on the grounds of cruelty we caught the steam tram back to Warneton, the terminus, sat tight when we got there, and so eventually back to Ypres."

Will and May visited more war memorials and some of the vast military cemeteries that blanketed the landscape—the resting places of hundreds of thousands of young men.

"On the following day we accompanied an old Lancashire couple in the Field- Major's car to a distant cemetery where their son lies buried. It was

pathetic and distressing and brought home to both of us once again what anguish war brings in its train. The old couple come once a year. She said to me, 'He was a good lad. He just went away so bright and we never saw him again.' They were anxious we should see his grave. We went with them, but had to go soon, it was more than we could stand.

"At one cemetery we noticed an Australian grave with the following words cut at the bottom of the stone: 'Stars shine down on the grave I shall never see'. What a world of anguish and longing in those few words.

"From the cemetery the Field Major, at my special request, drove us down to the Somme. I wanted to find the Memorial of my old Division, the 3rd A.I.F. We found it at Sailly le Sec, and I took some photos of it. From there we travelled along the Bapaume road, passing Pozieres, where there is a Memorial to the 1st Division A.I.F., Charles' old Division."

Paris was their last stop. After enjoying its most popular sights they caught a train to Boulogne, and a ferry across the channel. They returned home by rail to the welcoming arms of their three young children.

Photos of May, possibly taken in Paris in August 1930

By late August the family was on the move again, following another step in Will's career. May's mother Agnes Holdaway was making preparations for her return trip to Australia. May writes,

"We have secured a furnished house at Fawley, about thirteen miles from Southampton, and two from Calshot, the seaplane station where Will will be doing his navigation course. It is right on the edge of the New Forest, and wonderfully pretty country..."

"It's a big job moving round with a family, but I'd rather have that job than stay here by myself for three months, especially as the summer will soon be over, and the dreary winter beginning once more. We are getting quite excited about our new move. It is rather a good thing that I will be very busy packing as soon as Mother departs, as I will miss her very much of course."

In Java on 8th September, Will's mother sat down to write him a letter filled with love and optimism. His 39th birthday would fall on 8th October, and the mail would take weeks to travel by steamship from Indonesia to England, so she ensured she would be able to post her letter early.

My dear Will,

I do hope, that today a month, this letter will promptly come in your hand, so that my hearty congratulations with your birthday be just in time. Again on such a day we feel full of gratefulness for the Lords preserving mercy and the many blessing received. May it be a very happy day spent with dear May and the children, and may many of them follow. . . Shall we be together next year? . . .

However we keep believing. Who knows, that after all the end of the year will bring the whole family here. . .

EXTREME MODIFICATIONS TO THE R101

Soon after the completion of both R100 and R101, it was obvious to all concerned that neither airship was capable of lifting its specified payload. The R101 in particular needed more lifting power, if she were to be commercially viable. The airship was "flying heavy", and something had to be done before the well-publicised trip to India could take place on schedule in October.

The Royal Airship Works tried loosening the gasbag wires to increase the gas capacity. This modification proved insufficient to fix the problem, so the design team decided on some extreme structural alterations. They would cut the airship in two across her central section, insert an extra bay to provide greater volume, and put her back together again.

The new 45 foot long bay would give an additional gross lift of 15.2 tons.

Thus, in June 1930, after the R101 flew over London during the Royal Air Force's Air Display, she returned to Cardington, where work commenced on lengthening her. Other alterations included two new reversible Beardmore Tornado diesel engines so, for the first time, all five engines could provide forward thrust while two engines could provide reverse thrust as well.

The modifications increased R101's total length to 777 feet (237 metres), while maximum diameter remained just under 132 feet. Her hydrogen capacity was now 5,508,800 cubic feet (approximately 155,992 cubic metres) in 17 bags, and her theoretical maximum flight speed was 71mph (114.2kph). The designers at the Royal Airship Works calculated that she could now lift a much heavier payload.

The R100, however, remained at her original size, with a gas capacity of around 5,000,000 cubic feet (approx. 144,400 cubic metres).

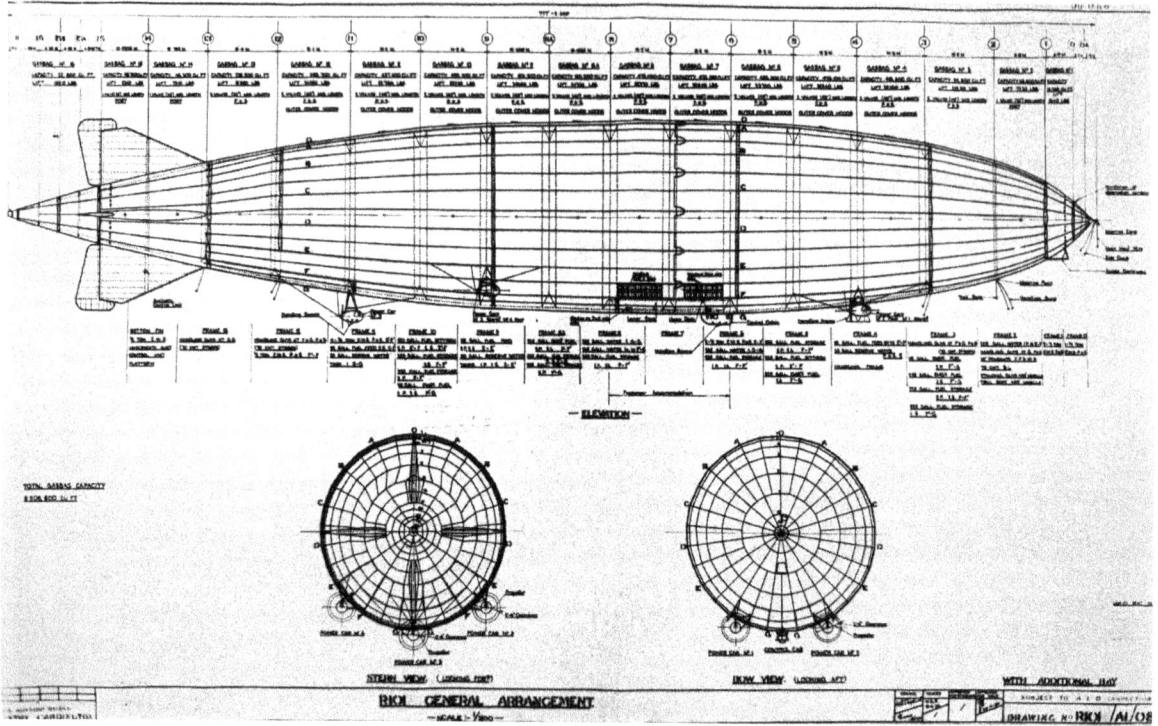

R101: Plan of General Arrangment in 1930, with additional bay.
Image courtesy of Airships Online, the website of the Airship Heritage Trust.

PLANS FOR THE FUTURE OF AIRSHIP TRAVEL

The craze for long-distance airship travel was reaching its peak. Everyone was talking about the R101, Britain's claim to long-distance travel, and her ambitious flight to India with which the Air Ministry would inaugurate a new Commonwealth Transport Service. Few doubted that during the coming decade, international airship services would fly back and forth along routes across the globe.

Flushed with success and optimism, the British government was already busy making plans for two more airships, bigger and better than R100 and R101, and a third, larger airship hangar at Cardington; Shed No.3.

In *To Ride the Storm*, Peter Masefield records that the Air Ministry decided to construct two more airships, R102 and R103, of 7,500,000 cubic feet (210,000 m3) capacity. It was expected that these enormous aircraft would be capable of carrying 50 passengers and ten tons of cargo for 4,000 mi (6,400 km).

They proposed that the R102 would enter service in 1934, and the R103 would follow in 1935, making a total of four airships in the Imperial Airship Service. Monthly return services to Montreal and Karachi would be offered, and there would be a weekly service to Ismailia in Egypt. In 1936 the service would be extended to Australia, for which an even larger airship, the R104, would be constructed.

According to the Airship Heritage Trust's online article *The Future: as at 1930 (R102, R103, R104): Imperial Airship Programme 1931-33*:

> "With the new ships being tested, plans were underway for the design concepts of the new class of Airships. Funding had been agreed and the design specifications drawn up. The budgets and plans had been agreed up to 1935. At Cardington the design team had already started plans for the next generation."

Airship expert C.P. Hall II adds, "R.102 and R.103 would be 7,500,000 cubic feet sister-ships based upon R.101 engineering enlarged. Hydrogen inflated, they would carry 50 passengers plus mail and freight 4,000 miles. For comparison LZ-129 Hindenburg containing 7,000,000 cubic feet of hydrogen could carry 50 passengers plus mail and freight over 6,000 miles in 1936."

Sir Peter Masefield wrote of the still larger proposed airship R104, "This ship would be capable of regular operations with a non stop travel to Egypt with a substantial payload. The ship would then move on with stops at Karachi, Rangoon and Singapore to Australia. It was expected to reach westwards to Montreal non stop in all weathers".

The Airship Heritage Trust's *The Future* article continues,

However it was agreed that Project H (R102) could carry out the same duties being a smaller ship, if additional masts were built for refuelling. Plans and land surveys were carried out at Malta and Baghdad on the India route, and at Monkton, New Brunswick on the Canadian route.

The future plans also included the lengthening of the Cardington sheds, and the building of one new shed capable of accommodating two ships side by side. An additional mast would also have to be built so that the R100 and R101 could run and operate services concurrently. This would also be backed up by a mobile transporter tower and supported by a second transporter tower at the Karachi base with its own shed and mooring mast. Recent research has confirmed that some three farms near Cape Town in South Africa had already been purchased by the Air Ministry with the intention to turn them in to an airfield with its own mooring mast.

The pressure for haste

Wing Commander Reginald B. B. Colemore, RAW Director of Airship Development, reported on 11th July 1930, "Every effort will be made to complete the [R101] as quickly as possible but we have no allowance in our programme to cover unforeseen delays."

In spite of all Lord Thomson's previous assurances that he would put safety first and never exert pressure on the team constructing and testing the airship, he did just that, writing on 14th July 1930:

> "As long as R.101 is ready to go to India by the last week in September this further delay in getting her altered may pass. I must insist on the programme for the Indian flight being adhered to, as I have made my plans accordingly."

Later, he grudgingly allowed the date of the Indian flight to be pushed back one week, to 4 October.

The R101's appearance and design might even have been superior to that of her rival, the R100. Her 777-foot hull was elegantly streamlined, but her power and steerage were complicated and significantly less efficient. Developmental issues like these could be expected with any adventurous project, and had the design team been given more time, they would probably have rectified most of them. The political pressure was enormous, however, and time was running out.

On 30 August Squadron Leader Palstra travelled as the official Australian delegate to the Hague in the The Netherlands for an RAF Aeronautical conference. Once again, it was almost as if he were coming full circle. The Hague is a city on the western coast of The Netherlands on the North Sea. Will now found himself only about 150km away from his birthplace in Zwolle. Many of his uncles and aunts and cousins, especially on Jacoba's side, still lived in this country, which they called "Holland".

Will's six-month job as Liaison Officer at Australia House in London came to an end on 22 September, 1930.

The single test flight

After all her modifications, the R101 did not fly again until October. In those final hectic months she was not only stretched, but the outer skin, particularly around the curved nose, was doped in place rather than replaced. The construction team had inserted the extra bay and fitted the reversible engines.

The new version of R101 was ready on 25 September, but bad weather postponed the final test flight. High winds delayed the airship's move from Number One Shed to the mooring mast. At last, on the evening of 30 September, the skies cleared sufficiently for a last-minute trial run the next day.

On 1 October the altered version[42] of the R101 took to the air for her one and only test flight before setting off for India. She was captained by Flight Lieutenant Herbert Carmichael "Bird" Irwin, one of the most experienced airshipmen in the British Isles.

It was originally intended that this would be a twenty-four-hour endurance flight, so that engine and other tests could be completed. Before the departure, however, Royal Airship Works officials agreed that if Scott[43] was satisfied that the ship was behaving as expected, then he could cut the flight short. This would allow more time to prepare the airship for the important flight to India in just two days' time.

This test flight was the only opportunity for a full speed trial of the newly installed reversible engines. However, due to mechanical problems in the forward starboard engine, the airship was unable to undertake that test. The sunny, calm weather conditions throughout the flight were perfect. The flight lasted only 16 hours 51 minutes, during which the calm weather conditions were close to ideal.

The R101 returned to her mooring mast next morning, 2 October. That same day the Aeronautical Inspection Department (AID) issued a Certificate of Airworthiness, in recognition that all was well with the empire's mightiest airship.

During all her eleven trial flights before her embarkation for India, the R101 had never undertaken a full-power test, or flown in bad weather. There is no doubt that the experts working on the airship knew the tests had been insufficient. Strangely, nonetheless, they did not show much evidence—at least in public—of being worried about it. Perhaps, either the overwhelming optimism of Thomson and his cronies somehow gave them a false sense of security, or they had blind faith in British ingenuity, or they trusted in the luck that had so far helped them survive the Great War and their subsequent daring aviation feats. Or perhaps they simply felt powerless in the face of such strong political pressure.

---

42 "The initial ship was described as R.101a; following the weight reduction it became R.101b; and finally R.101c with the extra bay and reversing engines." Source: Davison, 2015

43 Irwin was R.101's Captain, not Scott; however, Scott was on board, and his okay would be the operational deciding factor as to the airship's readiness, listened to by the officers above him.

Whether the R101 was actually ready for the long flight to India was open to dispute, but Lord Thomson was determined that Britain's airship was going to leave on the arranged date—4 October 1930—with himself on board. Only the elite were to accompany him on the trip—the highly trained airship crew and some of the top "brass" of the RAF. There were to be four specially privileged passengers. One of them, representing the Royal Australian Air Force, was Squadron Leader William Palstra.

```
The Canberra Times (ACT: 1926—1954)
page 4 Saturday 4 October 1930
FLIGHT TO INDIA
R.101 Now Ready TRIALS SUCCEED
LONDON, Thursday.
Flight-Lieutenant [sic] William Palstra, liaison officer
of the R.A.A.F., at present carrying on a three months
navigation course at Calshot, will represent Australia
aboard the airship R.101 on its flight to India.
He will report to the Government the aspects of the
flight of interest to Australia.
```

Preparations for the flight to India

For two days the R101 remained on her mooring mast at Cardington, while the crews busied themselves with last-minute preparations for her historic journey to India.

As the hour of the R101's departure approached, further evidence of the lack of communication between engineers and ministers, or general lack of comprehension of the weight problem, became apparent.

It was reported that visitors inspecting the airship—possibly members of Parliament—had commented on the lack of carpet in passenger areas.

Thus, at the request of the Secretary of State, the Royal Airship Works laid 2,630 square feet of pale blue Axminster carpet on the entrance gangway and in the lounge. That fitted carpet weighed 1,052 pounds. The weight of this heavy floor-covering counteracted many of the earlier weight-reduction initiatives.

It is extraordinary that after all the efforts to lighten the ship by lengthening it and jettisoning some non-vital mechanical devices, the R101 prepared to set off on her first official voyage bulging with bric-a-brac. In addition to the Axminster carpeting, heavy silver dining sets and cutlery were carried aboard. Elegant potted plants adorned the bamboo-furnished lounge and smoking room.

The luxury of the fitments can hardly be imagined in the modern age of streamlined plastic jet- travel. To compensate for additional weight, the crew had to leave their parachutes behind.

How could these luxuries have been permitted to weigh down the already overweight airship? Publicity was partly to blame, for at the Imperial Conference in London in November 1929, when the airship service had been announced, one reporter proudly claimed; "The R.101 will provide luxuries undreamed of by Jules Verne and H.G. Wells. It will positively be an aerial hotel."

Will's feelings about the trip

As for Squadron Leader Palstra—how did he feel about his forthcoming intercontinental voyage aboard the biggest airship in the world?

Will does not expand upon his feelings about the trip in his letters. This is not surprising, considering he rarely committed to paper the inner workings of his mind.

"[The Australian Government has] also agreed that I may travel in R.101 to India and back in the autumn," he wrote in July 1930. His words indicate that this flight was something he wanted, not something he had been ordered to do against his better judgement. The idea that he was keen to undertake a long journey in an airship is reinforced by his mother-in-law Agnes Holdaway's comment in her letter of April 1930, "Will has just come home and is saying he might get a chance to go in this new airship to Canada next month. He would like it..."

One of Will's fellow officers (probably Flight-Lieutenant Charles J. Harman) later revealed that he did have some reservations, nonetheless. Will was a realistic and practical man, and he was fully aware that the airship was experimental. He was fully aware, too, of the much-publicised airship tragedies of the past.

```
The Armidale Express and New England General Advertiser
(NSW: 1856—1861; 1863—1889; 1891—1954)
Wed 8 Oct 1930 Page 8
Mastery of the Air.
Australian's premonition.


. . . Squadron Leader William Palstra, Royal Australian
Air Force Air Liaison officer (ALO) to the British
Air Ministry . . . like all airmen . . .  would face
anything in the spirit of adventure but the Australian
Press Association understands that he did not approach
the present task in the same wholehearted enthusiasm.
A fellow officer said: "He was one of the most daring
chaps that I know. Give him any old bus and he would go
up and do anything that you asked him, but he was chary
about air-ships.
"I said to him, 'I would give my last farthing to swap
places with you'. Palstra smiled reflectively and said,
'You know I don't like the idea of that five million
cubic feet of gas above me.'"
```

PART XII:
STEPPING ABOARD THE R101

STEPPING ABOARD THE R101

The dawning of the day

On the morning of Saturday 4 October, Will awoke in the home of his friend and colleague Charlie Harman, in south-east London, where he had stayed overnight. The previous evening, he and Charlie had held a meeting with Senator "Harry" Foll, an Australian politician who served as a Senator for Queensland, to discuss aviation problems.

More than a hundred miles away, May opened her eyes to find herself alone in the double bed at the family's newly rented home. The house was at Ashley Meade, Fawley, Hampshire, near RAF Calshot, where Will had been studying. No doubt she fondly recalled the previous afternoon, when he had kissed her and the children goodbye at the garden gate, his suitcase in his hand.

May missed her husband dreadfully when he was away. She could not help worrying, and feeling impatient for his return from India, which was scheduled for 19 October. There was little time to dwell on her anxieties, however; most likely the three children were already awake. May's mother and her friend Mrs Harlow had long since departed on their return journey to Australia, so there were fewer hands to help May with the endless duties of looking after the little ones and doing the housework (which in 1930 was a good deal harder and more time-consuming than it is in the 21st century).

After getting out of bed and donning her clothes, May began dressing the younger children and preparing breakfast. On the other side of the world in Australia (where night was falling), *The Age* newspaper had already announced,

```
The Age, Saturday 4 October 1930
BEFORE THE FLIGHT

The flight of the R.101 to India will begin at dusk this
evening. Egypt will be reached by way of France and
```

the Mediterranean, the precise route depending on the meteorological conditions. The Ismailia airship base is equipped with a mooring tower similar in all respects to that at Cardington and a hydrogen plant capable of an output of 60,000 cubic feet per hour. Her stay there will be short, and after a few hours the journey will be resumed via Aleppo, Baghdad and Basra to Karachi.

In addition to a mooring tower and hydrogen plant, there is also at Karachi a housing shed which is the largest in the British Empire, being slightly bigger than either of the sheds at Cardington. On each section of the flight, from Cardington to Ismailia and from Ismailia to Karachi, four days rations will be carried, consisting of two days ordinary ration, one days reserve ration and one days emergency ration. Lord Thompson hopes to complete the round trip by 19th inst, so that he may attend the Imperial Conference discussions on transport. The mooring of the airship at Ismailia will be marked by an air banquet, at which the Air Minister and the Acting High Commissioner in Egypt will entertain a number of guests in the spacious dining room of the R.101.

This will be the first flight of any airship to either Egypt or India. It is being undertaken on an experimental basis to test the behavior of the airship over a long distance, and more especially under severe tropical conditions.

The weather forecast

The weather forecast on the morning of 4 October was generally favourable, predicting south to south-westerly winds of between 20 and 30 m.p.h. (32 and 48 km/h) at 2,000 ft (610 m) over northern France, with conditions improving over southern France and the Mediterranean Sea.[44]

R101's meteorological officer Maurice Alfred Giblett was keeping a close eye on the weather reports emanating from the meteorological office. The mid-day forecast indicated that the weather conditions over Cardington and Northern France would begin to deteriorate during the evening, although the wind was not expected to rise significantly.

He passed on the news to Captain Irwin. Though not ideal, these predictions were not considered alarming enough to postpone the voyage. The captain decided to hurry the passengers on board, complete the loading of the ship, and begin the voyage in the hope of bypassing the worst of the weather. He planned to fly R101 over London, Paris and Toulouse, crossing the French coast near Narbonne.

Baggage and last letters

On 4 October 1930, after rising at 6:30, Will boarded the 9:25 steam-train to Bedford at busy St Pancras Station in London. After his arrival at Bedford Railway Station he made his way to the Royal Airship Works airbase in Cardington, arriving late in the morning. He had lunch there, chatted to some of the officers and strolled around, taking in the sights.

"We held a weather conference this morning," Major Nixon told him. "The weather conditions over northern France are predicted to become cloudy with moderate winds. It's been agreed that the ship will depart between 4pm and 8pm this evening."

In his typical conscientious fashion Will viewed the flight to India not as a pleasure jaunt, but as a fact-finding mission. He was already composing, in his mind, the detailed report and 'useful information' he would give to his commander on his return. With his

---
44   Masefield, 1982 p. 337

trusty camera he took some photos of the R101 docked at the mooring mast. He planned to get them developed upon his return, so that he could show them to his family, as well as his colleagues.

He also sat down and also wrote a letter to his beloved wife. One of his comments implies that on this voyage he was relying on luck as much as anything, and that perhaps he had discussed the potential risks of airship travel with May, and was trying to reassure her that good luck was on their side.

Airship Base Cardington

Beds

4th Oct 1930

Darling girl,

I did well to leave Calshot yesterday afternoon, for though as it now turns out R.101 will not leave until 7pm tonight, there was yesterday afternoon a possibility that she might have left that evening. As it is, we have to be on board at 4pm this afternoon which has left me just enough time to do some scouting round here and obtain information which will be very useful for my report.

On arrival at Australia House yesterday I put through a trunk call to Cardington and got the latest about sailing time. I spent the night at Harman's Hotel somewhere in South Norwood near the Crystal Palace. You have to get out there by bus. First of all we had to wait fully 1/2 an hour to get on a bus as these are packed about 6pm. When we did get on it must have taken us an hour and a half to get to the Hotel. Fancy having to put up with this sort of thing in Winter. I had a bath and went to bed early as I had to be up at 6.30 am in order to catch a train at St. Pancras at 9.25.

I am the first of the 4 passengers to arrive here. Major Nixon one of the Technical directors made me welcome, and as I said I got some useful information from him. After a cold lunch strolled over to the Mooring Tower and took a snapshot. She looks fine. They expect she will be back on the 18th or 19th. The other passengers are Lord Thompson, Secretary of State for Air, Sir Sefton Brancker Director of Civil Aviation and Squadron Leader O'Neill representing the Indian Office. So I am one of 4 celebrities. The crew consists of 5 Officers and 37 others. In addition there will be 7 Air Ministry Technical people making a total of 53. Weather reports are favourable. Apparently I should have taken an overcoat as it may be cold at altitudes. Also a coat is not counted in the 30 lbs luggage. Major Nixon came to the rescue and has lent me his own leather overcoat, so the luck holds.

Excuse the random manner in which this letter is put together. It is written in a hurry. I know you would like something from me. Don't get feeling too lonely whilst I am away. It won't be long.

Give the kiddies each a kiss from Daddy.

All my love to you

Will.

Will's 39th birthday would be on 8th October, by which date he expected to be well on the way to India. He was not the only passenger putting pen to paper on that morning, and hoping for good luck. First Officer of the R101, Lieutenant Commander Atherstone, made an entry in his diary on October 4, 1930:

"Everybody is rather keyed up now, as we all feel that the future of airships very largely depends on what sort of show we put up. There are very many unknown factors and I feel that the thing called "Luck" will figure rather conspicuously in our flight. Let's hope for good luck and do our best."

Lord Thomson, too, was busy writing.

```
The Herald (Melbourne, 3 January 1840—)
LAST MINUTE WILL OF AIR MINISTER.
Scribbled at desk before boarding airship. (Herald
Special Representative)
London Oct 6 –

The Daily Mail says that just before leaving to board
R.101 the Secretary for Air Lord Thompson [sic] sat down
at his desk at the Air Ministry and hurriedly scribbled
a will on a slip of note-paper as though he had realised
at the last moment the hazards of the flight.
The will read, 'I am setting out for a flight to India
and in case anything may happen to me I leave all my
property and possessions to my brother Colonel Roger
Gordon Thompson.'
Two officials witnessed the will, which Lord Thompson
instructed should be locked up and returned to him, to
be torn up on his return.
```

On the morning before the flight, Sir Sefton Brancker, who was never known to be nervous, seemed fidgety. Friends noticed that his manner was different, and afterwards his private letters showed that he knew all was not well with the airship.

The airship's Chief Coxswain, William George Hunt, lived with his family in a house next door to the Cardington air base. In the BBC documentary "R.101: Ship of Dreams" (BBC, 2001) Hunt's son describes his father's departure for the flight to India, after the family sat down together for their midday meal.

"...we ... had our dinner and then [my father] got up and picked up his flight bag and [all] that, and kissed my mother goodbye, and said goodbye to my sister, and I walked down the road with him a little way until we got to the Number One Shed, but then he stopped, and he took his bag from me, and he said to me, 'Now look lad, I want you to make me two promises.'

"So I said, 'Yes, Dad.'

"So he said, 'One is that you'll join the Navy, if they want you to, and the other one is you'll promise me that you'll look after your mother and your sister.

"Because,' he said, "I may not be coming back off of this flight'. "And with that he turned and walked off."

Despite the fact that the crew and passengers feared for their lives, they considered it their duty to fly in the R101.

Late in the afternoon of October 4, at Cardington air base, workers had finished loading the last of the heavy luggage and supplies—bed linen and other assorted oddments—into the storage units of the accommodation section. Fifty-four people prepared to go aboard, including the cream of British aviation development engineers—men like Atherstone, Major G. H.. Scott, Wing Commander Colmore and the Captain, Flight Lieutenant Irwin, one of the most senior and experienced airship fliers in the country.

They expected—or hoped—to be back in about two weeks.

The passengers and crew

At Cardington on the afternoon of Saturday, 4 October 1930, the electric lift would carry the passengers, crew and Air Ministry technicians up the mooring mast, to step inside the R101—the pride of the British aviation industry—ready for her long-distance flight.

> "I am one of 4 celebrities," Will had written in the letter he posted to May just before he boarded the airship. "The crew consists of 5 Officers and 37 others. In addition there will be 7 Air Ministry Technical people making a total of 53."

In fact there would be 54 men on board. Without prior notification, and weight issues notwithstanding, The Right Hon. Lord Thomson, Secretary of State for Air, insisted on bringing his valet.

Officers of R101 in front of control cabin (when the airship was in her shed)

The crew of the R101. Image: www.airshipsonline.com

Lord Thompson's luggage

It was Lord Thomson's pressure that hastened the R101's departure on 4 October 1930. It appears he had convinced himself there were no risks. In his eagerness to share in the scheme's success, Thomson inadvertently contributed to its failure by smuggling his young valet aboard, and by taking with him, on the day of departure, several crates of champagne and a roll of (yet more) heavy carpet.

In the 21st century, the protocol of weighing baggage before boarding an aeroplane is taken for granted. It seems amazing that no effort was made to tally the total weight of the people and items lugged aboard the R101. Lord Thomson's effects alone were reported to weigh as much as 24 people. Whether this was a later exaggeration of the truth will never be known.

Due to an attempt to limit the weight carried by R101, the crew were subject to severe baggage limitations. Nonetheless, on the very day of departure, Lord Thomson arrived with quantities of food and champagne for his reception banquet at Ismailia, a large quantity of other unexpected baggage and a 'lucky charm' roll of Persian carpet weighing 149 pounds (67.5kg), apparently to impress the guests at the banquet. The baggage handlers had to manhandle the heavy carpet up the stairs of the mooring tower, since it would not fit inside the lift cage. The roll was too long for the available stowage area, and was reportedly laid in the forward companionway.

Thomson proclaimed that for him, this carpet had a romantic connection with his pen-friend the celebrated Romanian-French writer, socialite, style icon and political hostess Princess Marthe Bibesco. She had lost a similar piece in a fire at Posada, in Romania. Bizarrely, Thomson had also hidden a personal item—one of the princess's shoes—in his baggage.

The airship

Dominating the landscape, the huge, silver, cigar-shaped airship, 777 feet long, floats high in the air like some monstrous fish, parallel to the ground. She seems to dwarf the cottages on the edge of the aerodrome. Her body is secured to ground-anchors by long steel cables. Her nose is tethered to the tip of her mooring mast; she has not left it since she docked here after her trial flight three days ago, on October 1st.

A ring of small, round portholes seems to encircle her nose. Her name, "R101", is painted in large letters on each side, near her nose, and also near her delicately-pointed stern. On her rudders, also called vertical stabilizers, or fins, is painted the letter "G". (The horizontal fins are called elevators.) Her aircraft registration sign "G-FAAW" is displayed on her flanks at her mid-section.[45]

---

45   For aircraft call signs, the Paris International Conference of 1919 had allocated the British Empire the prefix G followed by four other letters. The Air Ministry decided to use the G-Exxx sequence for heavier-than-air aircraft (for example G-EAAA) and "G-FAAA to G-FZZZ" for lighter-than-air aircraft.

The R101 floats at her mooring mast, Alamy ID:G3B972

Crowds assemble outside the Cardington Air Base to see the giant airship, 1930
Alamy ID: 2M9700B

The engine cars

Suspended by metal girders beneath R101's sleek bulk are five engine cars or power cars, each fitted with a front and rear propeller, or air screw. Because of their elliptical shape, the crew referred to these cars as "power eggs". They look like the airship's tiny feet.

The airship's driving machinery is carried in these independent power units. Each holds a Beardmore Diesel Tornado engine of 585 h.p., and a small auxiliary engine by which the main engine is started.

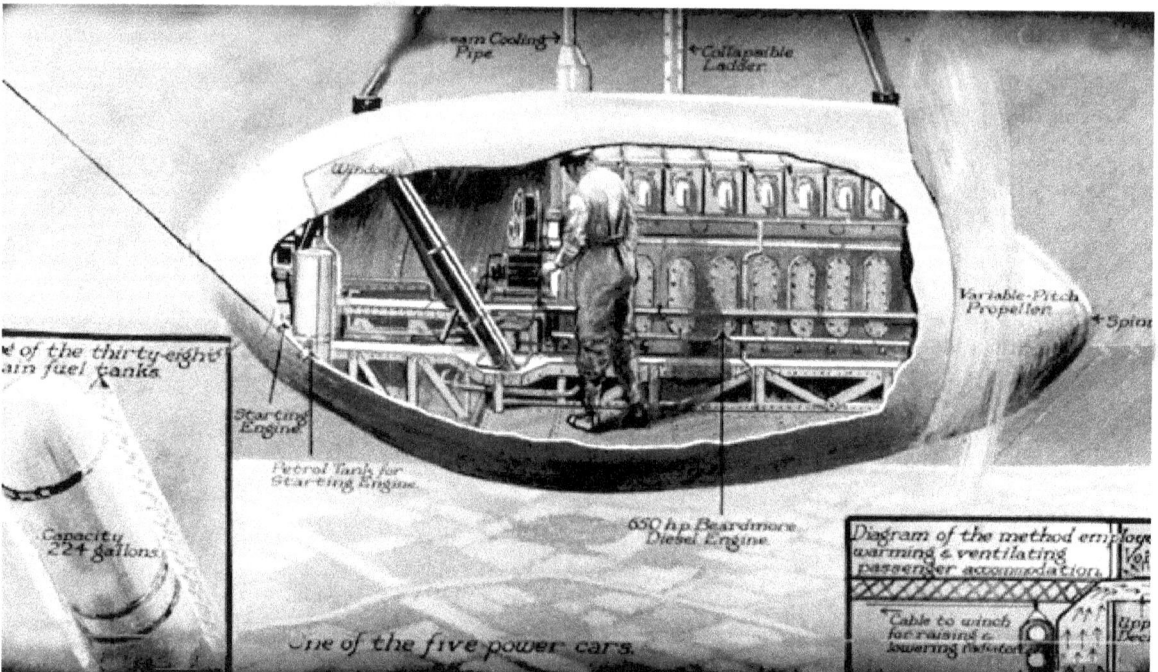

Cutaway of an airship engine car. London Illustrated News.

The engineers who man the outboard cars have to dress themselves in full leather flying suits, complete with tight-fitting caps and goggles. It is cold in those cramped cubicles. Besides, access to the cars is by way of a metal ladder completely exposed to the elements, and winds can be icy at altitudes of thousands of feet.

Being in charge of an engine car was probably the worst job on an airship. For eight hours at a time the crewman had to keep his engine in repair, while always remaining on the alert for the bell that signalled orders being telegraphed from the control car. When orders arrived, he must immediately adjust the engine settings.

Conditions inside an engine car were uncomfortable. The ceiling was so low that the engineer on duty couldn't stand up to his full height. Nor was there much sideways room, there being only a narrow space around the engine, between it and the car's walls; just enough room for a man to squeeze himself in to work around the engine.

This meant that the engineer was never more than about a forearm's length away from the thundering, exhaust-belching 585 horsepower engine in his care.

Relief engineer going down from inside the ship to take his watch in the port forward power car. London Illustrated News.

The roar of the diesel Tornadoes was almost deafening. It's possible that the attendants usually plugged their ears to protect their hearing, although first hand accounts inform us that two engineers were able to hold a conversation inside a fully operating engine car.

During a change of watch, the crewman on duty in an engine car would have to wait for the new man to turn up. Then, after exchanging information about how the engine was running, he would somehow squeeze past him and out of the car, onto the vertiginous ladder leading through the clouds, up into the airship's belly.

The cars were affixed to rigid struts that held them away from the ship's outer envelope. They could only be reached by a metal ladder that led down from a hatchway in the lower deck, outside into the elements.

A rigger examining the under-fabric of the hull from the ladder of the rear power car. London Illustrated News.

Anyone descending the slippery rungs to the engine cars found themselves suspended on a spindly ladder in the sky, vulnerable to hail, clouds, rain, fog, or whatever weather conditions the airship happened to be flying through. The propeller mounted on the rear of the car rotated with such force that the air it disturbed (the "prop wash" would be able to swing him sideways off the ladder if he was not careful.

If wind gusts were strong enough to make the airship lurch, a man clinging to the ladder would be at further risk. There is no evidence that crew members on these dizzying ladders had safety harnesses to save them if they slipped and lost their grip. It was akin to the dangers of being in the rigging of a great sailing ship, high above the deck and the boiling ocean.

The control car

An exterior "control cabin" or "control car" is slung beneath the R101's underside, right in the centre. This plays the same role as the cockpit of an aeroplane. From here, the airship will be navigated and conned, conning being the act of controlling a ship's movements by way of the engines, rudder, elevators etc.

Inside the control car of the R101. Alamy ID: ETXPE0

Living quarters

Directly above the control cabin, in the middle of the airship, lie the quarters for passengers and crew.

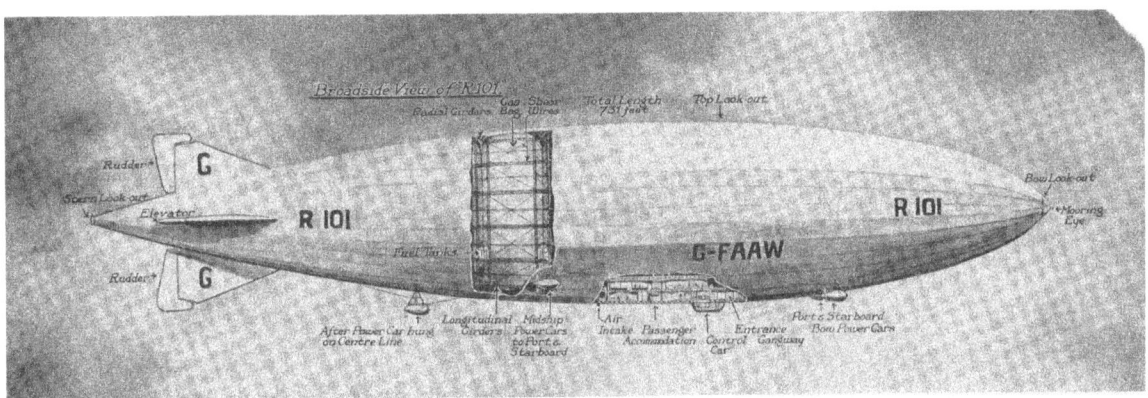

Cutaway image of R101 showing the added gasbag bay and positions of living quarters.

Alamy ID: 2BEATNF

The mooring mast and its lift

The web-like metal structure of the cylindrical mooring mast encloses a lift shaft and a zig- zag metal staircase. The design of the mast echoes that of a lighthouse, with its roughly domed roof, and a balcony encircling it near the top.

The R101 anchored to her mooring mast at Cardington Air Base.
The two airship sheds are in the foreground. Alamy ID: DRFJ4A

At the base of the mast, stewards load last-minute supplies into the lift—wooden crates filled with fresh milk in glass bottles. The lift looks as though it would hold up to about twenty passengers. A large, highly polished brass bell hangs near the lift entrance, its clapper dangling within arm's reach. The lift (or "elevator" in American terminology) is a metal box entered through steel scissor gates that are manually slid shut before the box starts to ascend swiftly and smoothly, straight up the centre of the mast.

The stewards disappear, and now outside the lift doors the senior officers pause, smiling, to allow photographers to take a group photo. The hair of these early twentieth century men is cut short, and although there are plenty of moustaches, there are no beards. Everybody wears a hat except the lift boy. The officers wear their R101 uniforms; dark blue reefer pattern jackets with eight shiny buttons—gold for officers and black for men—wide lapels, the white collars of shirts showing beneath, and dark neckties. Their peaked caps are banded with ribbon, and a glinting badge is pinned at the front, showing the airship's special insignia. This consists of a circle surmounted by a crown, in the centre of which are the words "R101" and on the circle, "R.A.W. Cardington".

A groundsman wearing a flat cap stands aside respectfully as the young lift attendant ushers the officers into the lift. The attendant adroitly uses his knee to push the last officer's protruding luggage inside the cage, then steps inside with the men and slides the scissor gates closed. The lift rises.

The weather

The afternoon is darkening as the sky becomes overcast with heavy cloud. Rain drizzles lightly, and a cold wind blows in strong gusts. It is autumn in England.

The dignitaries arrive

It is 3.30 pm on the afternoon of 4th October. Standing on the concrete apron just below the mooring mast, Lord Christopher "C.B." Thomson confidently faces the cinematographers. You can view this moment on YouTube.

Tall, spare, and sporting a small, fashionable moustache, Thomson smiles benignly. His hair and moustache are greying. At fifty-five years of age he is the oldest passenger. Thomson is wearing a black fedora, a double breasted knee-length overcoat with wide lapels and large round buttons, dark trousers, a scarf partly tucked beneath the overcoat, and a necktie. A white handkerchief protrudes from his breast pocket, and white shirt cuffs neatly peep from beneath his coat sleeves. In his leather-gloved hands he is carrying a swagger stick.

Asked by a reporter if he thinks the trip will be the forerunner of a regular service to India, Lord Thomson laughingly replies, "I will not prophesy." He expresses great confidence, and says the conditions seem quite satisfactory.[46]

Sir Sefton Brancker stands beside Thomson, with his trademark monocle screwed to his right eye. He is wearing a three piece single-breasted suit and a pale fedora with a contrasting hat band. Like Thomson he has a white handkerchief projecting from his breast pocket and crisp white cuffs jutting from beneath his coat sleeves.

Standing to the left of Thomson during this brief pause for photographs is thirty-seven year old Lieutenant-Colonel Vincent Crane Richmond, engineer and R101 airship designer, in a three-piece pin-striped suit and fedora. His bluff face is wreathed in smiles of genuine pleasure at the excitement of this momentous occasion.

To the right of Brancker, looking highly pleased but slightly self-conscious amidst the glare of publicity, stands Flight Lieutenant Irwin, aged 36, the airship's commander. He is wearing the double-breasted uniform of the R101 with its shiny buttons and cap- badge. The Irishman exchanges a few pleasantries with Sir Sefton.

Clearly, they are discreetly excited, these distinguished airmen and civil servants.

Here comes a lean, sprightly, and neatly dressed figure; the Liaison Officer for the Royal Australian Air Force with the British Air Ministry, Squadron Leader William Palstra, a few days short of his thirty-ninth birthday. Like the other passengers, he is wearing a dark coloured suit and a fedora hat. Over his arm he carries a bulky overcoat. He and his fellow Dominion Representative, Bill O'Neill, remain in the background while the cameras are focussing on the politicians and the senior officers. It is not for them to claim the limelight, nor do they wish for it. They are here to do their jobs.

---

46   The Age (Melbourne, Vic.: 1854—1954) Mon 6 Oct 1930, Page 9

Important personages filmed just before they enter the lift to take them up the mooring mast on 4 October 1930. Left to right: Squ. Ldr, E.L. Johnston, Sir Sefton Brancker, Major Lewis G. S. Reynolds, Lord Thomson, Lt-Col. Richmond.

Into the lift. . .

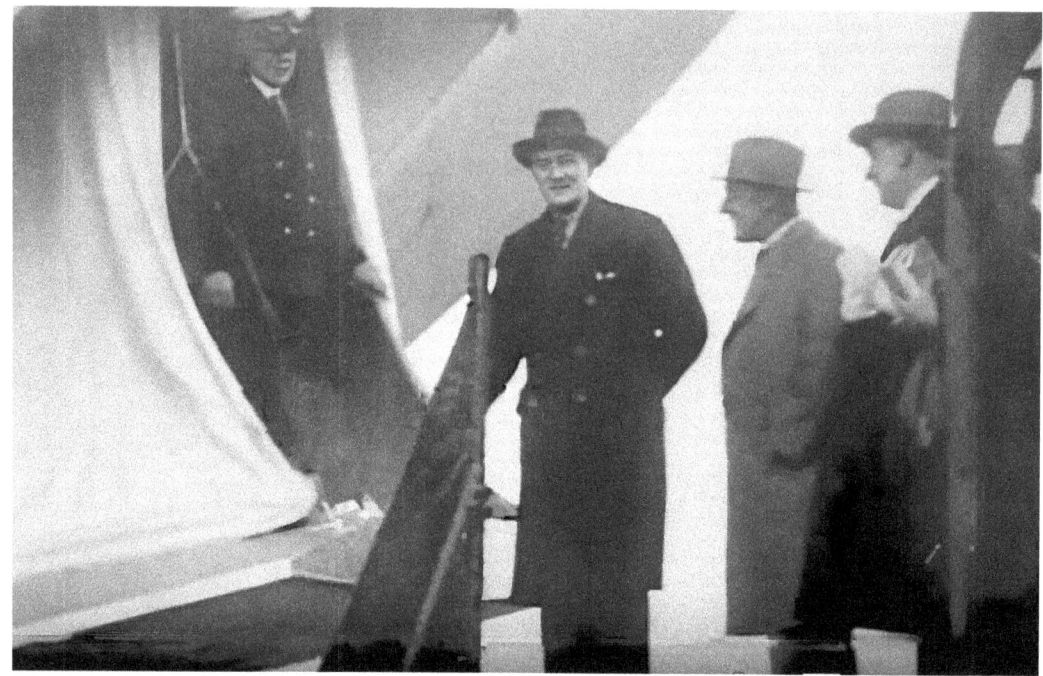

The captain welcomes Lord Thomson aboard, on the bridge between the mooring mast and the airship.

Boarding the R101. Image: www.curlysairships.com

The onlookers

The airship base is busy with hundreds of people going to and fro. Selected visitors mill respectfully in the background while photographs are snapped. As well as newspaper reporters, photographers, and cinematographers, they include friends and family of the passengers and crew, come to bid farewell. Onlookers include smiling women in chic cloche hats and waist-belted coats with fur collars, and men in fedoras and bowler hats wearing suits and neckties.

The dignitaries and observers turn away from the photographers and journalists. They enter the lift and the scissor gates clang shut. Thomson is carrying a newspaper. His swagger stick is nowhere to be seen—perhaps he has passed it to his valet. The lift rises smoothly. At the top of the mooring mast the passengers emerge, one by one, from a doorway that leads onto the open-air balcony. A passenger boarding-bridge with canvas sides has been let down out of the front of the airship, like a little hinged jaw, the mouth of a fish, whose lower lip meets this aerial platform.

The airship's commander is standing just inside the gangway to welcome the dignitaries and observers aboard. And possibly, also, to help them step up onto the bridge, which hovers somewhat higher than the platform, perhaps as much as three feet (one metre), and sways a little as the featherweight airship trembles in the wind gusts.

By the time the distinguished passengers arrive, the R101's crew is already busy aboard the airship; the cooks in their white clothes with their tall, puffy chefs hats on, the stewards in their crisp, black uniforms. Thomson climbs aboard, then turns around while standing on the bridge, aiming one last smile in the direction of the photographers. He is holding onto a cable with his gloved left hand while the folded broadsheet is held against his body with his right. He turns and makes his way into the vessel, disappearing from the range of the photographers' lenses.

The last couple of passengers step out onto the metal balcony. Carrying Major Nixon's leather overcoat over one arm, Will extends the other arm and grips a handrail to help pull him up. With one energetic step, he bounds into the airship.

TO RIDE THE STORM

Imagine stepping aboard the R101 as she floats horizontally, her nose tethered to her mooring mast. As you plant your foot on the deck for the first time, you might feel a slight quiver, a ripple shifting beneath your feet. It's as if the airship were alive. This feels like no other form of transport you've ever experienced. It is akin, perhaps, to stepping aboard a boat, but instead of water, a gulf of air fills the space between you and the ground, and the soughing of the wind is unbroken by any lapping of waves.

It is like those childhood dreams of flying.

Inside the airship

You can take a virtual look inside the R101 on YouTube: "Welcome Aboard the R101" on the Airship Heritage Trust's channel.

In the company of the other passengers, RAW personnel and some of the airship's officers, Squadron Leader Palstra descended a short flight of stairs. They walked down a gradually sloping interior walkway on the lower deck; a corridor that extended the length of the airship, illuminated by small windows. Probably Squadron Leader Bill O'Neill kept pace with Will, and we can imagine the two officers occasionally exchanging convivial comments as they went.

The floor flexed beneath their feet, creaking at every step, a sensation these newcomers must have found somewhat disconcerting at first. If RAW airship designer Lieutenant Colonel Richmond noted any looks of surprise, he would have reassured them that the floors, despite being made of three-ply wood to reduce weight, were stiffened with spruce. They were stronger than they felt underfoot, and the men could be confident that they would not break through and plummet to the ground.

A staircase led to the upper deck, which housed the main passenger accommodation, public spaces, lounge, dining room and promenades. At the top of the stair the men found themselves on a wide landing lit by softly glowing, frosted wall-sconces clustered near the ceiling.

Passenger cabins

To one side, narrow corridors led to the main passenger sleeping accommodation. The walls consisted of square pillars with doped, double-thickness white-painted linen panels stretched between them. Each metal pillar was covered with a veneer of fine 2mm (1/8 inch) thick spruce cladding whose fluting was painted gold, as were the edges of the cloth panels.

Airship expert C.P. Hall estimates that some 12 passenger bedrooms or 'roomettes' were available, with two berths per room.[47] Given the extremely low temperatures experienced at high altitudes, they used to be warmed by a heating vent set into the floor under the bunks. Regrettably, this system—along with half the number of original roomettes—had been removed to save weight. (Since the ship was flying to India, who needed heating?)

Image from "The London Illustrated News" 9 March 1929
showing an artist's impressions of the interior of the R101, "the world's largest airship".

---

47   C.P. Hall writes, "As a 'perk' for Lord Thomson the cabin just outside the dining room doorway and the adjacent cabin forward were converted into a one-bed 'suite' for him." Hall goes on to speculate, " Brancker, Palstra and O'Neill each had a room, as did Colmore, Scott, Richmond and Rope. Bishop, Leech and meteorologist Giblett each had a room and presumably James Buck had a room close to Lord Thomson. That left one room to store Thomson's excess baggage …"

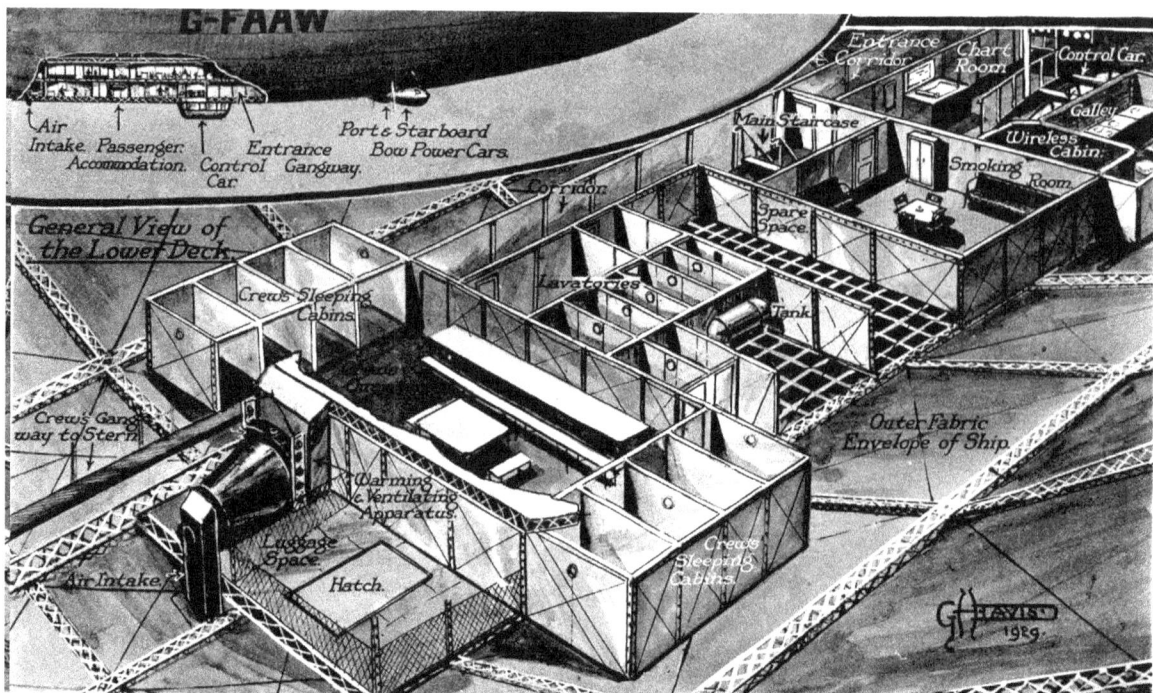

"General view of the lower deck" (London Illustrated News)[48]

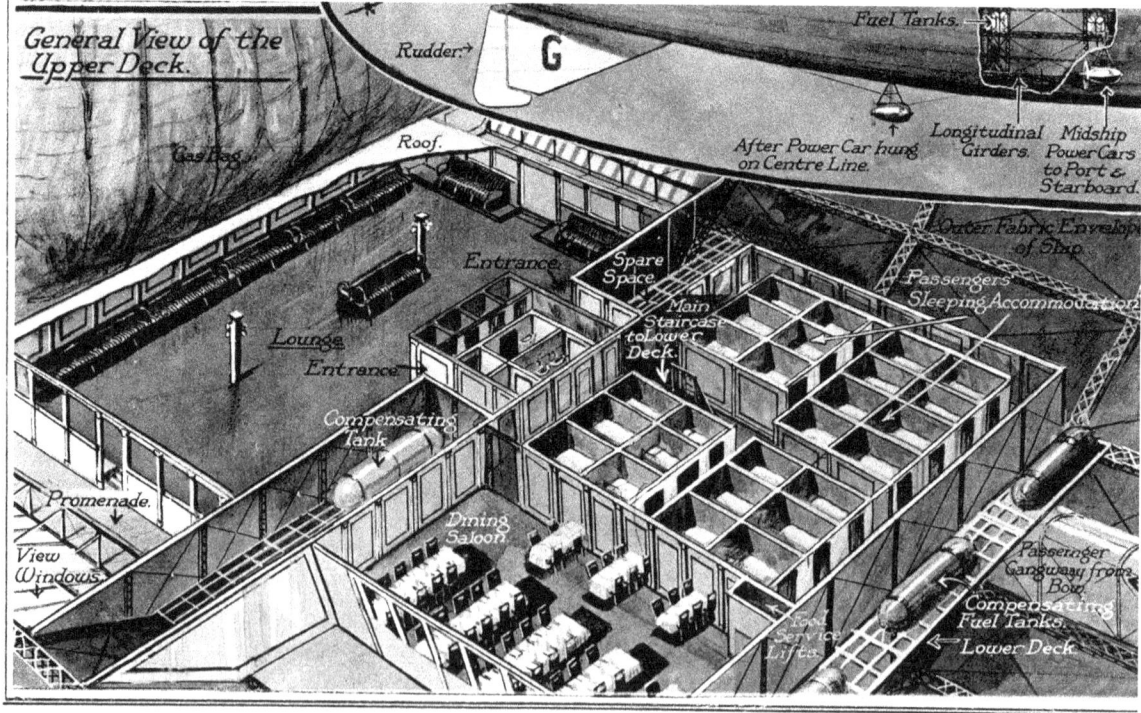

"General view of the upper deck" (London Illustrated News)

48 C.P. Hall comments: "The G. H. Davis illustration is quite inaccurate as a guide. For example there is a separate, starboard side walkway from crews' quarters to galley. The 'switch room' is off this walkway as well, radio room access is inside upper control car. The five compartments port and starboard ends of crews' quarters hung over the outer cover simply were not there."

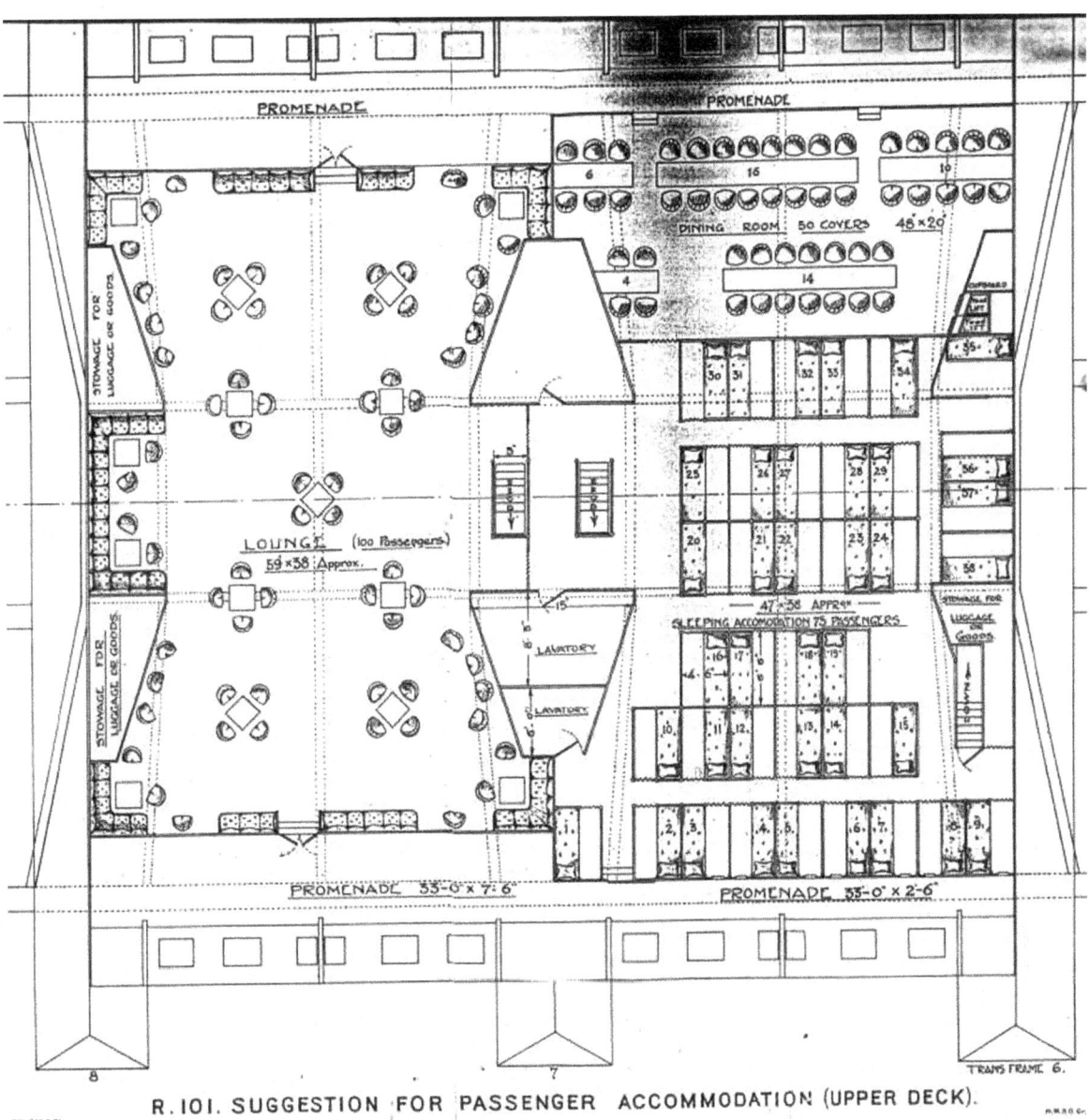

"R101 suggestions for passenger accommodation" Airship Heritage Trust

"Typical two-berth cabin" (London Illustrated News)

A two-berth passenger cabin on the R100, similar to those on R101. Airship Heritage Trust

To begin with, the passengers probably made their way to their quarters to offload their luggage. A long, dark-blue curtain divided each cabin from the corridor, in place of a solid door. Cool shades of blue belonged to the R101. The heavy curtain could be tied back with a ribbon, allowing passengers to pass through without having to brush it aside.

The main electric light in Will's gold and white bedroom was an imitation porthole, fitted to the wall with a small blind which could be drawn over it. This typified the nautical style of the R101's interior decor. A small reading light was attached to the wall above his duralumin berth.

The renowned Belfast Linen company had supplied all the brand new sheets, pillowcases and towels. There was no space to hang up one's clothes, but a compact foldable stool squatted on the small blue patterned rug, providing a location for cabin bags. Conceivably, Will folded up his borrowed leather greatcoat and arranged it on the stool. One wall displayed a printed notice explaining the protocols of airship life, including details for summoning a steward.

Hallway in the passengers' quarters on the R101.

Through the thin partitions between the cabins drifted the sounds of footsteps and voices. Will could feel faint vibrations through the floor and walls, as his fellow passengers moved around their cabins.

With so few passengers, and being an invited VIP, Will was able to enjoy the privacy of a stateroom all to himself.

Corridor in the passengers' quarters.
Airship Heritage Trust

Imagine:

He places his suitcase on the bunk's blue coverlet, and opens it. The half-finished letter to May lies on top of his belongings. Extricating a compact washbag from his luggage, he sets it aside. It contains his toothbrush, toothpaste, razor—Wilkinson Sword Company— and shaving brush. He also takes out his camera and places it atop the greatcoat, so that it will be close at hand. He'll surely want too take some snaps during the voyage, and he has plenty of film left, even after taking a couple of photos of the R101 floating at the mooring mast. Then he snaps shut the suitcase and stows it beneath his berth...

Communal washrooms for passengers were available close by, just as they were aboard passenger ships and in most hotels during the early 20th century; ensuite bathrooms did not become prevalent until the 1950s. The washrooms were fitted with aluminium sinks. On the wall behind the sinks, long, half-length mirrors hung suspended on two wires. The washrooms being on the lower deck, passengers must go down a set of stairs to use them.

The passenger lounge

Having settled in, the passengers would have made their way to the lounge area, to take refreshment.

The design of the R101's upper deck was influenced by nautical architecture, so that the passengers almost felt as though they were aboard a ship of the ocean. But what a luxurious vessel!

According to the Airship Heritage Trust, "The R101 interior was one of the most magnificent collections of rooms ever constructed in an airship. The fittings of the airship were luxurious—an attempt to equal the splendour of the ocean liners."

The "saloon lounge" of the R101 was the largest open space ever included on any airship, stretching right across the hull and measuring 33 feet (approx. 10 metres) by 62 feet (approx. 19 metres). The colour scheme of white wall panels with gold-painted inlay continued. The dark green fronds of potted plants peeped from the corners. Much of the Cambridge-blue upholstered seating was installed against the walls, but in the centre of the lounge, wicker armchairs with buttoned padding and seat cushions clustered around small, lightweight wooden tables. Square pillars punctuated this airy space, and leafy indoor plants in circular planters peeped from their bases.

White-frosted electric lamps bunched around their tops glowed like small moons. Framed watercolours of English country scenes and cloudscapes adorned the walls. At each end of the left hand side of the lounge, writing desks ran along the wall. Here, the Air Ministry had provided complimentary R101-headed stationery for the passengers' use.

The passenger lounge of the R101. You can see one of the 'promenade decks' at the far end. There was a promenade deck at either end of the lounge. Alamy ETXWC7

Drawing of passengers dancing in the lounge area of the R101. London Illustrated News.

Gentlemen relaxing in the lounge of the R101. www.airshipsonline.com

The lounge with the Promenade Deck in the background. Curtained windows allow light into the lounge from the airship's windows. www.airshipsonline.com

The Promenade Deck

On both sides of the lounge, passenger could mount three small steps to either of the two promenade decks. There were two such decks extending along either side of the airship between two of the middle bays, one to port and one to starboard. These were, in the words of the Airship Heritage Trust, "one of the most striking features of an airship. The promenade decks on the R101 had floor to ceiling windows flush to the hull of the side of the ship. The view would have been wonderful."

The row of large windows sloped away on an angle. A safety railing separated the deck from the window panes which were made of light-weight cellon safety glass. Gazing down and out, Will and his companions could see the darkening airfield below, the upturned faces of the watching crowds lit by floodlights and the headlamps of cars.

On the promenade deck of the R101. Hilda Lyons in a deck chair, with Squadron Leader Ernest Johnston. The chair was rented for one day for publicity photo purposes in 1929.
www.airshipsonline.com

When leaning on the hand-rail that ran the length of the promenade deck, passengers would be able to enjoy the bird's-eye view of the landscape passing far below, sometimes veiled by clouds.

Waning daylight seeped from the promenade deck through a row of windows separating the deck from the saloon lounge. Curtains dyed Cambridge blue (a bluish spring-green) could be opened during the day, or closed at nights to allow people on the promenade deck to have a better view.

An artist's impression of the "viewing lounge" on the promenade deck.
London Illustrated News.

R101 forward, portside promenade (opposite the dining room on starboard side). Photo discovered by C.P. Hall in Richard Van Treuren's archive and submitted to Dirigible Magazine, where it was published for the first time. www.airshipsonline.com

The dining room

A corridor led from the lounge into the R101's dining room. Windows down one side looked out upon the other promenade deck, which could be accessed through a door. Here, where up to 50 people could be seated on wicker chairs, the stewards had placed vases of fresh flowers on the spotless white tablecloths. A batten was fitted down the centre of each dining table, and the tables' edges were deeply beaded, to prevent any utensils from falling off during rough weather. The chairs and tables, nonetheless, were not bolted down—there was no need to do so when airship flight was usually so smooth and calm. Silver cutlery, emblazoned with the crest of the Royal Airship Works, was laid out formally. Snowy white serviettes lay in readiness beside each decorative china plate, also bearing the crest of the RAW. Everything was meticulously appointed.

MP's enjoying a meal in the dining room of the R101 in 1929. Alamy ID:2BW2GNX

A small lift set into the wall, known as a "dumb-waiter" could hoist dishes of food to the dining room from the galley below. The two stewards would then serve the food to the passengers. Diners could listen to music while they enjoyed their meal, because a wireless set had been installed high on another wall.

It's likely that in the dining room, refreshments were now served to the passengers, who would also have been advised that 'The smoke room is open'. Not being interested in either alcohol or nicotine, Will probably leaned back in his comfortable wicker chair sipping a cup of tea and eating a slice of cake served on one of the airship's custom-made blue-and-white china plates.

Final Route of the R101. www.airshipsonline.com

Artist's impression of the R101's "dining saloon".
London Illustrated News.

Albert Savidge, Chief Steward Airship R101 in the dining room. Alamy ID:2RG9GKG

R101 dining saloon. www.airshipsonline.com

Chief Steward, Airship R101, In the dining room with the blinds rolled up. www.airshipsonline.com

The Smoke Room

There was one noticeable difference, here, from the dining rooms and lounges of most public spaces in the 1920s and 30s. No smell of stale cigarette or cigar smoke clung to the walls or permeated the floor coverings. Nearby staircases led down to the fireproof 'smoke room' on the lower deck; a feature that was unique to the R101.

The Airship Heritage Trust's website explains that, "The floor and ceiling of the smoke room were made of light asbestos, with a thin sheet of metal reinforcing the floor. The walls were the same construction as the rest of the ship, being made of linen cloth. The smoking room was not considered a hazard to the ship, because all precautions had been taken with materials in construction. This is where you could retire after dinner and enjoy a cigar and postprandial drink."

No lighted cigar or cigarette was permitted to be taken from this room.

Comfortable settees, sufficient to seat 24 people, were arranged around the walls. Some of the small cane tables, with individual chairs, were furnished with decanters and glasses.

Artist's impression of the R101's "smoke room". Alamy Image ID:2M3NJ79

The galley

The passengers and crew had finished boarding around 4pm, but the airship was not yet ready to depart. Quite possibly, during the next few hours before dinner, R101's designers Squadron Leader Reginald Colmore and Lieutenant-Colonel V.C. Richmond gave the passengers a tour of the lower deck. Will would have been interested in the crew's living quarters, the cargo hold, the navigation chart and meteorological room, the wireless room and the galley with its all-electric oven, vegetable steamer, stainless steel cooking ranges, work benches and storage shelves.

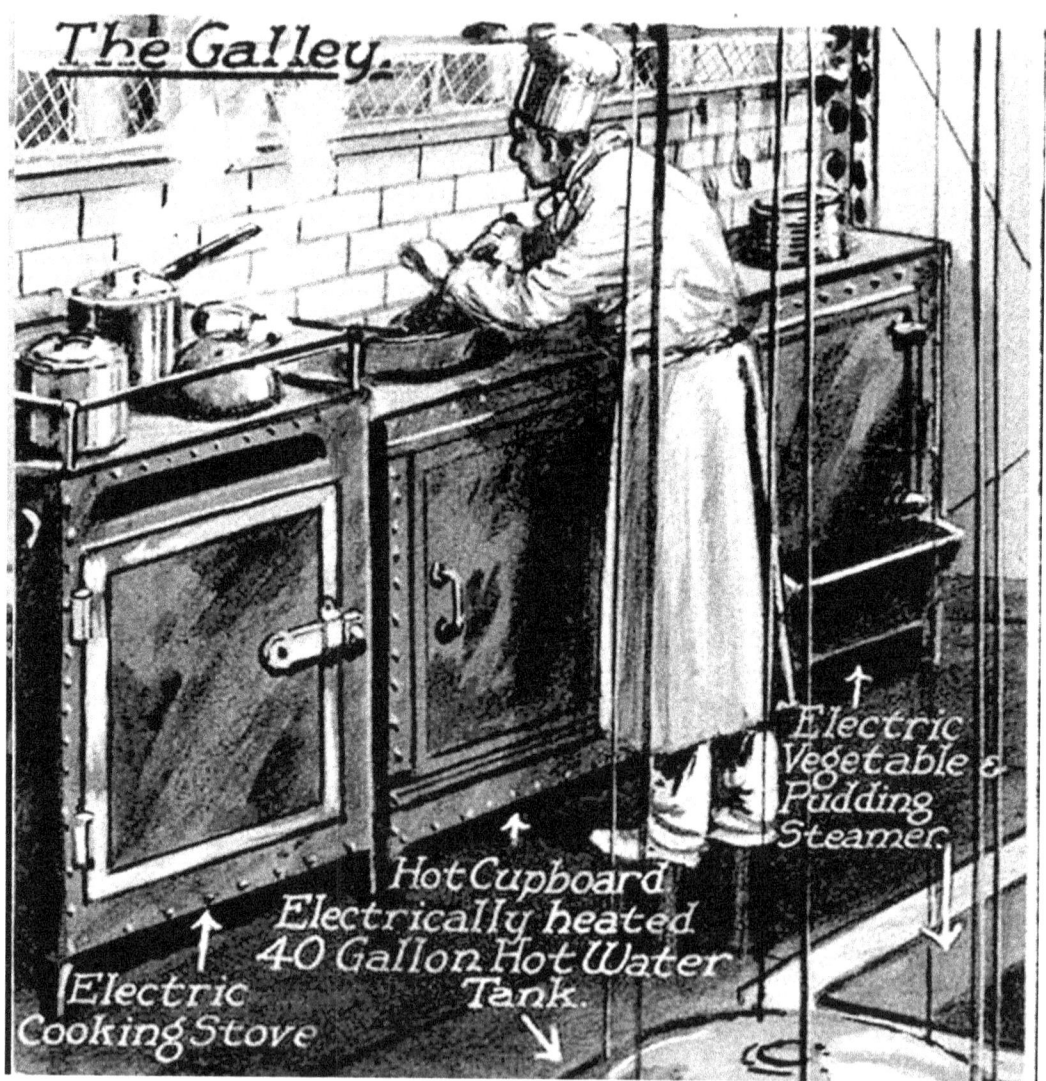

Amenities of the R101: the galley. Alamy Image ID:2M3NJ79

Galley of the R101. www.airshipsonline.com

A visit to the control car

Will and his companions probably also descended the short ladder in the middle of the ship that lead down into the control car where the men of the first watch were on duty, all wearing warm woollen pullovers. From here, suspended below the airship's envelope, the view through the many windows was extensive.

The car was lined with flight instruments, and there were two steering wheels, exactly like the spoked helm-wheels of ocean-going ships. One, situated in the nose of the control car, was to be used by the steering coxswain. The other wheel, jutting from the side, was the province of the height coxswain.

Meanwhile in the steam-filled galley the cook and the young galley boy were hard at work putting the finishing touches to the sumptuous evening meal.

In the engine cars—

Five engineers of the first watch had already climbed down the open-air ladders into the five engine cars, those egg-shaped capsules dangling from metal struts outside the main hull. Carefully checking and rechecking that all was well, Foreman Engineer Harry Leech had been moving between the port and starboard midship engine cars, the aft car, and the cars on the port and starboard bows. Riggers were patrolling and inspecting the entire ship at frequent intervals. They were monitoring the temperatures and pressures of the gas bags, to ensure the stability of the airship's pitch, trim and elevation.

Above the heads of 54 men those massive gas bags, filled with five million cubic feet of hydrogen gas, shifted slightly in their wire cradles as the airship floated at the mast.

Diagram showing the crew's duties aboard the R101. Alamy Image ID:2M3PCBR

THE FLIGHT

The departure of the world's biggest airship on its first intercontinental flight was a major public attraction. On the afternoon of Saturday October 4, vast crowds of people thronged to the Royal Airship Works at Cardington, despite the darkening skies and gloomy weather. From all over the United Kingdom they came, by motor car, train and bus, on motorcycles and bicycles, or on foot. The Age newspaper reported that "Several thousand spectators lined the nearby roads, which were ablaze with the head lamps of motor-cars."

The Bedfordshire council had provided thousands of temporary parking spaces around the air base. Notwithstanding, the car-parks were overflowing into the roads around the air base. Motorists deposited their vehicles along the verges of the narrow byways. Policemen patrolled, keeping order.

As the afternoon waned, fine rain drizzled down. Raindrops twinkled in the light that streamed from the row of windows along the airship's promenade deck, where Will and his fellow passengers congregated, looking down across the crowded air base. From the mooring mast, the strong beams of searchlights dramatically illuminated the scene below.

The airship's crew reported to base at half past six; "We're about to cast off."

At the appointed hour, amid cheers from the multitudes gathered around the airfield, the R101 freed herself from her anchoring guy ropes, uncoupled from the mooring mast and rose majestically into the cloud-heavy sky. Through her expansive windows, the men lining the R101s promenade deck watched as the ground receded. They experienced very little sensation of movement. When the noisy diesel engines in the "power eggs" spluttered to life, they were, perhaps, not bothersomely loud for those aboard. Three of the engines were far aft of the accommodation, and two were far forward, so that their chugging may have sounded a long way off.

The faces of the watching crowd tilted up, as all eyes followed the progress of the R101. "There she goes," shouted someone. "She's away!"

As one, the spectators let out a lusty, jubilant cheer. "Hurrah! Hurrah!" Their mingled voices rose to reach the ears of the passengers and crew. Many crew-members flashed their torches to loved ones on the ground.

The Age (Melbourne, Vic.)
Mon 6 Oct 1930.
Page 9

The crew evidently heard the cheering, and replied by flashing their lamps. None had the slightest thought of tragedy when the R.101, the biggest airship in the world, with the brilliance of a monster flood lamp gleaming on the silver of her massive hull, left Cardington. The highest hopes were entertained for the success of the flight, which was recognised as a most momentous one, marking a definite advance in the history of aviation and full of potentialities in regard to the quickening of the Empire's communications.

Inside the control car of the R101, with the two giant hangars visible through the windows.

As light as a butterfly the gigantic airship floated away, her vast bulk contrasting surreally with her weightlessness.

And that was all there was to it.

To the earth-bound onlookers, the chuggetty-chug of the R101's diesels as they turned the air screws was rough, deep and guttural, like the growl of a powerful motorcycle.

Water ballast had been dropped to trim the airship just before departure. As the R101 backed gently away from the mooring tower, the onlookers could clearly see the last of the water draining from the line below the control car.[49]

The lighted windows of the promenade deck shone forth like a row of square-cut jewels as the R101 cruised over the two enormous airship sheds. With her engines opened up to about half power, the airship slowly began to climb away to the northwest. On reaching Bedford she circled around it, in a salute to her home town. She rose to around 1,000 feet, then higher, heading south-east towards London. From the promenade deck the passengers could see the tiny lights of villages twinkling below, strewn across the dark landscape.

Moving steadily south, R101 sent out regular radio messages so that her course could be followed. When she passed over Hitchin, Hertfordshire, householders peered out of their upper- storey windows, eager to catch a glimpse of the airship's lights as she went by overhead.

---

49   "R.101 was fitted with two independent prototype systems for catching rain water in flight. So at least some of the lost ballast would be recovered by the time they got across the Channel." [Dr Giles Camplin, Airship Heritage Trust.]

The R101 over the English village of Hinckley during the day, October 1930.
Supplied: www.hinckleypastpresent.org

The R101 in flight. Alamy Image ID:2JPTBP0

7.30 pm to 8.30 pm

By around twenty past seven, the R101 had flown 29 miles (47 km) but was still only 8 miles (13 km) from Cardington. She set her course for London.

The passengers and Royal Airship Works senior officers gathered at the tables of the dining room where, behind the hum of genial conversation, the music of the BBC Dance Orchestra might have emanated from the wireless on the wall, and the dumb-waiter rattled faintly as it hoisted up a tray of hot food from the galley. The two stewards served dinner.

It is not known what foods the diners consumed at this meal but an undated R101 lunch menu (probably from the visit by 50 MPs on November 23rd, 1929) and a wine list from 6 November 1929 give an idea of what might have been on the menu this evening.[50] (With thanks to the Airship Heritage Trust for collecting and saving such ephemera and generously making it available to the public.)

---

50   The Airship Heritage Trust. https://www.airshipsonline.com/airships/R.101/

H.M. AIRSHIP R. 1 0 1 Menu

LUNCHEON

Oxtail soup

Chicken with Bacon, Bread Sauce Rice Potatoes, Green Peas

Jam Tart or

Milk Rice Custard Cheese

Fruit

Coffee will be served in the lounge. The Smoke room will be open.

H.M. AIRSHIP R. 1 0 1 WINE LIST

Empire Wines Australian Sherry South African Paarl

South African Draakenstein Australian Ophir

South African Veldt Burgundy Australian Muscatel

Liqueurs

South African Van der Hum Beer

At 8:21pm, after passing over Potters Bar, R101 sent her second routine wireless message to Cardington:

"Over London. All well. Moderate rain. Base of low clouds 1,500ft. Wind 240 degrees [west south west] 25mph. Course now set for Paris. Intend to proceed via Paris, Tours, Toulouse and Narbonne."

By then the weather conditions had deteriorated, and it was raining heavily. The wind was rising. Like a sailing ship pushing against strong ocean currents, the airship was flying with her nose pointing some 30 degrees to the right of her track.

```
The Age (Melbourne, Vic.: 1854-1954)
Mon 6 Oct 1930, Page 9
R.101 passed over London shortly after 9 p.m. Thousands
of people waited for hours in the streets to get a
glimpse of her, but owing to the overcast sky only a few
saw her lights.
```

```
Mirror (Perth, WA: 1921-1956)
Sat 13 Dec 1952 Page 9
A dismal rain was falling over London as the airship
passed over the capital, cruising at 54 knots. But if
it were dismal outside, the tinkling of ice in glasses
and the hum of happy voices in the lounge caused it to
pass unnoticed.
```

The evening meal proved most satisfactory. After it was over the smokers retired to the smoke-room to enjoy port and cigars.

8.40 pm

The meteorological office at Cardington sent out a wireless update of the weather situation at twenty minutes to nine. The forecast was a lot worse than had been expected. South-westerly winds of up to 50 mph (80 km/h) with low cloud and rain were predicted for northern France, with similar conditions over central France.

The weather on that 4th October night was the worst ever encountered in a flight over land by a British rigid airship. The R101 was so long—almost 800 feet in length—that wind gusts could differ between bow and stern, buffeting her from several directions simultaneously.

9.30 Crossing the English coast

Around half past nine the airship crossed the English coast near Hastings. The airship transmitted another routine progress report to Cardington:

Code: CROW "At 21.35 GMT (9.35) crossing coast in the vicinity of Hastings. It is raining hard and there is a strong South Westerly wind. Cloud base is at 1,500 feet. After a good getaway from the Mooring Tower at 18.30 hours ship circled Bedford before setting course. Course was set for London at 18.54. Engines running well at cruising speed giving 54.2 knots. Reached London at 2000 hours and then set course for Paris. Gradually increasing height so as to avoid high land. Ship is behaving well generally and we have already begun to recover water ballast."

A few minutes later the airship sent out another routine message:

'Crossed the Sussex coast at 1,000 ft and, against a 26 knot headwind, set course for Pointe St Quentin, a 57 mile crossing.'

An impression of the R101 at night, flying over Hastings
(from an original painting by Ken Marschall). Airship Heritage Trust.

As the airship passed over the English Channel the wind picked up and a moderately serious engine problem occurred.

The R101 slowly lost height, until she reached the alarmingly low level of about 750 feet on the altimeter. The passengers, looking out from the promenade deck windows, could see the white foam on the wave-tops glimmering faintly.

Down in the control cabin at 10 p.m., Commander Atherstone took the elevator wheel from the height coxswain and pulled the airship up to 1,000 feet. When he handed back the controls to the coxswain, he warned him not to let the R101 go below 1,000 feet again.

Anyone able to watch the R101 flying through that stormy night would have seen intense bursts of light, like miniature stars, springing into existence one by one in the water beneath her as she passed. Navigator Major Johnston was taking drift readings, leaning out of a control cabin window to let calcium flares fall into the Channel. In contact with water, calcium phosphide produces a bright light without an explosion. Using the flares as markers, Johnston calculated how fast and in what direction the airship was moving.

11 pm

In the dining room, the R101's passengers and senior officers were being treated to supper, which might have comprised a cup of hot cocoa and a biscuit, or other light refreshment.

After this snack and another sojourn in the smoking room, they probably enjoyed one final look out of the windows. They knew they must be approaching the French coast and perhaps, through the darkness and the rain, they glimpsed the long line of the shore pass below them. Then they bade each other 'Good night' and made their way to their sleeping quarters.

It can be imagined that Will laved his face and hands in the washrooms of the passengers' quarters, and cleaned his teeth, before making his way to his cabin where he put on his pyjamas and slipped between the fresh, new sheets of Irish linen. It had been a long and exciting day, and he must have been tired. As he drifted into sleep, soft vibrations rippled through the airship. She trembled softly, cradling her burden as gently as a mother's arms.

11.30pm

It was raining hard over the English Channel and, burdened beneath the weight of the downpour, she fought her way with some difficulty, a thirty-five mile an hour sou-wester hammering on her starboard beam.

The surface area of airships was so enormous that in a rain-shower, the cumulative weight of thousands of droplets could exert significant downward pressure.

As the Royal Airship Works designers had noted in 1923 with reference to an earlier dirigible, "No reliable measurement of the weight effect of rain on an airship has been made so far in England. This effect is naturally less in a wind than in stagnant air, but in either case it rapidly reaches an equilibrium value. The maximum heaviness caused in R33 at the mast by rain appears to have been about 1.5 tons."[51]

The doped linen cover of the R101 was letting in the rain, and the gasbag material—goldbeaters' skin—was fragile. The rain was not only getting in, it was also weighing the airship down.

Despite difficulties, the R101 reached the French coast, and by that time the engineers had corrected the mechanical problem. The Channel crossing took two hours, for at 11.36 pm the airship reported:

> Code: CENT[52] "Crossing French coast at Pointe de St Quentin. Wind 245 true. 35mph"

---

51 Scott & Richmond, 1923.

52 Code word CROW meant 'running on four engines', Code word CENT meant 'running on five engines'..With thanks to C.P. Hall for insights about the Secret List of Code Words.

Midnight

At midnight, the R101 sent out a further message, one that later became famous, passing into history. In spite of the rough weather conditions and serious trouble in maintaining height, the words betrayed no real fears on the part of the airship's guests and crew.

> Code: CENT To Cardington from R101. 2400 GMT
>
> 15 miles SW of Abbeville speed 33 knots. Wind 243 degrees [West South West] 35 miles per hour. Altimeter height 1,500 feet. Air temperature 51 degrees Fahrenheit. Weather—intermittent rain. Cloud nimbus at 500 feet.
>
> After an excellent supper our distinguished passengers smoked a final cigar and having sighted the French coast have now gone to bed to rest after the excitement of their leavetaking. All essential services are functioning satisfactorily. The crew have settled down to watch-keeping routine.

Airship historian Peter Davison writes, "This was the last message from the R101 giving speed and position. The airship continued to send out directional wireless signals to check her position or to test the strength of the signals.

"The last directional signal R101 addressed to Cardington was at 1.28 am. A final signal was sent from Cardington to the Croydon Station and relayed via ship at Le Bourget at 01.51am. An acknowledgement at 01.52am was the last signal ever sent by the R101."[53]

The planned course would have taken the R101 four miles west of Beauvais, but Johnston's estimations of wind speed and direction were not entirely accurate. Consequently, the airship was tracking to the east of its intended route.

This mistake must have become clear to Johnston when, at about 01:00, R101 passed over Poix-de-Picardie, a hilltop town easily distinguished by its unique architectural characteristics. Then airship therefore changed course. Her new route would take her directly over the 770 ft (230 m) Beauvais Ridge, a landform well-known among aviators for its turbulent atmospheric conditions.[54]

---

53   Davison, 2015

54   Masefield, 1982, p. 396

Approaching Beauvais

As she travelled into France, the R101 met with pummeling winds and battering rain.

Battling this onslaught, she was forced to slow down to a ground-speed of around thirty miles per hour. Across the north-west of France that night, many people saw her pass. Some thought she seemed to be struggling against the weather.

R101 sent out that regular position report at 1.28. At 1.30 she appeared to pass so low over the village of Saint-Valery-sur-Somme that the inhabitants scrambled from their beds, certain she would scrape the rooves off their houses. Slowly, the row of lights that was all that was visible of the airship in the pitch-darkness, roared away into the night.

Despite the pressure of the raindrops and the force of the wind squalls tearing at her outer envelope; despite being weighed down by yards of carpet and luggage, the R101 continued to persevere through the storm.

```
Mirror (Perth, WA: 1921–1956)
Sat 13 Dec 1952 Page 9
The R.101 roared over the town of Beauvais at less than
400ft., and the sound of her engines, like the thunder
of a train, brought the startled French citizens out of
their beds peering at the flashing lights in the darkness
above them. The time was 6 minutes past two on the
morning of Oct. 5.
```

2am change of watch

The weather conditions continued to deteriorate, with rising winds and pouring rain. Despite this, in line with standard procedure the airship's watch was changed at 0200 hours on the morning of 5th October.

Nick Le Neve Walmsley, Airship historian says, "... at about two o'clock in the morning they were just changing over the watches, and two of the engineers who were changing over in the engine cars had to look out of of the car and saw the pinnacles of a great Gothic church [sic] going past at eye level—which is when they realized something was wrong, and they were much too low down, and this was actually the town of Beauvais . . ."

Although the R101 was carrying only direction lights, the people of Beauvais, looking out of their windows, could clearly see her shape during the ten minutes she was over their homes.

The airship's course took her east of the municipality. She began to approach the infamous Beauvais Ridge, whose air turbulence frequently caused problems for aircraft on the London-Paris route.

If the engineers were worried, they said nothing of it. To everyone else, all appeared to be in order, despite the weather being the worst ever encountered by a British rigid airship over land. The departing watch retired to rest. All engines were running smoothly and they were on course, albeit slightly late due to the headwind.

The crewman who had not gone to bed was Foreman Engineer Harry Leech.[55] He had smoke-room privileges, and returned there for a last cigarette before turning in. All seemed well. Leech thought the airship was gliding along quite smoothly, in spite of the gusting wind.

THE FALL

Allonne Wood

A small woodland of hazel and oak trees grows outside the village of Allonne and the hamlet of Bongenoult, about 2.5 miles (4 km) southeast of Beauvais, in France. It is called 'Le Bois d'Allonne' (Allonne Wood).[56] In 1930 a hedgerow of hawthorn or blackthorn formed a fence between the wood and an adjacent apple orchard. The season being autumn, the leaves of the apple trees, bronze and yellow, had begun to fall.

---

55   Leech enjoyed an unusual status which C.P. Hall perceives as an 'honorary second class passenger'.

56   One corner of it bears the name 'Le Bois des Coutumes' (Customs Wood).

On that October night of wild wind and rain only one small, grey-haired man was abroad in Le Bois d'Allonne, moving somewhat stealthily among the trees. A 56 year old employee at a factory near Beauvais, his name was Monsieur Rabouille. He went about his business discreetly, for he was laying snares to catch rabbits, and poaching was illegal.

Shortly before 2 a.m., the poacher heard a strange throbbing roar in the sky, behind the din of the wind and rain. It grew louder, as if approaching. He climbed to the top of a hillock. Straining his eyes through the gloom, he made out the huge form of an airship coming towards him, her onboard lights ablaze. She was flying very low and, as he thought, circling over the nearby village of Allonne.

"She was drifting on the violent westerly wind, and I had the impression that she was having a hard fight against the wind and drenching rain. Then, steadily losing height, she approached the place where I was standing, moving very slowly, although her engines seemed to be running flat out.

"...she crossed the wood at a height of about 150 feet, coming lower and lower all the time. I said to myself, 'Something is going to happen.'..."

Monsieur Rabouille, his head tilted back, heedless of the pouring rain, stared as the airship approached through the stormy sky.

"I clearly saw the passengers' quarters, well-lit, and the green and red lights on the right and left of the airship. I noticed that the airship was not going steadily," said the poacher, "and I saw the lights go out twice.

"Suddenly there was a violent squall. The airship dipped by the nose several times.."

Time: 02:07 + 24 seconds: The first dive

What were they like for Will, those last moments? We can only imagine, then turn away.

* * *

At 02:07 + 24 seconds, Squadron Leader Palstra starts from a deep slumber as he is rocked violently in his berth. He rolls hard against the wall. The luggage stool slides across the floor, spilling its burden.

He springs out of bed, befuddled by sleep, trying to collect his thoughts. A well-known sensation of lightness tells him he is rapidly losing altitude. Instinctively, every nerve snaps to alertness. For an instant he wonders where he is, then he recalls—he is aboard an airship.

What is happening? He can hear telegraph bells ringing, and the sound of answering gongs. The whole cabin is on a steep tilt. There are no windows, and the cabin is dimly lit by slender strips of radiance seeping around the door-curtain from the corridor. He fumbles for a light switch, trying to recall where it is. Through the thin walls he can hear men's voices, the other passengers, mumbling, "Good lord, what the devil is going on?"

* * *

At seven minutes past two, with no warning at all, the airship had gone into a steep dive. As she lost altitude, she was hit by a gust that forced her nose further down. She tilted so sharply that the engineers manning the ship were thrown off balance, and furniture shot forward across the decks.

The abrupt change of attitude, and the sounds of telegraph bells and gongs, woke some of the crew, and probably many or all of the passengers. Conceivably, some people had even been tipped out of their berths.

Harry Leech, the Foreman Engineer from Cardington, was still in the smoke-room.

Afterwards he recalled, "I had been there 10-15 minutes when the ship's nose went down very rapidly to an angle of 40 degrees. Tables and all loose articles slipped down towards the forward bulkhead. I slipped from the centre of my settee to the front end which was against the bulkhead."[57] Leech attributed the rolling and pitching of the vessel to weather conditions.

Twenty-five year old rigger Sam Church, coming off first-watch duty, was walking back to his bunk in the crew's quarters. He staggered and reached out for support as the floor suddenly dipped.

In the R101's aft engine car, engineers Joe Binks and Arthur Victor Bell were having a chat. All at once the floor changed pitch, sloping down towards the front of the car, and the men flung out their arms to steady themselves. They felt the airship rapidly losing height.

It is difficult to imagine, but there was no general panic among the crew. Airship flight is normally so smooth and buoyant, and altitude changes so much a part of the pattern that few people would leap to the idea of "crashing" in the way that modern aircraft passengers might. The men on board were trained to be calm in dangerous situations. Besides, their faith in God and the British Air Ministry was profound, and of course, it was just not "done" to panic in front of one's peers.

The R101 was now flying only 584 feet above the ground, buffeted by violent gusts. For an aircraft her size, this was far too low.

In the control car Second Officer Maurice Steff, who was in charge of the second watch, knew he had to reduce the ship's angle by lightening the load at the front and raising the elevators. The only remaining ballast that could be released automatically, from the control car, was four tons of diesel fuel stored forward of the control car. He pulled some levers, and the fuel was discharged from frames 3 and 5.

Meanwhile the height coxswain was trying to right the airship. He pulled hard on the wheel controlling the elevators, raising them until they were almost fully up.

This first dive may have lasted for half-a-minute, but it brought the airship many hundreds of feet nearer the ground.

---

57   Harry Leech, Foreman Engineer, Statement AIR5/903 Source: Davison , 2015

Time: 02:07 + 37 seconds: recovery

A few seconds after the dive had occurred, Will felt the airship straighten. The floor of his cabin slowly levelled out. The R101's nose slowly tilted up, until she was almost on an even keel again. It appeared she had recovered from the dive. She was now tilted only 6 degrees nose down, and had almost returned to being horizontal.

Will must have felt relieved, hoping the crew had managed to fix whatever had caused the ship to fall like that. It seemed that everything was all right.

Or was it?

Another telegraph bell jangled. The floors and walls trembled and bounced. From beyond Will's thin-walled cabin came the distant rumble of engines, the steady patter of rain, the ringing of bells, men's voices…

In the smoke-room Chief Engineer Harry Leech took the opportunity to start tidying the mess.

The ship, though almost horizontal now, was still descending at a rate of 290 feet per minute.

And then she made a second dive.

Lech recalled,

> "The ship dived a considerable distance before resuming on an even keel. Remained on an even keel for a minute or less, engine still running at cruising speed: then dived again same angle as before. Between first and second dive I picked up some glasses and a siphon and laid them on table.
>
> "Just before the ship started her second dive I heard the telegraph bell."[58]

---

58   Harry Leech, Foreman Engineer, Statement AIR5/903 Source: Davison, 2015

The crew in the control car realised that the elevator was 'hard up' and yet the airship's nose was only three degrees above the artificial horizon on the instruments panel. "This meant that the nose was now extremely heavy and hence a serious loss of gas from the forward bags must have occurred."[59]

They also realised that R101 was dropping to the ground, and they commenced to make preparations for an emergency landing.

Over the course of the next minute Second Officer Steff, in the control car, transmitted orders by the engine-room telegraph, telling the men in charge of each engine-car to reduce the power of the engines. His aim was to minimise any forward impact by decelerating from the original cruising speed.

Throughout the airship passengers and crew could hear the engine telegraph bells ringing at each of the engine cars in turn, followed by acknowledgement gongs. The telegraphic signals took a few seconds to transmit, since each engine car had a separate system. The engineers heard the bells and acted upon their instructions.

In the left-hand midships engine car, twenty seven year old engineer Alfred J. Cook heard the telegraph ring the signal for reducing speed. "I had got an order by Engine Telegraphs to 'slow' (450 rpm)". He acknowledged the order and began to comply.

Second Officer Steff had slowed the descent, but he may not have known precisely what caused this dive. He dispatched the Chief Coxswain, George Hunt, to alert Irwin, and to order a rigger to manually drop some ballast. Hunt spotted Sam Church, who was just returning to the crew's quarters after finishing his watch, and told him to hurry forward to manually release one of two remaining half tons of emergency ballast in the airship's nose. Some of the R101's ballast bags could be operated from the control car, but not the forward emergency bags, which is why Church was told to go and do the job. Dumping a load of liquid ballast from the front of the ship should cause her nose to rise again. Church was on his way to the mooring platform when he felt the floor of the airship begin to slope once more, nosing down in a steep gradient.

---

59   The Airship Heritage Trust: "The R101 Crash" https://www.airshipsonline.com/airships/R.101/Crash/R.101_Crash.htm

Meanwhile, Irwin instructed Hunt to awaken the crew, which he was doing when disaster overtook them. Rigger Church was, for wahever reason, unable to carry out his task. Both ballast bags were, no doubt, ruptured on impact, thus helping the bow to lift briefly before it settled to earth.

Time: 02:07 + 40 seconds.

In the switch room, Chief Electrician Arthur Disley lying on his bunk, and his colleague seated at the switch board, were wide awake. The vessel had just resumed an even keel when the Hunt came by. He popped his head into the switch room and announced, "We're down, lads."

This famous comment by one of the most experienced airship crew members showed that the R101 was not going to be able to continue flying, and that an executive decision had been made make an emergency landing.[60]

Hunt did not seem panicky or excited. He gave Disley the impression that he was warning them to get ready to leave.

In the switch room, just as Disley was rising from his berth, the ship went into a second steep dive, throwing him back onto his bunk. As the "SLOW" engine telegraph gongs began to sound he managed to get to his feet and 'trip' one of the field switches. This disconnected one of the two main electrical circuits, as a safety precaution in an emergency landing.

Still, there was no sense of panic or real urgency.

The Second Dive and Landing

At the edge of the dark, rain-soaked wood, the watching Frenchman Monsieur Rabouille had seen the airship level off. "... she dipped," he said, "descended a short way, then seemed to straighten out. Then she tilted again and sank slowly to earth, still moving gradually forward and pointing her nose downwards…"

---

60   ibid

As the ship descended to the earth she was brilliantly illuminated, especially the control car, which was all lit up. Within seconds of the brief recovery the airship had lunged downwards again, and this time the height coxswain could do nothing to pull her out of the dive. Steff, the officer in command, could see what was coming. He ordered all engines to reduce power, and warning bells were rung throughout the airship. Before some of the engineers could respond to the new orders, the airship touched the ground.

Her forepart crashed into the northwest edge of the Bois des Coutumes [Customs Wood]. The lights went out immediately she came into contact with the earth.

Time: 02:08 + 32 seconds

The airship tipped on an angle, and vibrations shuddered through the floor. The two engineers Binks and Bell felt a slight shock as their engine car landed quite lightly on the ground and skidded along for a short distance.

In the switch room, Chief Electrician Arthur Disley felt the final dive and the "crunch" of a relatively gentle impact.

Fearing that something serious was happening, engineer Cook peered out of the door of his engine car. "… and while I looked," he said, "the ship struck the ground."

The airship seemed to rebound after the first bump. The young man immediately stopped his engine. Some seconds occurred between the first and second striking of the ground, then the airship slid to rest at the edge of the wood outside Allonne 2.5 miles (4 km) southeast of Beauvais. Simultaneously with the impact, the lights went out.

Imagine:

> At 02:08 + 32 seconds, Will is momentarily flung off balance again as the whole cabin lists a second time. Something brushes across his face—the folds of the door-curtain billowing into the room. Bells are jangling, this time like a warning alarm. The throbbing of the engines slows. He feels the floor falling away from beneath his feet followed by a gentle impact; hears the

scrape and howl of buckling metal accompanied by the feeling of slackening momentum, as if the airship is shuddering to a halt. The lights go out, and for an instant the cabin is pitch dark...

Wind and rain tossed the boughs of the trees at the edge of the wood. At 02:08 + 50 seconds, with a great grinding noise of engines slowing and metal grating on metal, the R101 grounded softly at 18.1 degrees nose down, with a forward speed of around 12 miles per hour. She bumped forward along the ground for about 60 feet and, with her tail still 258 feet in the air, finally came to rest.

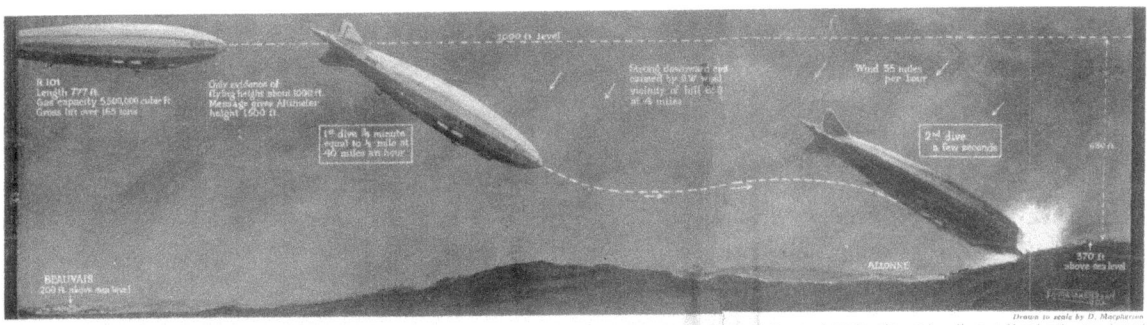

A diagram showing how the British R101 airship dived twice and crashed on a hillside of Allonne, near Beauvais, France on 5th October 1930 on its maiden voyage.
Alamy Image ID:2M3NJ7E

She had spent only seven hours in the air.

The impact with which the nose of the ship struck the earth seems to have been less severe than might have been expected. One witness described it as a "crunch".

According to Davison, "The force of the landing broke the mooring cone and buckled the nose, and the whole ship compressed 88 feet longitudinally before settling almost vertically with the aft section staying clear of the ground."

The Airship Heritage Trust records, "There was no violent jarring. The only impact mark in the ground was a two foot deep by nine foot long [0.6m by 2.74m] groove which was cut by the nose cone, in which soil was later found."[61]

With the forward engines set at 'Slow', the propellers were still revolving on impact. Those on the starboard forward engine car dug grooves in the wet earth. The engine car itself twisted completely around on its struts and was forced up and into the hull.

Peter Davison explains, "A single sapling was left standing within the frame. The crunch crushed the nose access corridor, trapping all the passengers, and the forward starboard engine gondola was pushed up into the hull structure.

> "The main longitudinal girders seem to have stayed intact though the forward section compressed as the short girder sections of the intermediate reefing girders acted like crumple zones, popping out at each frame intersection."[62]

C.P.Hall elucidates, 'The R.101's bow fitting hit first, digging the trench described. This bent the nose backwards and probably crushed the two half-ton emergency water ballast bags located under the winch platform. The bow lifted and moved forward about 60 feet, coming to rest at a shallower angle—initial contact point forward of the engine. As the ship came to rest, it settled (the stern declined). When the forward engines came to ground, the

---

61 ibid
62 Davison, 2015

forward, starboard engine rotated 180 degrees into the side of the ship, likely resulting in the ignition of the fire. As the airship continued to settle, the control car was crushed upward into the hull.

Imagine:

> Trapped in the blacked-out passenger quarters, Will holds his nerve. The darkness is confusing, threatening, cacophonous, The floor and walls quiver. Shocks ripple through the structure as the airship touches down.
>
> He refuses to panic. After all, there might be no reason to worry. Everything is probably all right.
>
> Yet if, for some reason, the hydrogen gas ignites as has happened on other airships, he will have no chance. What if the worst should happen?
>
> Beneath his feet the floor jars and judders a second time. It heaves up with a sudden lunge, throwing him off balance. He steadies himself, and the familiar, comforting words he first learned as a child spring to his mind. Quietly, he prays.
>
> "The Lord is my shepherd…"
>
> As he whispers the words, in this final extremity his thoughts turn with full intensity to the people dearest to him.
>
> May. Margaret. Jocelyn. Bill. Dad. Mum. . . .
>
> He yearns to be with them, his loved ones; longs for them with every particle of his being. Next, the world explodes.

The R101 had pointed her bow to the earth and suddenly disappeared behind a rise. She touched the ground so lightly that almost everyone on board lived through the landing.

Without what happened next, the crash would probably have been survivable, but almost immediately after the airship came to rest, she burst into flames. A bellow of thunder erupted through the valley as five million cubic feet of hydrogen ignited.

Rabouille could scarcely believe what he was seeing.

"As she was settling on the ground, the middle collapsed as if she had broken her back. The engines continued to run for a second or two after the crash. I had the airship in sight all the time from first hearing it to the moment of the catastrophe.

"The first part of the ship to touch the earth was the body close up to the nose. That part of the ship which is half way between the nose and the middle touched the ground, and immediately there was a tremendous explosion. The noise almost broke my ear drums. The sound came from the fore part of the ship. Simultaneously a giant burst of flame swept the envelope from front to tail, scorching me, even 100 yards away. I was blown down by the force of the explosion, knocked onto my back. As I picked myself up, two more explosions of much less violence followed, and the whole of the ship burst into flames.

"Soon flames rose into the sky to a great height—perhaps 300 feet. Everything was enveloped by them. There was a terrific glare. I saw human figures running about like madmen in the wreck.

"I heard people in the wreckage crying out for help, but did not see anyone."

Artist's impression of the disaster. Image: www.planetminecraft.com

CATASTROPHE

The explosion shook the houses of Allonne and Beauvais to their foundations, and smashed windows nine miles away. People in the vicinity of Beauvais were awakened by loud noises and streaks of light soaring across the sky. Then followed flames that burned fiercely and brightly for five to seven minutes, casting a ghastly yellow light over the countryside.

The dark night turned into a kind of lurid day.

```
Mirror (Perth, WA: 1921—1956)
Sat 13 Dec 1952 Page 9
The woods of Bougenoult lit up as the R.101 glowed like
some terrible, huge lantern. Flames from the blazing
gasbags shot high into the air, and scorched the trees.
As Rabouille ran away in fright he could hear the
agonised screams of wounded men being burnt to death as
they lay trapped in the wreckage.

But if the poacher of Beauvais lacked courage there
were men who did not. Some fortunate survivors had
been flung clear at the moment of impact, and as soon as
they had recovered their wits they ploughed through the
scattered burning wreckage to drag out less lucky crew
members and passengers.
```

Arthur Disley, the twenty-eight year old wireless operator, later gave his account;

"I was lying in my bunk when a terrific, stunning crash occurred. Everything went dark. Then there was a tremendous burst of flame.[63]

"There was a crash, a series of explosions, and blinding flashes all round, and the whole ship flared up from stem to stern. I do not know where the fire started, but I believe the

---

63   Examiner (Launceston, Tas. : 1900 - 1954) Tue 7 Oct 1930, Page 9 "A Miraculous Escape"

amidships were just a mass of flames roaring like a furnace. I threw myself against the fabric in an effort to break through, but failed."[64]

"I rushed out and attacked the fabric, using my teeth and nails, but it withstood. The flames were rushing towards me, and I sank down in the corridor exhausted. Then the flooring gave way, and I fell through on to the grass."[65]

"I sat down trying to collect my wits, and found myself sitting on wet grass. Then I discovered myself under the airship, where the fabric was torn. I crawled along the ground, following the tear, and emerged in the open air."[66]

"I got out just in time. Leech and Binks rushed towards me, and dragged me to safety."[67]

"I went to see if I could rescue anybody, but it was over in a minute or two."[68]

Inside the smoke room, Harry Leech had felt the shock of impact. It was ". . . not great—more a crunch than a crash—I was not even shaken. Simultaneously with the impact the lights went out . . . I counted a second or two between the crash and the explosion, followed by a roar of flame.

"Within two seconds of striking, a blinding flash of fire appeared to originate from above the control car. I saw the mass of flame through the door of the smoke room.

"The upper passenger deck collapsed on to the tops of the settee backs, leaving me a space of three feet full of fumes and smoke, but no flames. I heard people screaming and moaning in the crews quarters and upper passenger deck, which was then blazing."

Leech managed to escape through the damaged wooden wall of the smoke room.

"I tore a settee away from the bulkhead and scrambled through the opening, and found myself inside the hull on the starboard side. The outer cover had then been completely burnt

---

64 The Register News-Pictorial (Adelaide, SA : 1929 - 1931) Tue 7 Oct 1930 Page 3.

65 Examiner (Launceston, Tas. : 1900 - 1954) Tue 7 Oct 1930, Page 9 A Miraculous Escape

66 The Register News-Pictorial (Adelaide, SA : 1929 - 1931) Tue 7 Oct 1930 Page 3.

67 Examiner (Launceston, Tas. : 1900 - 1954) Tue 7 Oct 1930, Page 9 A Miraculous Escape

68 The Register News-Pictorial (Adelaide, SA : 1929 - 1931) Tue 7 Oct 1930 Page 3.

away from that section, except for the cellon windows which were still blazing and through which I had to force my way."[69]

The Foreman Engineer literally jumped through the burning body of the ship, escaping through the framework to safety. He landed in the branches of a tree, and as it was raining, the leaves showered water all over him. In his own words, "this cooled me off."

Engineer Joe Binks described his experience in the aft engine car, when he and Arthur Bell felt the R101 touch the earth. To him, it felt as if the airship had taken on a malevolent life of its own. "Car does not strike ground heavily, but in the ship's effort to telescope the car, is bumped all along the ground causing the bottom to cave in."

Bell said to his friend, "Looks as though all is up."[70]

Both engineers were convinced they were doomed.

Just after the airship struck the hill for the second time they heard a deafening crash as fire broke out. Flames seemed to be roaring all around them, but next moment some overhead service water-tanks for the engine burst apart. Water flooded their engine car and temporarily dampened the flames.

Binks and Bell remained in the car for a short while until the flames slightly subsided, then wrapped their heads in wet cloths and rushed through a small opening in the port quarter on the left side of the stern. Once free of the car, they picked their way out of the wreckage through the crumpled girders.

Being drenched with water helped to protect them from the intense heat of the surrounding fire, but the metal girders through which they navigated were white-hot, and the men sustained painful burns.

Engineer Alfred Cook was in the port midship car. He felt the jarring of the first impact, then the rebound of the airship, before she crashed again and almost immediately became enveloped in flames.

---

[69] Harry Leech, Foreman Engineer, Statement AIR5/903 Source: Davison, 2015

[70] Examiner (Launceston, Tas. : 1900 - 1954) Tue 7 Oct 1930, Page 9

A minute or two after the ship struck the hillside, his engine car sank to the ground. He had time to stop the engine, while pieces of structure were falling onto and around the car.

"I tried to get out of the car through the door, but there was a mass of flame, and the heat was terrific. I turned to the sliding doors on the exterior side, and found that a girder had fallen across the opening. The cellular[71] door was blazing."

Cook's first attempt to get out of the burning wreckage was unsuccessful. He tried again, diving into a wall of fire.

"I thought I was completely trapped, and became desperate. I thrust the girder up and jumped out. I landed on the grass, and tore off my burning overalls. My hands were hurting terribly. At the same time I heard minor explosions."[72]

Ultimately he made his escape, but with life-threatening injuries.

Later, as he lay bandaged and dying in hospital, he said with heart-breaking gallantry, "It was terrible, but it adds another page to British heroism. Captain Irwin was a hero. As I fought my way through the flames I saw him standing at his post, giving orders. He made no attempt to save his life. That was the last we saw of him. He died there."[73]

Rigger Walter George Radcliffe, a Bedford resident aged thirty one, was also in one of the engine cars. All the cars were located outside the main hull, so when the airship landed, he too was able to escape, either through the windows or the door, and flee from the burning airship.

One of the first people to arrive on the scene of the disaster was an Englishman called George Darling. He tried to help.

---

71   "Cellular door": Cook was referring to the material "cellon", from which the R.101's windows were made.

72   The Northern Miner (Charters Towers, Qld. : 1874 - 1954) Mon 3 Nov 1930 Page 2 "R.101 DISASTER"

73   Examiner (Launceston, Tas. : 1900 - 1954) Tue 7 Oct 1930, Page 9 and The Register News-Pictorial (Adelaide, SA : 1929 - 1931) Tue 7 Oct 1930 Page 3. "Commander Of R.101 Meets Death At Post Calmly Giving Orders."

Examiner (Launceston, Tas.: 1900–1954)
Tue 7 Oct 1930, Page 9
"Rising and Falling"

A former resident of Leeds, George Darling, now residing at Beauvais, states that he saw the airship overhead at 1.45 am. She was rising and falling ominously, and he realised that she was in difficulties, so he decided to follow her in his motor car. He was some distance behind when she came down with a terrible crash. Flames instantly appeared at one end, but they had not a substantial hold.

"When I arrived I was amazed to see a man in a blue tunic standing dazed," says Darling. "It was Leech, who said that nobody was aware that the R.101 was in difficulties till a few minutes before the crash. He knew that the captain was trying to communicate with the engine room to stop the engines."

Two More Survivors
Then Bell and Binks appeared from nowhere. Darling broke the mica door and with Leech and others penetrated the mechanical control room and tried to reach the cabin, but the flames repelled them. They saw one man, terribly burned, frantically trying to escape, but he collapsed into the inferno.
Later they found Church, whose hair was burned off.

[East Anglian Daily Times 6/10/1930]

```
Darling said, "I managed to climb into that end of the
airship which was farthest from the fire by breaking a
glass door, and got as far as I could along the inside
of the structure. Ultimately I got to the cabin where
the machinery was. This was quite intact, and was not on
fire, so I went further on through the ship to see if I
could save anyone. But it was burning furiously at the
other end, and the flames drove me back.
"Leech and the other men joined me inside the airship,
but it was hopeless to do anything for the victims. We
saw one man, who was evidently trying to get out of a
cabin, but he was terribly burned, and we saw him fall
back helpless into the flames."
```

Though injured, Bell, Binks and Leech re-entered the burning airship in an effort to save others. They showed true bravery. Darling, too, demonstrated immense courage.

The force of the explosions hurled fragments of the R101 into the sky. According to the a witness statement statement of a fourteen-year-old French girl, Mademoiselle Moillez, "After the explosion the sky was filled with pieces of burning wreckage and these floated away from the spot slowly sinking; it looked like a large firework going off."[74]

Attracted by the explosions and the great flaring light of the blaze, citizens and policemen soon arrived at the edge of the wood.

---

74 Davison, 2015

Examiner (Launceston, Tas.: 1900—1954)
Tue 7 Oct 1930, Page 9

Monsieur Sourin, commanding the Gendarmerie of the Oise Department, who was first to arrive at the scene, says: "It was a terrible sight. I heard groans, but in spite of all efforts, I could not get close to the airship, from which the flames were shooting to a great height."

Examiner (Launceston, Tas.: 1900—1954)
Tue 7 Oct 1930, Page 9
A Blazing Mass

Village people at Beauvais say that there was a misty rain when the airship passed over. She seemed in difficulties, and there was soon a terrific explosion and a blinding flash. Allonne peasants scampered to the scene in their night clothes, but the inferno prevented their approach to the R.101, which was a twisted, blazing mass, from which charred remnants of fabric were incessantly dropping. One engine could be seen deeply embedded in the mud.

The Age (Melbourne, Vic.: 1854—1954)
Mon 6 Oct 1930 Page 9
R.101 DESTROYED. STRIKES HILL & BURSTS INTO FLAMES.
DISASTER IN FRANCE EN ROUTE TO INDIA.
FIFTY-THREE ABOARD-ONLY SEVEN SURVIVE. VICTIMS INCLUDE AIR MINISTER.
LONDON, 5th October.

> The wreckage burnt fiercely, and was unapproachable till
> near daylight. The French authorities rushed troops,
> doctors, nurses and ambulances to the scene. When at last
> the rescuers managed to approach the wreckage, though
> it was still hot, only twelve bodies were recovered. All
> the remains were so badly charred as to be unrecognis-
> able. It was a dreadful scene — the weather was stormy
> and rain was falling.

The hydrogen-fuelled inferno consumed almost every part of the R101 and her contents; her acres of outer coverings, the R101 letterhead notepaper, the Irish linen bed-sheets, the Axminster carpet, Lord Thomson's Persian carpet, the tablecloths, curtains, potted plants, cane furniture, suits, pyjamas, handkerchiefs, neckties and other clothing; the crew's blue R101 uniforms, and most of the people she was carrying...

WRECKAGE AND SURVIVORS

The first light of dawn on Sunday October 5th illuminated a dismal scene.

Like the charred skeleton of some prehistoric monster, the blackened metalwork of the R101 lay across the wood. The inferno had vapourised the delicate gold-beater's skin gas bags and the doped-linen envelope. The main skeleton had survived, apart from the central section, which had almost completely collapsed. Amongst the tangle of twisted girders, flames were still leaping, and smoke climbed into the grey morning air. It was still raining. So hot was the wreckage of the R101 that the raindrops evaporated, hissing, as soon as they touched it.[75]

---

75 "The main skeletal form survived apart from between frames 6 and 8A where the weight and flammability of the centre section caused almost complete collapse." Davison, 2015

```
Mirror (Perth, WA: 1921-1956)
Sat 13 Dec 1952 Page 9
```

"The tail stood intact for hours; a little fabric remained on the elevators. These were still wound fully up, and a tattered and scorched R.A.F. ensign still fluttered forlornly at the stern. Of all the non-metallic parts, this was the only thing not burnt to ashes. Nothing else remained of the glorious R.101 but a massive tangle of scorched metal, the twisted, burnt and charred framework.
She was completely gutted by fire."[76]

The wreckage of the R101 airship which crashed at Allonne, Beauvais, near Paris, France. Firemen holding up the scorched ensign, which was found flying at the stern. 5th October 1930. Alamy Image ID:2HHKA51

---

[76] Footage of the immediate aftermath of the crash can be seen on YouTube: "R100 and R.101 Airships. Archive film 99490" on the Huntley Film Archives channel. See also "R.101 Disaster witness interview 1930" on the channel belonging to "Bomberguy".

Examiner (Launceston, Tas.: 1900–1954)

Tue 7 Oct 1930, Page 9

Aerial photographs have been taken of the wreck. Which was so sudden that one of the engineers who was burned almost to cinders still clutched a spanner. The photos show the airship with the envelope stripped, like the twisted skeleton of a giant whale.

THE TIMES Monday October 6 1930 THE SHIP'S SKELETON

. . . I found the wreck of R.101 near the village of Allonne, a few miles south of Beauvais. As I approached the scene of the accident through the Bois Seck (a woodland) I caught sight of what looked at first like the half-built roof of a railway station standing up on the horizon beyond the trees. This was the framework of the unhappy airship.

Getting nearer still, a delicate network of girders could be made out against the sky. It was one of the vertical fins of the ship. All the fabric had disappeared, and as one began to realise the immense size of the structure, which from a distance of a quarter of a mile already towered over the surrounding trees, it was difficult to believe that these were the remains of an aircraft fallen by accident into this windswept landscape, and not the framework of some gigantic building intended to stand permanently in this place.

. . . All the gasbags and the outer envelope had vanished, but through and over the distorted framework wire stays and gasbag nettings made a fine and elaborate tracery as though an army of gigantic spiders had already covered the useless skeleton of R.101 with their webs.

. . . Near the very centre of the ship a denser mass of wreckage indicated the quarters of the ill-fated passengers. Here domestic fittings such as staircases and water-tanks could be distinguished, and on the starboard side a row of gilded pillars, - all that remained of the promenade deck - seemed to grin garishly like false teeth in a skull. A few flames still flickered on the ground, twelve hours after the wreck. Into this part of the wreckage men had to cut their way with blow-lamp, chisel and hacksaw to look for possible survivors and to get at the bodies of the dead.
The ridge on which the airship struck is thinly wooded with hazel and oak bushes, and among these the forward portion lies. . .

. . . SHATTERED FRAMEWORK

The extreme nose of the airship lay on the summit of a hill. From this point, looking back down the hill, the whole carcass of the airship lay before me, a mute witness to the tragedy of hopes shattered and lives sacrificed. The long, twisted girders writhed on the ground in parallel lines. On each side the remains of the cross-frames rose like broken ribs, and in the distance over the arched skeleton of the airship's tail, itself as large as the entrance to an ordinary railway station, the frame of her vertical fin rose mournfully against the sky and the balance rudder, still rocking on its hinges, swung aimlessly like an indifferent weathercock in the wind.

Here and there among the contorted steel beams lay a few charred personal items such as clothing, watches, rings and keys. The only known exit from the sleeping quarters of passengers and crew was crushed when the airship landed. There was no escape for the occupants. The accommodation area collapsed completely in the fire.

The R.101 Airship after making two unexpected dives over Beauvais, near Paris, hits the ground with only six survivors from the 54 passengers. 5th October 1930.
Alamy Image ID:2HHK63R

Alamy ID:2JPTBNH

AIRSHIP/R101 CRASH/1930 Alamy ID:K05KFY

Alamy ID:2ACYKG4

RECOVERY OF BODIES

Image supplied

Of the fifty-four crew and passengers only eight men made it out of the burning wreck alive—five engineers, two riggers and a wireless operator. They were taken to hospital in Beauvais and treated for burns. The two riggers perished during the following days, bringing the death toll to forty-eight.

The bodies of all the victims, recovered within hours by the local gendarmerie, pompiers (firefighters) and townsfolk, were burnt beyond recognition.

```
Examiner (Launceston, Tas. : 1900 - 1954)
Tue 7 Oct 1930, Page 9
Recovery of Bodies


The firemen were able to begin operations at dawn. They
quickly discovered four charred, unrecognisable bodies,
and then a score of others were extricated from the
ruins of the central cabin. The engineers are working
frantically with oxy-acetylene blow pipes to sever the
tangled metal.
```

French police search through the wreckage of the British R101 airship that crashed near Beauvais in France on 5th October 1930. Alamy Image ID:2M3NJ8G

French soldiers at the scene of the crash of the British airship R101 in the French village of Beauvais;October 1930. Alamy Image ID:B571GX

THE TIMES
Monday October 6 1930
WORK OF IDENTIFICATION

Directly after the crash all the available police and troops at Beauvais hurried to the rescue. As fast as the bodies could be got out of the wreck, they were laid in a row along the outskirts of the wood and sheets were thrown over them. Eight bodies were still there this afternoon.

All of them, as far as I could see, were practically unrecognisable. In some cases rings, keys and small belongings were found on or near the bodies and these may help in identification. These things were laid temporarily with the bodies. Near one I saw a watch which was still going.

Arrangements for the identification of the bodies, as far as it is possible, have been made for tomorrow. The identification will be based in almost every case on the personal belongings of the victims. These will be shown to the relatives and others whose testimony is required, and the bodies which have been identified will immediately be placed in coffins and sent to England.

Examiner (Launceston, Tas. : 1900 - 1954)
Tue 7 Oct 1930, Page 9
RUSH TO HELP

Assistance came promptly from the villagers at Allonne, and from Beauvais, police, military and doctors hurrying to the scene.

Parts of the airship has been scattered in all directions and the debris continued to smoke until late today. The few survivors were quickly hurried to hospital and this morning the remains of the 46 victims, many unidentified, were collected.

LIKE A FURNACE

The clothes had been burnt off most of them, but some of the bodies were identified by rings and watches, among them being that of Lord Thompson [sic], the Secretary for Air.
Today the French Air Minister (M. Laurent Eynac) and other French officials were early on the scene . . .

Scene of Destruction
The wreckage lies in a hollow athwart a high hedge. The forepart, twisted beyond recognition, lies in an apple orchard, and the stern and about one-third of the ship's length are standing up in the air. The metal-work is practically undamaged.
A half-burned Union Jack fluttered at the stern for many hours after the crash. It was hauled down in the afternoon and handed over to the British military attaché.
Some of the bodies of the victims were so shrivelled that they would fit into a child's coffin. They were laid out in the shelter of the hedge. Many were completely unrecognisable. Sir Sefton Brancker's body was known by his monocle.

Enormous crowds arrived at the spot throughout the day, mounted police and firemen keeping them at a distance to prevent pilfering of mementoes, although scarcely anything of value remains.

The airship might have been a gigantic furnace, so completely was everything consumed.

Policemen carrying bodies from the wreckage on stretchers.
"R101 Rescue Operation" By Hulton Deutsch.
Getty Image ID 613462436

Beside the hedge, sheets cover some of the bodies recovered from the wreckage.
Getty Image ID 80749532

Bodies of the victims, in coffins, being taken to the schoolroom at nearby Allonne on horse-drawn carts. Alamy Image ID: GAFP7W

The Argus,
Wednesday October 8th 1930 Page 7
LOSS OF R.101
BODIES OF VICTIMS HONOURED BY FRENCH BODIES PLACED IN COFFINS
London, Oct 6
Messages from Beauvais state that a special committee of identification, including a senior officer of the Air Force and an officer from Cardington who knew all the members of the crew of the R.101, after working all day failed to establish the identity of the majority of the bodies of the men who were killed when the airship struck a hill and was burnt near Beauvais on Sunday morning. All the bodies have now been enclosed in lead lined coffins which will be screwed up in order to spare thee feelings of the relatives who will be shown clothes and other articles such as rings and keys, which were taken from the bodies.

Examiner (Launceston, Tas. : 1900 - 1954)
Mon 6 Oct 1930 Page 7
TERRIBLE AIRSHIP DISASTER.
The airship is lying on the side of a hillock in a desolate stretch of country. One portion stands straight to a height of a hundred feet. Fires are still smouldering in several places. Identification of the bodies will probably be established only by articles. For instance, one man had a bracelet in each hand, another a photograph, compass, key; and pair of scissors, and another a box of cigarettes and a cigarette-making machine.

The News Travels

Messengers hurried away from the scene of the disaster to spread the news.

So much faith and confidence had been placed in the R100 and R101 that at first, newsmen on night duty refused to believe the reports of the Beauvais crash. Only the Express ran the story in their Sunday edition.

After the reality eventually sank in, news of the terrible accident travelled fast. It reached Australia by telegraph.

```
The Age (Melbourne, Vic.: 1854-1954)
Mon 6 Oct 1930 Page 9
R.101 DESTROYED
The News Arrives in London.
The Sunday papers had long gone to press, and all
England was enjoying an hour's extra sleep owing to
the lapse of summer time, when, with a startling flash
the tape machines announced the explosion of R.101. The
first message was followed immediately by the following
from Paris.
'Announced explosion occurred aboard R.101 2.30. this
morning whilst a few miles from Beauvais.'
"This was obviously the route of R.101, which Londoners
a few hours previously had been trying to see through the
rainclouds, would be pursuing. An anxious hour passed
before a message was received from Beauvais definitely
stating that R.101 had exploded. Another hour passed, and
at 5 a.m. came the terrible news that the air-ship had
crashed in flames and that only seven of the 53 aboard[77]
had survived. All the survivors were badly injured. The
victims were burnt to death.
```

---

[77] Note that at this time it was generally believed there were 53 passengers and crew aboard. Later it become known that Lord Thomson's valet was the 54th.

1930 Daily Sketch front page reporting R101 airship disaster. Alamy Image ID:TXJ75A

> The Age,
> Monday October 6th 1930
> R.101 DESTROYED
> STRIKES HILL & BURSTS INTO FLAMES DISASTER IN FRANCE EN ROUTE TO INDIA FIFTY-THREE ABOARD - ONLY EIGHT SURVIVE VICTIMS INCLUDE AIR MINISTER
> London 5th October.
> A ghastly disaster, the worst in the aviation history of Great Britain, occurred in France early this morning. The airship R.101, which set out for India at 7.30 last night, crashed near Beauvais, forty miles north of Paris, burst into flames, and was completely destroyed...

A few journalists were cruel and sensationalist enough to publish the following reports. It is to be hoped that they were never read by those who knew and loved the victims of the disaster. Some newspapers even published photos of the burned corpses before they were respectfully covered with sheets. Policemen, mindful of the devastating effect on families, tried to shield the victims from photographers.

> The Register News-Pictorial (Adelaide, SA: 1929—1931)
> Tue 7 Oct 1930 Page 3
> Practically all of the bodies were found with clenched hands and arms pulled back, indicating that death was not immediate. All the men had fought hard for life.

> The Register News-Pictorial (Adelaide, SA: 1929—1931)
> Tue 7 Oct 1930 Page 3
> "Village girls placed wildflowers near the bodies of the victims, all of which were dreadfully contorted by the agonising deaths."

THE FRENCH PAY TRIBUTE

Allonne

By farm cart to Allonne.

That Sunday, the scene of the accident was swarming with people including reporters, politicians, policemen, firemen and gawkers. Carpenters were busy on site hammering together wooden coffins and lining them with lead. The bodies of the victims were extracted from the wreckage, placed in the coffins and carried in horse-drawn farm carts to the only large public hall in the nearby tiny village of Allonne—the school room. Men unloaded them, one by one, and carried them inside. Soon, the makeshift coffins were covered with flowers from local gardens, brought in armfuls by the villagers.

Of the dead, only twenty-six could be identified.

```
Chronicle (Adelaide, SA : 1895 - 1954.
Thu 9 Oct 1930. Page 45
BODIES UNRECOGNISABLE.
Sir John Salmond's Grim Task.
SOME OF VICTIMS SUFFOCATED.
PARIS. October 5.


To-night thirty bodies lie in unadorned coffins in the
Allonne village school room. They arrived there in farm
carts. Ten other bodies are still lying in a field
adjoining the wreckage, where carpenters are hurriedly
preparing coffins for them.
Late this afternoon Air Marshal Sir John Salmond began
the task of trying to identify the dead, but he had to
discontinue it owing to the disfigurement of the bodies.
He placed a tab with the word 'unrecognisable' on each
```

coffin examined, and the relatives will be asked to come to France to assist in the identification. Meanwhile the personal possessions found on or near the bodies have been placed in envelopes and attached to the coffins. This work is being carried out by the British military-attaches in Paris. . . .

The Register News-Pictorial (Adelaide, SA : 1929 - 1931)
Tue 7 Oct 1930 Page 3
Enormous crowds arrived at the scene throughout Sunday, but mounted police and firemen kept them at a distance, and frustrated souvenir hunters and pilferers, although scarcely anything of value remained.
Visitors to the scene of the disaster say the wreckage resembles a skeleton of a fantastic, mediaeval dragon or a prehistoric monster. The ship's oil tanks were still spouting flame and smoke through the rain.

Warwick Daily News (Qld. : 1919 -1954)
Thu 9 Oct 1930 Page 5
Not a flower was left in Allonne gardens. Every one was picked and placed on the coffins of the British dead. . .

LONDON October 5 1930 Examiner
(Launceston, Tas. : 1900 - 1954)
Tue 7 Oct 1930, Page 9
Special Prayers
Prayers for the bereaved were offered in all the churches this evening. The King and Queen joined the village people in special prayers at the parish church at Sandringham. The congregation at Westminster Abbey knelt in silence

for three minutes. The Dean said that the disaster had stricken the whole country.

The Herald, Melbourne, October 1930.
MESSAGES OF SYMPATHY
King Horrified at News (British Official Wireless)
LONDON October 5.
- Innumerable messages of sympathy have been received from all parts of the world.
The King, in a message to the Prime Minister (Mr. McDonald), says: 'I am horrified to hear of this national disaster and the consequent serious loss of life, including that of Lord Thompson [sic], my Air Minister. The Queen and I sympathise deeply with the relatives and friends of those who have perished in the service of their country and also with the injured survivors.'
The Prime Minister, in a message, said that he was 'grieved beyond words at the loss of so many splendid men, whose sacrifice has been added to the glorious list of Englishmen who, on uncharted seas and in unexplored lands, have gone into the unknown as pioneers and pathfinders and have met death.'

Vigil at Allonne[78]

An ancient custom in some countries involves mourners keeping watch, or vigil, over their dead until they are buried. Loved ones and friends took turns to sit up all night with the deceased, the practice being called a "wake". 21

At Allonne, on the night of October 5 1930, the villagers kept vigil through the hours of darkness.

---

78   A "wake for the dead" evolved from the vigil, "watch" or "guard" of earlier times. "Wake" in this sense stems from ancient words, including the Old English -wacu (in nihtwacu "night watch"),

The Times, Wednesday October 8, 1930
In the small village of Allonne, where the bodies of the dead found their first shelter, every man and woman, from the mayor to the poorest peasant labourer, made his contribution to the common tribute. They gave up sleep and leisure; they volunteered to watch the coffins through the night.

The Memorial at Allonne

Reuter. The Sunday Times (London, England)
Sunday, October 12, 1930; pg. 17;
Issue 5609.
MEMORIAL AT ALLONNE
"On Monday the French Engineers will remove the middle of the port engine of the airship with a view to transferring it to England. To do so they must cut a way through the wreckage by means of oxyacetylene blow-lamps. The engine, which weighs about 3 1/2 tons, will then be drawn out over the field by Caterpillar tractors.
The newspaper "Liberte" understands that Monsieur Laurent Eynac, the French Air Minister, will propose at the next meeting of the French Cabinet that a memorial to those who lost their lives in the disaster be erected at Allonne.

A few months later, the building of a memorial did indeed commence at the site of the crash, near Beauvais. It was officially unveiled in 1933. If you type 'R101 memorial crash site' into Google Maps you will see the spot. It's just off the Chemin du Bois de Coutumes, or Customs Wood Road, and it's marked by an engraved stone.

Official unveiling of the R101 memorial at Allonne in 1933. Image supplied.
"A la memoire des victimes de la catastrophe du dirigeable R101 5 Octobre - 1930"

Allonne Village School Monday 6th October 1930:

```
Northampton Chronicle and Echo
Monday 06 October 1930.
AT BEAUVAIS.
The Horror on the Hill Side.
MOVING THE BODIES.
BEAUVAIS, Monday.


A glare like a beacon, on the hillside near the small
village of Allonne, still flickered late last night to
mark the spot where lies the mangled wreckage of R.101.
Fed by remnants of the dirigible's fuel, the blaze
illuminated with its grim light the giant carcase of
```

```
twisted metal that lies sprawling across the mud.
For a time visitors stood and watched the French troops
on guard slithering round the debris and then withdrew.
Many remained till a late hour outside the little hall
adjoining the Mairie [town hall], where the draped coffins
of 47 victims lie closely packed together.[79]
```

In the humble village schoolroom, forty-six rudimentary wooden coffins lay wherever space could be found for them. To each was attached a tab, bearing a number. Five tabs had a handwritten name beside the number. The rest bore the word "unrecognisable". Will's name was not on any of the name-tabs.

To each and every coffin was also affixed a manila envelope containing small, blackened personal items. People brought in yards of black crepe, which they draped over the coffins to show respect and give them some vestige of dignity. Villagers brought home-made bunches and wreaths of colourful autumn flowers to place atop the crepe.

```
Northern Whig
 - Tuesday 07 October 1930
SPECIAL TRAIN
A train will convey the bodies to Boulogne, where they
will be transferred on gun-carriages to H.M. destroyers
Tempest and Tribune for their last journey across the
Channel.
Military honours will be rendered. Throughout France
the tricolour will be meanwhile flown at half-mast. . .
```

---

[79] https://www.britishnewspaperarchive.co.uk/viewer/bl/0002130/19301006/095/0004

Strange finds, four days later:

```
The Sydney Morning Herald (NSW: 1842—1954)
Thu 9 Oct 1930 Page 11
THE R.101.
LONDON, Oct. 7.

Curious discoveries made by searchers among the wreckage
lead to the hope that official documents, and, perhaps,
even the logbook, may be found. Sheets of ruled paper,
used for passing orders from one cabin to another, were
found to-day. They owe their survival to the fact that
they were buried in debris after the crash. Boxes of
cornbeef [sic], bottles of jam and pickles, and other
edibles were found in the kitchen, practically intact.
```

REACTIONS TO
THE WORST AVIATION DISASTER IN HISTORY

The tragedy of the R101 grabbed instant attention around the globe. Tributes poured in. Typical of the newspaper headlines and sub-heads are these from regional Australian newspapers, syndicated from British newspapers:

```
Examiner (Launceston, Tas.: 1900—1954)
Tue 7 Oct 1930 Page 9.
DISASTER OF THE AIRSHIP R.101.
EMPIRE SHOCKED BY THE WORLD'S WORST AVIATION TRAGEDY
"The Daily Herald" says:—"Not since the Titanic
disaster has peace time witnessed such an overwhelming
catastrophe, such a thunderbolt of death."
```

The Narracoorte Herald (SA: 1875—1954)
Fri 10 Oct 1930 Page 2
The British Airship Tragedy.
GREATEST DISASTER IN HISTORY OF AVIATION.
A HORRIFYING SPECTACLE.
WORLD-WIDE CONCERN AND SYMPATHY WITH BRITAIN.
LOSS OF GREAT AVIATION EXPERTS.

Western Argus (Kalgoorlie, WA : 1916 - 1938)
Tue 14 Oct 1930 Page 25
AIR DISASTER
WORLD WIDE SYMPATHY
Deep Feeling in France. London, Oct 6.

The one satisfactory feature of the disaster is the remarkable world-wide expressions of sympathy. Scarcely any civilised country in the world has not cabled to London or instructed its representative personally to express his regrets. . .

The emotion in France is even greater today than yesterday. Pages in the newspapers are entirely devoted to details and photographs of the disaster. The most striking aspect of the French reaction is the real and profound sympathy felt for England. It is safe to assert that on no other occasion since the war has there been so deep and widespread a feeling. . .

```
[Examiner (Launceston, Tas.: 1900—1954)
Tue 7 Oct 1930, Page 9]
THE NATION MOURNS
Shocked and Astounded LONDON, Oct. 5.
The whole of Britain is shocked and astounded by the
R.101 airship catastrophe, feeling that the numerous
deaths are almost a personal loss . . .
```

In Britain, tributes flowed from every quarter, including from the prime minister, the Secretary of State for Air Sir Samuel Hoare, and delegates at the Imperial Conference in London and the Labour Conference in Wales.

```
Examiner (Launceston, Tas.: 1900—1954)
Tue 7 Oct 1930, Page 9
British Prime Minister Mr. MacDonald in a message from
Downing-street says: "I heard in the early hours of the
morning of the terrible disaster. It has grieved me
beyond words. The loss of so many splendid men, whose
sacrifice has added to the glorious list of Englishmen
who on unchartered seas and in unexplored lands have
gone into the unknown as pioneers and pathfinders, and
met their death.
My heartfelt sympathy goes out to the families in their
hour of bereavement."

Northern Star (Lismore, NSW : 1876 - 1954)
Wed 8 Oct 1930 Page 7
THE R.101 DISASTER. EMPIRE DELEGATES TRIBUTE
The Imperial Conference resolution read: "We members of
the Imperial conference desire to place, on record our
great sorrow at the disaster to the airship R.101 and the
```

```
loss, of so many brave and valuable lives. On behalf of
all parts of the British Commonwealth we pay homage to
the gallant men who have given their lives as pioneers
in the cause of progress, and we wish to express, our
heartfelt grief for their bereaved families. To our
chairman we offer our deep sympathy at the loss of a dis-
tinguished colleague and a well loved friend."
```

The fallout was international. Condolences were sent to Britain by the leaders of many countries, including France, Germany, Egypt, India, the USA, Australia, New Zealand, and the Pope in the Vatican.

```
THE HAWARA STAR AND SOUTH TARANAKI GAZETTE
Tuesday October 7, 1930 Page 5
U.S.A. SHOCKED
Offer of Helium Supply
WASHINGTON, Oct. 6.

The whole of the United States has been profoundly
shocked by the R101 disaster. The newspapers are filled
with an expression of sympathy from official and private
circles. The principal reaction to the disaster appears
to be the belief that helium is necessary to further
dirigible development. Rear Admiral Moffett proposed
that the United States make its helium supply available
to British and German air ships. He urged Congress to
repeal the law forbidding the export of helium, and
added that his confidence in rigid airships was not
shaken "one iota."
```

Mr. Adams (Secretary of the Navy) has sent a message to the Admiralty — 'We of the American navy express our deepest sympathy and concern in the loss of R101 and her gallant complement. We deplore a disaster which
has cost the valuable lives of those who are in the van of scientific advance, appreciating that the pioneer work of conquering the air must be carried forward.'

"The New York Times" leader stated:— "The destruction of the R101 comes with the special force of a cruel tragedy. The loss of so many precious lives, including useful public men, adds poignancy to the major air calamity. Aviation's advance cannot be checked, but just at present it must be confessed that there is an impression of the natural forces, grim and ruthless, delighting in the frustration of the pride of man."
The whole world will condole with Britain in her agony. It is suggested that American sympathy might take the form of a grant of helium or the right to import it from us. This might well receive serious consideration."

Not Shatter Faith
"The New York Herald-Tribune's" leader says:—"There is something about the dirigible disaster that shocks the imagination more powerfully than any comparable tragedy, yet we should be on guard against permitting the stunning catastrophe to shatter our faith in the dirigible.

SQUADRON LEADER PALSTRA'S BRILLIANT CAREER

Throughout Australia, people expressed sympathy for the families of the R101's passengers and crew. In particular, Australians awoke to the fact that one of their own had perished in the catastrophe.

```
Chronicle (Adelaide, SA: 1895—1954)
Thu 9 Oct 1930 Page 45
AUSTRALIA'S GRIEF
Expressed by Mr. Scullin
LONDON, October 5.


When the Australian Prime Minister (Mr. J. H. Scullin) who
is in London for the Imperial Conference, was informed
of the disaster he said:- 'I am horrified by the news. I
feel that the disaster has cast a shadow over the whole
of the Imperial Conference meetings. Only within the
past few days I had a long and interesting talk with
Lord Thomson and Sir Sefton Brancker on the general
question of Imperial air communications, and they struck
me as being men of a most forceful personality. I had
no opportunity of meeting Squadron-Leader Palstra, but
had been looking forward to his expert assistance when
the Conference discussed air matters.'


Mr. Scullin wrote to Mr. MacDonald, conveying the
sincerest sympathy of the Commonwealth Government and
people with the relatives of the victims.
  Mr. Scullin will also communicate with Palstra's
relatives.
```

Examiner (Launceston, Tas.: 1900–1954)
Tue 7 Oct 1930, Page 9
AUSTRALIA'S MESSAGES MELBOURNE, Monday.

His Excellency Lord Somers has sent the following message to his Majesty the King:-"With humble duty, I join the Government and people of Australia in sending this expression of our deep sorrow and sympathy at the tragic loss of R.101 and the victims of this disaster." Messages of sympathy have been sent to the widow of Squadron-Leader W. Palstra, who was an officer of the Royal Australian Air Force, by the Minister for Defence and by the Air Board.

Experienced Men Lost
BRILLIANT SQUADRON LEADER
MELBOURNE, Sunday.
Squadron Leader Wm. Palstra served with the Australian Flying Corps in France in No. 3 Squadron, and won the Military Cross. When he returned to Australia he was employed in the Registrar's office at the Melbourne University, and while there he completed his course for the B.A. degree.
In 1925 he joined the R.A.A.F., and was director of Manning at headquarters until 1928, when he was nominated for a course at the Royal Air Force College. He completed this course brilliantly last year, and was retained in London as liaison officer of the R.A.A.F. at Australia House.

Examiner (Launceston, Tas.: 1900–1954)
Mon 6 Oct 1930 Page 7
TERRIBLE AIRSHIP DISASTER

The Chief of the Air Staff (Air Commodore R. E. Williams) considered him the most suitable officer to be included among the passengers on the flight of the R.101. On a portion of the projected airship route from England to Australia he was to have reported to the Federal Government on the flight to India.
Squadron Leader Palstra spent his early life in South Africa, and came to Australia with his father, who was an officer in the Salvation Army, when he was aged six years {incorrect]. He is survived by a widow and three children in London [also incorrect].

The Age (Melbourne, Vic.: 1854–1954)
Mon 6 Oct 1930 Page 9
AN AUSTRALIAN OFFICER
Palstra's brilliant career

Squadron Leader Palstra, MC., the Australian officer on board the airship, had been granted leave of absence from his position as liaison officer between the Royal Air Force and the Royal Australian Air Force. He was due to leave London next month, and he was looking forward to returning to Australia with his wife and three children. He was one of the most brilliant of all Australian Air Force officers, and the deepest regret was expressed by his fellow officers at Point Cook last night when they heard of his death. He left Australia nearly two years ago to take a special course at the Royal Air Force College, Andover. About eleven months ago he took the position of liaison officer in London from Squadron Leader Wrigley, who is now in Melbourne. He was only recently promoted Squadron Leader.

He saw service with No 2 RAAF Squadron in France. It was Squadron Leader Palstra's intention to write a report for the Australian Air Board embodying his observations of the flight. Before he left Australia he was secretary of the air accidents investigation committee. . .

The Salvation Army "War Cry",
October 18th, 1930.
R.101 MEETS WITH DISASTER.
Australian Salvationists deeply moved.

The Empire stood aghast when it learned that England's wonder ship R.101 had crashed, and in an appallingly brief moment had burned to pitiful fragments amidst which were the charred remains of what were once England's leading airmen.

Salvation Army circles in Melbourne were profoundly moved when the news was received. Squadron-Leader Will Palstra, who is among the dead, was once a member of the Staff Band. He is the eldest son of our erstwhile Chief Secretary, now Lieutenant-Commissioner Palstra, Territorial Commander for the Dutch East Indies. He is son-in-law of Mrs. Brigadier Holdaway, who has just arrived home again from a visit to her daughter in their English home, and is brother to staff bandsmen Frank and John Palstra of Canterbury Corps.

```
Many other Salvationists are linked by various ties to
the relatives of this brilliant young aviation officer,
hence the widespread nature of the shock when the
dreadful news reached Australia.
Instantly the aged mother in Java was remembered, then
the young widow and her children in England, and loving
messages of sympathy were despatched to each by the
Chief Secretary in the name of the Salvation Army.
The great airship, "the last word" in that department of
activity, in her tragic end calls loud to us all; "When
men shall say peace and safety, then sudden destruction
cometh upon them."
```

ALLONNE TO BEAUVAIS

On 6 October, the day after the tragedy, a troop of uniformed French soldiers hoisted the forty-six screwed-shut coffins onto their shoulders and bore them, "with military honours", out of the Allonne village school-house. The storm had not abated; in fact, it had intensified. Thunder rolled in the cloudy skies and hailstones battered the men as they loaded their burdens on to a convoy of motor-lorries. The vehicles transported their burdens through the bleak weather to the nearest town, Beauvais.

Hours later the convoy halted in the enormous square outside the historic Mairie de Beauvais (Beauvais Town Hall), an imposing mid-eighteenth century building.

```
The Argus (Melbourne, Vic. : 1848 - 1957)
Wed 8 Oct 1930 Page 7
LOSS OF R.101.

BODIES OF VICTIMS HONOURED BY FRENCH.
LONDON. Oct. 6.
The arrival of the coffins occupied 3 1/2 hours. During
```

```
this time a French guard of honour repeatedly presented
arms and townspeople stood bareheaded despite thunder
and hailstorms.
```

Hail and rain pattered down ceaselessly. Watched sombrely by a large gathering of French politicians, civil servants, military officers, mounted cavalrymen, platoons of soldiers and crowds of bare-headed townsfolk, the soldiers lifted the coffins off the lorries, shouldered them and bore them through the tall portal. Inside the town hall they laid out their burdens on rows of trestle tables that had been set up along black-draped walls.

As soon as the shocking news had arrived in England, dignitaries made ready to fly to France with their staff. They sent ahead to Beauvais a large quantity of Union Flags (Union Jacks), the national flag of the United Kingdom, brightly dyed red, white and dark blue. One of these flags was drawn over each wooden casket. Atop them rested wreaths of fresh flowers, gifted by the Beauvais townspeople.

Since Sunday morning, signals had been pulsing across the English Channel as telegraphed orders for large flowery wreaths were sent to French florists. These impressive floral tributes, from the British Army, Navy, and Air Force and the British government, international governments and other institutions, were placed in the middle of the floor.

Surrounded by black crepe and colourful flowers, guarded by former service-men, gendarmes and Red Cross nurses, and saluted by a passing procession of townsfolk paying their respects, the coffins lay all night in the state of "chapelle ardente".[80] The following day, Tuesday 7th October, was proclaimed a national day of mourning in France.

The forty-six coffins from Allonne were now joined by one more. It contained the body of 31- year-old rigger Radcliffe, who had died of his injuries in hospital in Beauvais.

---

80   'Chapelle ardente' translates directly as 'burning chapel'. The term is used to describe "a chapel or room in which the corpse of a sovereign or other exalted personage lies in state pending the funeral service. The name is in allusion to the many candles which are lighted round the catafalque." [Chisholm, Hugh, ed. (1911). "Chapelle Ardente". Encyclopædia Britannica. 5 (11th ed.). Cambridge University Press. p. 851.]

Beauvais

The Last Salute at Beauvais, 7th October.

The Great War had ended only twelve years earlier. Part of its military legacy was organisational efficiency; another part was the French people's enormous gratitude for the sacrifices made by their allies. During the three days that had passed since the airship disaster, the French government, the armed forces and the people of Beauvais had made arrangements for a spectacular tribute to be paid to the fallen men of the R101; citizens of the British Empire whose people had given their lives to defend France's liberty.

By now, the storm had finally petered out and the sun appeared from behind the clouds.

```
The Argus (Melbourne, Vic. : 1848 - 1957)
Wed 8 Oct 1930 Page 7
LOSS OF R.101.


BODIES OF VICTIMS HONOURED BY FRENCH. LONDON. Oct. 6.
The home-coming was invested with all the triumphant
pageantry of death. The heroes left Beauvais, the scene
of the disaster, to the solemn booming of gunfire, amid
scenes of military and civil mourning such as one nation
has rarely afforded in sympathy to another.


The Times, Wednesday October 8, 1930
FAREWELL OF FRANCE
LAST SALUTE AT BEAUVAIS
(From our special correspondent)


This morning the 47 coffins containing the bodies of those
who perished in R.101 began their journey home.
The coffins lay in state in the Town Hall at Beauvais
all night watched by gendarmes, soldiers and four Red
Cross nurses. Each was covered with the Union Jack,
```

and the large room in which they lay was so full with flowers that the coffins were almost hidden and the guards were faint with their perfume. There were wreaths from the British Government, The British Ambassador, the Royal Air Force, the Royal Navy, the British Army, the French Government and Services, and many others from the town of Beauvais and neighbouring villages, from all the local ex-soldiers and other associations, from the French Red Cross, and from individuals.

Early this morning the public were allowed to file through the main entrance to the Town Hall, past the open door of the mortuary. Thousands of people passed in a steady stream. Some made the sign of the Cross in the doorway; others threw single flowers into the room or stepped out of the ranks to lay wreaths or bouquets over the coffins.

In the meantime the troops who were to honour the dead were mustering in the great square outside. Two battalions of the 51st Infantry Regiment made a wall of horizon blue, topped with steel helmets and flashing bayonets, in front of the Town Hall. Facing them, opposite the main gateway, was a Colour party with the Colour of the Regiment uncased, and wearing the Cross of the Legion of Honour and the Croix de Guerre. The band of the regiment stood close by, and near them, a detachment of the French Marines in their seamen's dress, and a section of gendarmes with sabres bared. Along the sides of the square, most picturesque of all, two squadrons of Spahi cavalry[81], magnificent in their flowing robes, sat their fidgeting chargers waiting for the word to move.

---

81   Spahis were light cavalry regiments of the French army, recruited primarily from the indigenous populations of Algeria, Tunisia and Morocco. French military, naval and air officers gathered in groups, and, a little to one side of the square, a detachment from the naval airship base at Orly stood at ease. All the Services were present.

Beauvais town square. Troops and horses lined up outside the Town Hall, Tuesday 7 October 1930. Alamy Image ID:2MXACYD

French Infantrymen with wreaths waiting to join the funeral cortage at Beauvais. Image ID: B571HC

Spahi cavalrymen wait, and the French police (gendarmes) stand at attention with drawn sabres in front of the crowds, watching the procession of wagons bearing the flower-decked coffins. Photo by ullstein bild via Getty Images 542925939.

Alamy Image ID: 2MXA3K6

Image: supplied

BRINGING HOME THE DEAD OF "R 101": MILITARY HONOURS IN FRANCE.

FRENCH HOMAGE TO BRITAIN'S DEAD IN THE GREAT AIRSHIP DISASTER: THE MOVING FINAL SCENE AT BEAUVAIS—SPAHIS SALUTING THE COFFINS, BORNE ON FRENCH ARTILLERY WAGONS, AS THEY LEFT FOR BOULOGNE.

The remains of the dead from "R.101," only some of which could be identified from personal belongings, were placed in numbered coffins at Allonne, the village near the scene of the disaster, and thence conveyed in motor-vans to Beauvais, where they were received with military honours and lay-in-state during the night of October 6 in the Town Hall. "In most of the vans," writes a "Times" correspondent present, "the villagers had placed flowers, and indeed nothing could be more admirable than the kindness and devotion which the French population and authorities have shown. The British officers, whose task it has been to take care of the dead and living, have been overwhelmed with helpful sympathy." The British Ambassador, Lord Tyrrell, arrived at Beauvais on the 6th, and later came M. Tardieu, the French Premier, and M. Laurent-Eynac, French Minister for Air. The next morning the coffins, borne on artillery wagons lent by the French War Office, left Beauvais by special train for Boulogne. As the procession moved off from Beauvais Town Hall, batteries of "75's" fired a salute of 101 rounds, and a funeral peal was tolled from the Cathedral. Thousands of people lined the streets.

Alamy Image ID: 2M3NJ7B

```
BEAUVAIS TO BOULOGNE
FIRST PICTURE OF SCENE AFTER R.101 DISASTER
A tragic picture which arrived by airmail today of the
scene in the little town of Beauvais (France) where a
long line of military wagons were in waiting to receive
the remains of 47 of the official passengers and crew of
the ill-fated airship R.101 . . .
```

Newspaper photographs show a very wide street or city square, in which twenty-four gun- carriages, drawn up neatly in precise rows. Each is pulled by two mounted horses, or else one mounted horse with a rider ahead. Behind each gun-carriage stands a row of six soldiers at attention. An enormous brass band waits nearby; also more uniformed soldiers in neat rows, both infantry and cavalry. There are so many spectators that officials have installed a temporary fence to keep them back. On these gun-carriages the coffins were carried from Beauvais Town Hall to the railway station.

You can view filmed portions of the Beauvais tribute and other funeral ceremonies on YouTube: "Airship R.101 Crash, 1930's—Film 17489" on the Huntley Film Archives channel.

```
The Times, Wednesday October 8, 1930
FAREWELL OF FRANCE
LAST SALUTE AT BEAUVAIS
SURVIVORS PRESENT
IMPRESSIVE FRENCH TRIBUTE
Touching scenes marked the start of the last journey of
the airship victims. The simple townsfolk of Beauvais
were overwhelmed with grief as twenty-four munition
wagons removed the coffins to the railway station from
the Town Hall.
```

```
Soon after 10 o'clock the gates of the Town Hall were
closed, and the official personalities began to arrive.
. .
The greatest interest was caused by the appearance of
three survivors of R.101 - Messrs. Leech, Binks and Bell,
- who were to walk in the procession. All three were
hatless and dressed in the clothes they were wearing when
the airship crashed, and Mr. Leech had thick bandages on
his head and on one hand. They faced the crowd and the
photographers a little more nervously, perhaps, than
they had ever faced the air. Indeed the sang-froid of
the survivors and their fine spirit are the admiration
of their many French friends.
```

YouTube hosts remarkable footage of Disley, Cook and Savory, the "Survivors of the R.101", on the British Movietone channel. It was uploaded on 21 July, 2015.

```
The Times,
Wednesday October 8, 1930


Nothing was left undone for the honour of the British
dead, and one minute before 11 the first muffled boom of a
salute of 101 guns broke the waiting silence.
Twenty-four army gun-carriages, each drawn by four
horses, drew up in the inner court-yard. The coffins
were borne out, reverently placed on the vehicles, and
covered with Union Jacks and flowers. The cathedral-like
silence was broken only by the booming salute of the 101
guns, fired by a French battery.
As the Town Hall clock struck 11 the first wagon moved
out through the gate.
```

A flourish of trumpets – 'Aux Champs!' [Literally: To the fields!]– called the troops to the salute; it was followed by 'God Save the King' and the Marseillaise. As the music died away the roar of aircraft filled the air, and flight after flight of French war machines – Nieuport-Delage fighters and Breguet XIX, reconnaissance machines – soared overhead.

Wagon after wagon – there seemed to be no end to them – appeared in the archway. Each contained two coffins and a mass of flowers. A wagon with a single coffin came last. In the square nearby, 2,000 troops saluted, and every head was bared as the wagons took up their places in the cortege.

The procession slowly got under way, moving round three sides of the square. First came a company of gendarmes in their blue-and-black uniforms, gold-braided kepis, and white gloves. Then the band of the 51st Infantry Regiment, playing a Funeral March; the Colour, and the Infantry.

After the soldiers came the Beauvais firemen, who had vainly fought the flames of the R.101; next came a section of soldiers carrying wreaths, and then came the long, pathetic procession of wagons with their tragic burdens.

Eight French soldiers, with arms reversed, escorted each wagon. Here and there a French flying officer walked at the head.

Directly behind the coffins, and making a pitiful contrast to the numbers of their dead comrades, came the three survivors; Leech, Binks, and Bell, Leech's bandages conspicuous in the sun. Behind them, the many dignitaries. Then came a long succession of French civilians and ex-soldiers, Girl Guides, and nuns, with here and there the banner of an association. More infantry and the Marines and Spahis ended the procession.

The French Premier (M. Tardieu), the Air Minister (M. Laurent), and many other distinguished Frenchmen followed the procession, in company with the British Ambassador (Lord Tyrrell) the Secretary for India, the Under-Secretary for Air, Sir John Salmond and numerous other British officials and mourners, a long procession of French infantry and gendarmerie, and local societies.

First the gendarmes; next the Colour; then rank on rank of shining bayonets and horizon blue. The rhythmic clash of the French drums and the flourish of the glorious French trumpets went on and on, beating down the guards of men's hearts with their poignancy. The blue collars and red pom- poms of the Marines made a note of fresh colour in the watery sunshine. Last of all, a moving cloud of Spahi cavalry, with their wild dark faces, blue and white cloaks, bizarre tarbooshes and high white turbans, swept past.

A French military band, playing solemn music, led the sad procession. Kneeling crowds prayed as the cortege passed. The buildings were draped with crepe, and all shops in the town were closed, while overhead, aeroplanes circled.

Beauvais mothers' wreath

There were present also the Mayor of Beauvais and a deputation of citizens from the town which provided so much practical help after the crash.

One wreath on the gun-carriages came from 'The Mothers

of Beauvais to the sorrowing mothers of Britain'. Others were from the French and British services.

Near [Beauvais] railway Station, Flanders Poppies had been strewn by the children in the roadway.

The station was decorated with French flags and Union Jacks, draped with crepe. A train of nine empty vans stood in a siding. The wagons with the coffins drew up in a long line facing the train. . .

. . . The British Ambassador, officers and officials took their places on a platform facing the train to receive the farewells and condolences of the French Ministers and representatives, who filed past and shook their hands. The troops marched through to the far end of the yard, wheeled about, and marched past the coffins at the salute. The coffins were removed to a special train.

"Three R101 survivors following the last of the twenty-three ammunition wagons which conveyed the remains of the victims from Beauvais Town Hall to the station en route for Boulogne and England yesterday." The Daily Express, 8 October 1930

At Beauvais Railway Station, Tuesday 7 October 1930. Alamy GAFP80
The transfer of the coffins from the wagons to the special funeral train.

```
The Sydney Morning Herald (NSW: 1842—1954)
Wed 8 Oct 1930 Page 13
LONDON, Oct. 7.


The emotion in France is even greater to-day than
yesterday. Pages of the newspapers are entirely devoted
to details and photographs. The most striking aspect of
the French reaction is the profound sympathy felt for
England. On no other occasion since the war has so deep
and wide-spread a feeling existed.
```

BEAUVAIS TO BOULOGNE

The Argus (Melbourne, Vic.: 1848—1957)
Wed 8 Oct 1930 Page 7
HOMECOMING OF VICTIMS OF R.101 TRAGEDY
FRENCH TOWNS IN DEEP MOURNING ALL ALONG ROUTE
DENSE CROWDS AT VICTORIA STATION
PRIME MINISTER ON CONQUEST OF THE AIR

The last journey of the victims of the disaster began at Beauvais today. Heavy rain was falling as the distinguished mourners who had assembled at the station watched the entrainment of the remains. Troops filed slowly past the dead to the strains of the traditional slow march played by French forces.
Prayers were offered up by the Bishop of Beauvais and the Rev. Mr. Cardew, the pastor of the English Church in Paris, as the coffins were placed in railway wagons.

The Times,
Wednesday October 8, 1930
THE SOLEMN HUSH
Thousands stood in the rain at the railway station, the troops filing past the dead in the traditional slow march.
Dr. Carden (Paris English Church pastor), and the Bishop of Beauvais offered prayers, amidst a most solemn hush. Thereafter the coffins were gently placed on the sawdust covered floor of the railway vans, the doors were sealed and the train pulled out.

FAREWELL OF FRANCE A GRATEFUL MEMORY
Then the vans were loaded, closed, and their doors sealed, and they were coupled to a special train of four coaches, in which the official party travelled.

Three of the survivors of R101 and two senior officers of the Royal Air Force travelled with the special train.

It was a quarter past one when the long train drew out of Beauvais Station as the guns thundered and the bands played. The Mayor and Council of Beauvais and Allonne, the local ex-soldier's association, and about a hundred thousand people from Beauvais and elsewhere, massed about the station, waved a last salute.
The band wheeled into place and followed the procession away in silence, and the pageantry was over.
The British travellers in the train looked back gratefully at the historic town, quiet and grey, in its nest of trees. They had been through an experience which none of them will ever forget. Rarely indeed can there have been such a deep and spontaneous movement of sympathy between two great nations. Since British soldiers in their millions fought and suffered on French soil the population of these northern departments has held the friendly nation across the water in grateful memory. Everything which kindness and warm feeling could suggest was freely given to the victims of R.101, the survivors, and their countrymen.

The railway journey to Boulogne

On Tuesday 7th October, this day of national mourning, the French paid moving tributes to the dead at every stage of the funeral train's journey from Beauvais to Boulogne. In the towns through which the train passed, all flags flew at half mast to show that they were in deep mourning. At all wayside stations along the railway line to the Channel shore, citizens solemnly stood at the salute as the train slowly passed.

```
The Times,
Wednesday October 8, 1930.
HOMECOMING OF VICTIMS OF R.101 TRAGEDY AT BOULOGNE


The funeral train traversed a mournful landscape towards
the sea. Here and there along the line, groups of people
waited to see it pass. Station staffs lined up bareheaded
on their platforms. As we drew near the coast, heavy
clouds rolled in from the sea, as though England were
throwing a misty pall over the Channel. In the British
Military Cemetery at Etaples - the largest in France -
the Union Jack flew at half-mast.

The train moved slowly through the streets of Boulogne
towards the marine station. The town was in mourning.
Flags flew at half-mast on buildings and on the shipping
in the harbour. The quays were black with people, and
human clusters in masts and cranes.

The Prefect of the Department, the Sub-Prefect, the
Mayors and Councils of Boulogne and Calais, the military
and naval authorities, members of the Bar, and repre-
sentatives of every branch of the town's life waited
```

at the station. The Colour, the band and a company of the 110th Regiment were massed on the quay. Troops, presenting arms, lined the platform. Here and there a Tricolour banner rose from the dark mass. As the train drew in [the train arrived alongside the quay at Boulogne at 4.25pm], the forts fired a salute.

The destroyers Tempest and Tribune lay alongside the quay. The tide was dead low, and the tips of their funnels were level with the quay's edge. A broad carpeted gangway led from the platform to the waterside. On the right of this a guard of honour of British bluejackets stood with arms reversed. The White Ensign and the flag of the Boulogne branch of the British Legion, dipped in salute, swept the ground side by side.

In the French port of Boulogne, two British destroyers were waiting to take the coffins home to England, accompanied by a French naval escort. The French kept vigil at the quayside while the bodies were placed reverently aboard the vessels.

The Times, Wednesday October 8, 1930. HOMECOMING OF VICTIMS OF R.101 TRAGEDY AT BOULOGNE
A salvo of guns was fired when the special train reached Boulogne. The doors of the van were thrown open, and the band [of a French infantry regiment] struck up the Last Post and the Marseillaise, followed by the British National Anthem; "God Save the King", [while detachments of French soldiers and French and British Marines rendered military honours]. Then the long task of placing the coffins in the ships began.

Naval, military and civil authorities and a large crowd of spectators watched, with the greatest sympathy and reverence, the embarkation of the bodies, while the band played funeral marches.

In the presence of a great silent crowd, the coffins [each wrapped in its own Union Jack,] were carried to the waiting British destroyers.

Squads of firemen carried them from the vans across the quay. Here they laid them, one by one, on a cradle, and a crane swung them over the quayside and lowered them to the deck of the nearer destroyer. Bareheaded sailors carried them to the gun platforms of the ships, where guards were mounted. The great wreaths were set aside, to be heaped round the coffins when all were embarked, but the wilted bouquets of wild flowers and chrysanthemums which the peasants of Allonne and Beauvais had laid on the coffins were not disturbed. All the floral tributes were conveyed on to the destroyers, and soon the decks could not be seen beneath the vast sea of flowers. The gusting wind picked up the corners of the flags.

CROWD'S HOMAGE

It took an hour to carry the 47 coffins from train to ship. The band played funeral music, while the falling dusk slowly blotted out the people on the farther shore. The crowd stood patiently to the end. The three survivors stood a little apart, looking on sadly; and suddenly one of them - Bell - was overcome and collapsed, pitching forward on the platform. He was quickly carried away and recovered himself in a few minutes. Later he left for England.

SOIL OF FRANCE LEFT IN THE FALLING DUSK

At half past 5 [pm] the last coffin left French soil, and as it did so another salute crashed from the forts. It was now nearly dark, and from the blurred shapes of the destroyers the flags and flowers on the coffins stood out sharply under electric lights. The ships had to wait a little longer before they could go to sea.
They slipped away quietly soon after half-past 7 in pouring rain.[82]

Coffins of the victims are carried aboard HMS Tempest at Boulogne
Alamy ID:B5761R

---

82   A violent channel gale held up the French naval escort. After this delay the destroyers set out, but they had not sailed far before they had to turn back. The Times, Wednesday October 8, 1930: "GALE IN CHANNEL. LONDON, Wednesday,.— The destroyer Tribune damaged her propeller, shortly after leaving Boulogne, and had to return and transfer the coffins to the Tempest."

Coffins are loaded onto a British destroyer at Boulogne. Image supplied.

NEAR BEAUVAIS, REMOVING BODIES OF THE VICTIMS FROM THE WRECKAGE OF R101.

WARSHIP TO BRING VICTIMS HOME

MIDNIGHT SEARCH

Air Minister and Famous Pioneers of Flying Burned to Death

A WARSHIP is to be dispatched from Britain to bring home the bodies of the men who lost their lives when the R101 crashed and exploded yesterday morning at Beauvais, a village 40 miles from Paris.

The Air Ministry reported that 46 of the 54 persons lost their lives. A correspondent report from Beauvais early this morning insisted that 47 bodies had been recovered, and a search was being made for three more which were known to be in the wreckage. Eight are alive in hospital.

Two inquiries into the disaster will be held. One will begin at Beauvais to-day and the other will be held in London. Air Chief-Marshal Sir John Salmond, who flew to the scene to make investigations, returned to London last night and reported to the Air Council, which sat for two hours.

Air experts were last night investigating two theories as to the cause of the disaster. One is that the airship was forced down by her envelope becoming sodden with rainwater; the other is that the giant dirigible developed a defect in the storm.

Among those who perished in the disaster were Lord Thomson, Secretary of State for Air; Air Vice-Marshal Sir Sefton Brancker, Director of Civil Aviation; Wing-Commander

RETURN TO ENGLAND

Meanwhile in England on the evening of Wednesday 8 October, dense crowds of people began to assemble silently at the port of Dover and Victoria Station. Another violent October storm was, by now, lashing the coast.

```
The Times,
Wednesday October 8, 1930.
TO THE DEAD
Moving Tributes


Bodies Cross the Channel The R.101 Victims (Australian
Cable Service.) LONDON, Tuesday.
At Dover, and later at Victoria Station, where the
special train was due to arrive in the early morning,
representatives of the Government and services waited
to receive the honoured dead. Long before they were due
crowds began to silently assemble.
Crowds of thousands waited in the rain at Dover to await
the homecoming of the dead. One by one Air Force bearers
carried the flag-draped coffins to the special train. A
laurel wreath hung on the engine. Many thousands were
waiting in the rain at midnight at Victoria station for
the train's arrival.
DOVER. Tuesday night.

This is how our dead came home to England.

It is a cold night and the moon is hidden by low clouds.
Rain is falling, a south-westerly gale is blowing in
the Channel.
```

It is silent in Dover Harbour.

The day's work is over, the cross-Channel traffic has gone its way, and the cranes are silent on the dockside. The harbour is closed to the public, but a few officials have waited for three hours for the destroyer to come with her pitiful cargo (so writes H.V. Morton).

We look beyond the bar and see the Channel whitening in the storm. Every second the Dover lighthouse sweeps its sword over the water, and from the South Foreland comes an answering gleam.

Drawn up to the dockside is a train.. . [a purple wreath displayed on its smokebox]. It is more terrible than any hospital train that waited at Dover during the war. e stand awed before this train like frightened children. Men pass it on tiptoe, and when a railwayman enters it he removes his cap and walks as if in church.

[At either end of the train was a passenger coach, and between them were seven vans, normally used to carry the Indian mails from Cannon-street to Dover. Every van was draped inside with purple.]

There are seven long mail vans, of a kind known to workers in Southern Railway sheds as "Edith Cavell" vans. . . .

It was a van of this type in which Edith Cavell's[83] body was taken to Norwich. . . It was a van of this kind that took the Unknown Warrior to London.
Never before have seven of these sombre cars been coupled together to form a funeral train.

Hung With Purple.

Their barred windows are backed with purple cloth.
Each van is hung with purple from ceiling to floor, and down the length of each runs a strip of dark carpet.
Beside this train is posted a guard of honour of the Royal Air Force.

It is now ten o'clock.

A message is received to say that only one destroyer, the Tempest, is returning with the bodies. A propeller mishap had caused the Tribune to make for Portsmouth.
In ten minutes, as we look toward the sea, the tempest, long, low and dark, comes riding the swell and slips into Dover, her deck brightly lit.
But the storm is so severe that she cannot come alongside. Twice she makes the attempt, but is forced to back out again. As she swings round we see by the brilliant lights on her deck Union Jack after Union Jack, and garlands of bright flowers; but when the wind pulls aside a flag,

---

83 26 Edith Cavell 1865–1915 was a British nurse celebrated for saving the lives of soldiers from both sides without discrimination and for helping some 200 Allied soldiers escape from German-occupied Belgium during the First World War, for which the Germans arrested her. She was accused of treason, found guilty by a court-martial and sentenced to death. Despite international pressure for mercy, she was shot by a German firing squad. Her execution received worldwide condemnation and extensive press coverage.

we see beneath it the brass handles of a coffin.

On the third attempt she comes alongside. There is not a yard of room in her that does not hold its coffin. But they are banked high with flowers. It is strange to see the crew struggling with ropes, the rain shining on their oilskins, working against wind and tide in this sad garden.

The destroyer arrived at Dover when rain was falling like a benediction upon the coffins lying upon the deck in long rows covered with Union Jacks and wreaths from France.

Everything that could be done to make this sight beautiful has been done; but still the wind pulls the flags away.

The Homecoming.

The Times, Wednesday October 8, 1930
HOMECOMING BY NIGHT
THE ARRIVAL AT DOVER SILENT SYMPATHY
(FROM OUR SPECIAL CORRESPONDENT)

The guard of honour advanced arms, and then obeyed the order, 'Rest on your arms reversed'; a bugle sounded from the destroyer; one of the two great electric cranes on the pier gave a preliminary whirr, and the work of disembarking the coffins began.

The afterdeck of the destroyer was like a flower garden under the loads of wreaths which rested on the Union Jacks on each coffin. Here and there among them stood solitary bluejackets on guard with heads bent upon their rifles.

Other sailors in glistening oilskins stood in groups amidships and on the foredeck, and among them were three men with bandaged heads – the three survivors of the airship disaster who were well enough to travel from Beauvais today. The R.A.F. bearers went aboard the destroyer, and one by one the coffins were brought to shore, and carried to the train.

This train was bound for London's Victoria Station, where another crowd of silent people had been waiting for hours.

The Times, Wednesday October 8, 1930.

TO THE DEAD

Moving Tributes

Bodies Cross the Channel

The R.101 Victims (Australian Cable Service.)

LONDON, Tuesday.

Grim sentries stand with reversed arms beside the dead. The ship rises and falls with the swell. Two cranes dip down into the body of the destroyer and rise again. We look up and see a Union Jack against a dark sky, and the coffin swings round gently, describing an arc in the air; and behind it are the white cliffs of England, dim in mist. Our men have come home, as they went, in a storm.

Each coffin was borne upon the shoulders of eight airmen and soldiers and laid in the purple lined carriages of the special train for the journey to London.

As each coffin is placed in the funeral train a guard

salutes, and then stands above with reversed arms. Statesman, officer and private lie unknown and side by side in the purple coaches.

A Contrast

What a contrast to the public honours lavished in France is this silent, almost secret return to England! No sound but the rising storm; and as we hear the wind and see it lashing at the flags we shudder and remember.

Our feelings are dulled as they were during the war. It is no place for hysteria or easy emotion. We just stand bare-headed with the rain in our faces, grateful for the flowers that take the mind away from unhappy things.
Forty-seven coffins come out of the small grey ship, and then comes something that hurts as it lights almost brutally the reality of this tragedy. Men carry out forty- seven small numbered boxes, and we know that in these are the objects found beside each body.
An inspector travelled on the footplate with the driver and the fireman; officers of the R.A.F. were in the front coach; and the bearer party, an officer and ten men, travelled in the last coach.
The train of death moves out of Dover a few minutes after eleven.
There is not a sound but the howling of the wind.
So our men come home.

At Dover: "Forty-seven coffins come out of the small grey ship..."
on the shoulders of RAF bearers. Image: supplied.

Victoria Station

```
Warwick Daily News (Qld.: 1919 -1954)
Thu 9 Oct 1930 Page 5
AT VICTORIA STATION
VICTIMS' BODIES IN LONDON.
LONDON, Wednesday.


Crowds began invading [Victoria] station at 11 o'clock
last night. The gathering included working folk, men and
women in evening dress from the theatres, and many French
```

people resident in London. Shortly before midnight, the police cleared the station of all except ticket holders and travellers. The huge crowd, estimated at 10,000, waited patiently in the drizzling rain.

The Argus (Melbourne, Vic. : 1848 - 1957)
Wed 8 Oct 1930 Page 7
LOSS OF R.101.
LONDON. Oct. 8.

The return to London of the victims of the disaster on R.101 was a most poignant event, and the description herewith is taken from the London Daily express just to hand.
Crowds such as even London has rarely seen gathered in the early hours of this morning around Victoria Station for the home-coming of R.101's dead.
They waited for hours in the rain—many of them women in flimsy evening dresses—thronging every point of vantage along the route to Westminster mortuary, and time and again police and ambulance men had to link hands to regulate the surging masses.

Scene at Victoria London, Oct 8
Although it was 1.25 am when the special train with the coffins containing the remains of the victims of the R.101 disaster arrived at Victoria Station, the crowd which began to collect hours before had become swollen to an enormous size in spite of the rain and cold, and represented all classes and types. They were all there to do homage to the victims.

```
Probably there had never been such a crowd gathered at
a London Station before, except at the occasion of the
hurried home-coming of the Prince of Wales when the King
was ill.
The crowd lined the entrance to the station, while
a group of relatives and others headed by the Prime
Minister and his daughter Miss Ishbel MacDonald and 12
men wearing blue uniforms with caps inscribed "R-101",
who were members of the relief crew, waited on the
platform.
Slowly the long train pulled in - a train of darkness,
except for the lighted first coach where three survivors
who were able to leave hospital were travelling.
- Reuter.
```

October 8th was Will's birthday. He would have turned 39.

At Victoria Station, the group of notables and relatives stood with bowed heads. There was dead silence, as the forty-seven coffins were borne out and placed on twenty-four waiting Air Force tenders, which left the station in slow procession through the great, silent throng. The twelve members of the airship's relief crew, in their neat blue uniforms and peak caps bearing the badge of the R101, saluted the remains of their comrades as they passed. The vehicles made their way to the mortuary, where the bodies would remain until they lay in state in Westminster Hall.

```
The Times, Wednesday October 8, 1930


. . . Until the bodies are removed to Westminster Hall
they will lie in the Westminster Mortuary, in order
to facilitate the carrying out of certain statutory
formalities. Two special rooms, draped in purple hangings
```

and adorned with flowers, have been set aside for the purpose.

. . . To assist in identification personal belongings found near all the bodies have been carefully preserved and labelled. Relatives will probably be able to satisfy themselves with the help of these relics, in which case there will be no necessity to open the coffins.

Twenty-five year old crew member Sam Church had survived the disaster but, while in hospital at Beauvais, he succumbed to his terrible injuries. His family and fiance had rushed to Beauvais after receiving news of the accident, but Sam died on Wednesday October 8th, a few hours before they arrived. His body was brought to join the others in London. There were now forty-eight coffins.

Westminster Hall and St Paul's Cathedral

The Times, Wednesday October 8, 1930

It was officially announced last night that the King has given permission for Westminster Hall to be used for the lying in state of those who lost their lives in the disaster to R.101. The public will be admitted between 8 am and 10 pm on Friday.
The King will be represented by the Prince of Wales at the memorial service in St Paul's Cathedral at noon on Friday. Other members of the Royal Family will attend in person or be represented at the service. . . .

Lying-in-state

"Lying-in-State" is the formal occasion in which a coffin is placed on view to allow the public to pay their respects to the deceased before the funeral ceremony.

Westminster Hall, the oldest existing part of the Palace of Westminster, was erected in 1097 by King William II, becoming the largest hall in Europe. Over the centuries, the Hall served numerous functions, including as a place for lying-in-state during state and ceremonial funerals. Such an honour was usually reserved for the Sovereign and for his or her consort. Readers may recall that the lying-in-state in Westminster Hall of Queen Elizabeth II was televised across the globe. Before 1930, the only commoner to receive the honour in the twentieth century was Frederick Sleigh Roberts, 1st Earl Roberts.

On one historic occasion, however, this tradition was given to forty-eight commoners; men who were not members of the royal family and had (mostly) never held a political office.

From 8am on October 10, the public passed through Westminster Hall paying silent tribute to the memory of the victims of the R101. Scores of thousands of people paid their tribute of respect to the victims. At one point the queue stretched for more than two miles along the embankment.

Special police arrangements were necessary to control the traffic in the neighbourhood, particularly late in the evening, when the streets became very congested.

At 10 p.m., the official time for closing, it was estimated that more than 120,000 had passed through the hall, but waiting multitudes still were so great that the authorities, with the King's permission. decided not to close the doors until midnight.

The flower-covered coffins lay in a double row on the dais in the centre of the purple-carpeted hall, and the people passed solemnly on either side of them.

Men of the Royal Air Force, who had formed a guard over the dead since they reached England, continued to do so during the lying-in-state and would do so until the coffins were removed for burial at Cardington on Saturday.

In the end, the R101's dead were honoured by a hundred and fifty thousand people, who filed by in a continuous stream. The number of wreaths was almost countless, but among them one stood out, being noticed by more than one reporter. It carried a simple card, with a handwritten message. Evidences point to the strong possibility that it was written by May, for Will.

The Palstra family archives include a copy of the London Evening News, which May saved.

She has circled that message in pen. It reads:

"To Daddy, from us all."

```
London Evening News
Friday October 10th, 1930
A MILE-LONG QUEUE WAITS TO FILE PAST THE DEAD OF R.101
AS THEY LIE IN STATE.
AN ENDLESS LINE OF PEOPLE WHO MOURN.
So Great a Throng at Westminster Hall that Traffic has to
be Diverted.

In the ancient Hall of Westminster and in ancient St.
Paul's Cathedral the people of England - people of high
estate and lowly - today paid reverence to the men of
R.101 who perished in the most modern of man's struggles
against the elements, the struggle for the conquest of
the air.
From the time that the doors of Westminster Hall were
opened, at 8 o'clock this morning, an unending line
of people has filed past the flower-and-flag-bedecked
catafalques on which the 48 dead of R.101 lie in state.
During the afternoon more than ten thousand people stood
```

in a mile-long queue at the door, waiting their turn for admission. Traffic along Millbank had to be diverted.
Among the masses of flowers that decked the coffins in Westminster Hall or lay near them were wreaths of laurel and heather from the King and Queen, the Prince of Wales, and the Duke of York; a wreath from the King of Spain bore the words, "To the Heroic"; near it lay another wreath inscribed, "To Daddy, from us all".

ARMS REVERSED, HEADS BOWED.
By a Special Correspondent.

Softly, like the sad whispering of autumn leaves, sound the footfalls of pilgrims on the stone floor of Westminster Hall. Above their heads, beyond the stone steps, a great window of rich stained glass glows with a dark glory of scarlet and blue.
Through one little window, high up in the bare wall, the clear gold of the sunshine streams in slanting lines and passes gently from coffin to coffin as the hours pass.
That bright square of gold rests, for a few minutes on the figure of an airman, who stands like a statue beside his dead friends; his head is bent, and his hands are on the butt of his reversed rifle.
Softly it passes on.

THE PURPLE DAIS

It touches with sudden beauty the banks of flowers which lie round the purple dais – that unforgettable catafalque, which holds all that is mortal of the leaders and crew of the R.101.
It pours its light upon the endless files of Londoners, whose great pilgrimage began when Big Ben struck eight in the sunshine of this October morning and will not end until Big Ben strikes ten in the darkness of the night.
One by one they are vivid in the little patch of sunshine. A shop-girl, her face fresh with the bloom of youth, steps from the dimness, is clear in the light for a moment, and steps on into the shadow again. After her comes a member of Parliament in the formal black of mourning dress.
Then a workman, in corduroy trousers and an earth-stained coat, a woman with a little bunch of flowers, a boy who holds his cap in his hand – one by one they pass by, with bowed heads.
Watch them for a little while.

MARKS OF GRIEF

Standing in the shadow you can see the grief on the faces of them all.
Here all London is paying its homage to the men who died in the flames and twisted metal on the rain-swept hill of Beauvais. The people of London move slowly along in the dense lines outside the historic door of St. Stephen's;

they pass – ten thousand of them every hour – down the stone steps, between the purple ropes; they move endlessly past the tragic rows of flag-hidden coffins.

On that purple dais there is no distinction of rank among the dead; the man who was the chief of all the Air Force lies side by side with the humblest members of the airship's crew. And in this dim hall there is no distinction of rank among the pilgrims: lords follow commoners, and women from Mayfair in rich furs follow girls from the offices and shops.

A woman who has come in a big shining car lays a wreath of costly beauty at the foot of the dais. Beside it a girl from the poor streets places a simple posy of flowers.

For here is the democracy of death.

OUR ISLAND STORY

This ancient hall has known famous days in its long history.

It has seen King Charles of England facing his judges; it has seen King Edward lying in noble state; it has seen the gatherings of the old Parliaments centuries ago. But it has seen nothing so moving as this dead crew of a great modern airship, mourned by a nation.

On the walls, in their shadowed niches, stand the statues of the old kings and queens of England.

Under their eyes passes the London of today, sorrowing for a great new calamity.

Moving with the throng beside the banks of flowers, one

feels the full tragedy of that night at Beauvais.

The dead are heartbreaking in their very number: their narrow beds, with the covering of flags, stretch away in the dimness in an unbroken rank. Until this moment we had thought of the calamity only in numbers. Now we see before us the stark reality.

The flowers, which fill the cold air with a sweet fragrance, tell of the grief of the world.

LAUREL AND HEATHER

Here, at the head of them all, is the great laurel wreath sent by the King, with its sad adornment of white roses and white heather. Beside it rest the purple-draped laurel wreath sent by the Prince of Wales and the laurels sent by the Duke of York.

And around the dais, what a multitude of sad messages.

Here is one from Dr. Eckener, the commander of the Graf Zeppelin. Near it is a tiny bunch of flowers, which bears the simple words, "To my dear husband."

Shining in the cold light, which filters through the great door, is a big silver model of R.101 made by the men of the British Legion. It is poised above a model field of corn and poppies.

Beside it is another cluster of carnations, and half hidden among the blossoms are the words, "To Daddy, from us all."

Passing from the shadow of Westminster Hall into the daylight, one sees the vast multitude stretching away along Millbank in a dense, slowly moving throng.

People pour from the Underground stations and stream from the buses during the afternoon; there are 15,000 in that line which winds past Lambeth Bridge to the Tate Gallery.

Such a sight as this has not been seen since the nation mourned for the passing of King Edward the Peacemaker.

Traffic on Millbank has stopped.

It can no longer pass the multitude on the roadway, and mounted police have directed it round by other roads.

SALUTE

The scene is ever-changing and yet ever the same. When Big Ben strikes the hour of three the watchers in the quiet hall have seen 70,000 people pass softly through, and yet that picture in the shadows is the same picture that they saw seven hours before.

A picture ever memorable!

Women pass by with tears in their eyes. Here and there a woman faints with emotion, and is helped by ambulance men into a little room at the corner of the hall. A white- bearded man comes past with his walking stick held to his forehead in a strange gesture of salute.

A black-veiled woman kneels on the stone floor beside the moving file. She is the wife of a man who lies in one of those coffins – which one she does not know.

150,000

The vast multitude outside in the October sunshine moves steadily forward and is ever renewed.

Before Big Ben strikes ten tonight and the lying in state ends, 150,000 people will have filed through that hall, the tribute of a nation to the men who died in the cause of progress and died without a chance of being saved.

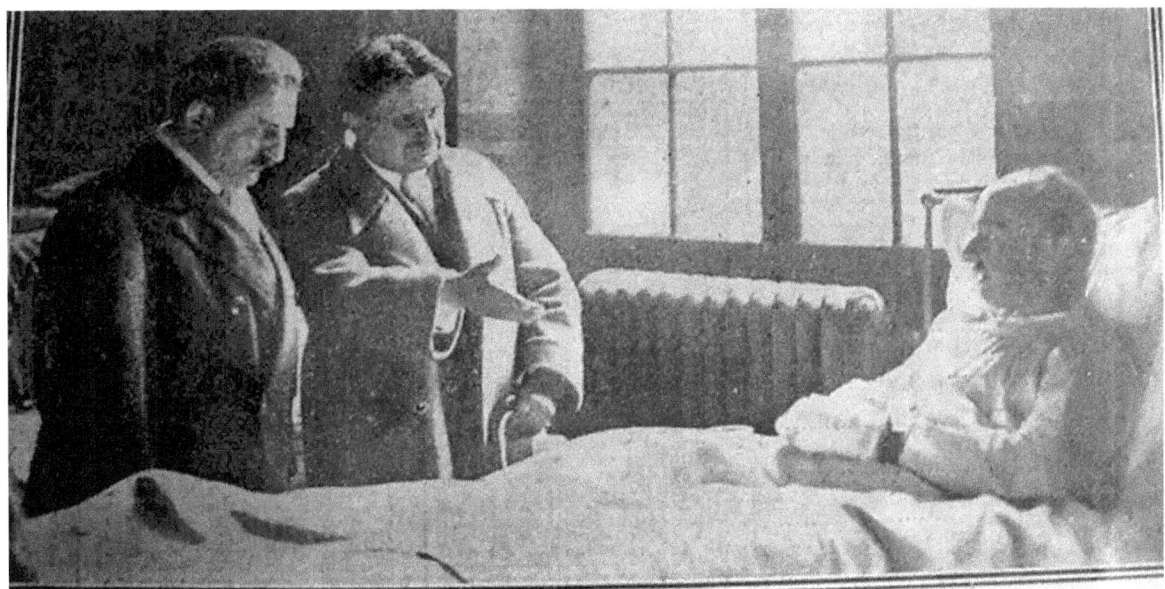

Mr. A.J. Cook, one of the injured survivors, in a French hospital, talking with the French Air Minister, M. Laurence Eynac.

Survivors of the R101 airship accident arrive at Croydon Airport, England. Alamy 2M3NJ83

"A Daily Mirror picture of the sad and impressive scene in historic Westminster Hall when the coffins of the forty-eight men killed in the R101 disaster lay in honoured state. An officer and men of the R.A.F., the latter with arms reversed, kept motionless guard beside the biers, around which were hundreds of beautiful wreaths, with that sent by the King and Queen at the head. An endless stream of people, numbering many thousands, passed in silent homage through the dimly-lit hall and paused reverently around the coffins, each of which was covered with the Union Jack. 10th October 1930." Alamy ID:2HHKGX8

The victims of the R101 airship disaster lying in state in Westminster Hall, London, 1930. Alamy ID:W7ENBF

A plaque in the Palace of Westminster commemorating the lying-in-state. [Wikipedia]

```
RELATIVES OF THE DEAD IN A MOTOR-BUS
By a Special Correspondent.


Through the stillness of a City strangely hushed, through
streets bare of traffic but lined with a silent multitude
of men and women, through avenues of mounted and foot
police, came to St, Paul's Cathedral today a slowly-
moving green motor-bus.
And as it passed, men raised their hats, women wiped
away their tears.
In that green motor-bus were the relatives of the dead
of R.101 on their way to the service at St. Paul's where
the nation was reverencing the men they had lost.


At the Steps
The bus swung round into the enclosure at the foot
of the Cathedral steps. A conductor in the uniform
of a Bedford motor-traction company helped his tragic
passengers down the steps from the upper deck.
```

Cathedral attendants gave their arms to the women in black who had halted when they saw the great crowd which encircled the Cathedral.

Stalwart sons helped grief-stricken mothers and sisters to climb up the steps of the cathedral to the doors, where vergers were waiting to take them to their seats near the altar.

Only a few yards behind this motor-bus was the Prince of Wales, who came to represent the King at this national service.

Words of Comfort

One part of the cathedral was reserved for the public, and a ring of mourners had encircled the building, waiting patiently for hours, for the opening of the doors leading to these seats.

On the pavements thousands who were unable to take part in the service listened to the organ notes and the singing.

At all streets leading to the cathedral giant barriers had been built, and all traffic was stopped during the service.

The service was a beautiful thing, full of wonderful words of comfort for the bereaved and praise for the men who gave their lives while on the service of their country.

The simple hymns, so familiar to all, "Rock of Ages" and "Jesu, Lover of My Soul", seemed to affect the elders among the mourners, and one mother and her grey-haired husband turned to look at one another and cried quietly

```
under the emotional spell of the music. Finally there
came the Benediction of the Archbishop of Canterbury,
the Dead March from "Saul", and the "Last Post" played
by trumpeters of the Royal Air Force.
There were few dry eyes in the whole Cathedral as that
"Last Post" was sounded.
Through the Windows


All the vast congregation stood perfectly still, with
bowed heads. No sound came from the street outside, but
sunlight streamed in . . .
```

Historian Nick Neve Walmsley said in an interview on YouTube: "The news of the disaster absolutely stunned people around the world. It totally shocked France as much as it shocked England. This was the biggest thing since the Titanic had gone down in 1912. Victims were brought back, and were the first civilians to lie in state in Westminster Hall. People queued from before eight o'clock in the morning until midnight to actually come and pay their respects. It just stunned the country. It was on such a vast scale and there were so many hopes been pinned on the airship, people were just numb."

The Memorial Service at St Paul's Cathedral

On that same day, a memorial service was held at St Paul's Cathedral, which British Pathé called, in their newsreel, "The Empire's Valhalla".

```
The Times, October 10, 1930
For the memorial service to be held at St. Paul's
Cathedral at midday, more than 20,000 applications have
already been received. There are seats for only 5,000,
although all possible extra accommodation is being
arranged.
```

Official representatives of all European and many other countries will attend, as well as members of the Cabinet and Dominion Prime Ministers and delegates in London for the Imperial Conference. The Prince of Wales will represent the King.

The Register News-Pictorial (Adelaide, SA : 1929 - 1931)
Mon 13 Oct 1930 Page 5
NATION HONOURS HEROES IN SERVICE AT ST. PAUL'S (REGISTER WORLD CABLES)
All Estates Of Realm Throng St. Paul's.

LONDON, Saturday.— The memorial service at St. Paul's Cathedral for the 48 victims of the R.101 was an impressive and touching example of a nation's paying honour to its dead heroes.
All estates of the realm thronged the great cathedral in solemn array. The service was broadcast throughout the world.

Dominion High Commissioners, Agents General, and a majority of Imperial Conference delegates were present, among the latter being Messrs. F. Brennan and Parker Moloney (Australia).
A motor bus brought the relatives of the victims through the reverent, bare-headed concourse, crowding the streets.
The Royal Air Force Band played a solemn march as the mourners. . . entered.

Symbol Of Flight

An almost eerie incident accompanied the brief invocation ending the first hymn, Rock of Ages. As the Amen sounded, a pigeon — one of those which flock outside the cathedral — took wing from the windowsill of the north transept, and flew straight down the main aisle toward the great door.

It was only less symbolic than a white dove. It was as if the soul of the airmen had taken flight.

A poignant touch at the memorial service was the pall draped over the altar.

It was the ensign of the R.101, which, tattered and charred, but glorious, had still floated over the shattered skeleton after the airship had plunged to destruction. Thousands of people passed in procession, two by two, to view it after the service.

London Evening News
Friday October 10th, 1930
At St. Paul's, where was held the memorial service which the Prince of Wales, members of our own Government and the Governments of many other lands, and the relatives of the officers and crew of R.101 attended, the multitude that sought admission was so great that 200 special police had to be sent to regulate the traffic.

"H.J. Leech, a survivor, with his wife after attending the memorial service at St. Paul's."
Photo from a British newspaper. Source: unknown.

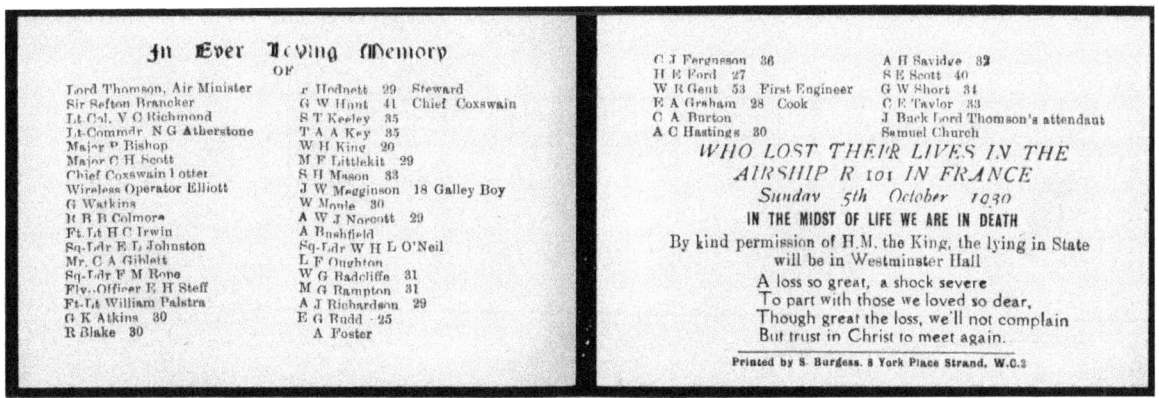

Mourning card with black edges, R101 airship. Alamy ID:RJB68A

```
Townsville Daily Bulletin (Qld. : 1907 - 1954)
Mon 13 Oct 1930
Page 7
R101 DISASTER.
THE R 101's FLAG.
LONDON, October 10.
The most poignant touch at the memorial service at
St. Paul's, which, as the Mother church of all three
services, is the Empire shrine, was the pall draped over
the altar. It was the R 101 ensign, whlch tattered and
charred, but glorious, had still floated over the shattered
skeleton after the airship had plunged to destruction.
Thousands passed in procession, two by two, to view it
after the servlce.
It will remain in its present position until it is sent
to Cardington for the funeral.

SQUADRON LEADER PALSTRA.
Squadron Leader Palstra's widow, although invited, was
unable to attend at the St. Paul's Service. His uncle
from Holland, and two other relatives were among the
mourners present.
```

In synchrony with the St Paul's Memorial service was a second service at Westminster Cathedral (nearer to Victoria Station) for those of the Catholic faith.

Readers who would like to "travel back in time" can view the newsreel of the Westminster Hall queues, the bus, and the dignitaries arriving at St Paul's on YouTube. The British Movietone channel has a video called *Sorrowing Crowds at Lying In State at Westminster Hall - R101* and another video called *Cortege Leaves Westminster Hall - (R101).*

. The British Pathé channel has *ENGLAND: DISASTER - Lying-in-state of R101 victims at Westminster Hall (1930)* and *London. The Nation bows its head—in poignant grief to pay homage at passing of the 48 victims of the ill-fated R-101*, uploaded Apr 13, 2014.

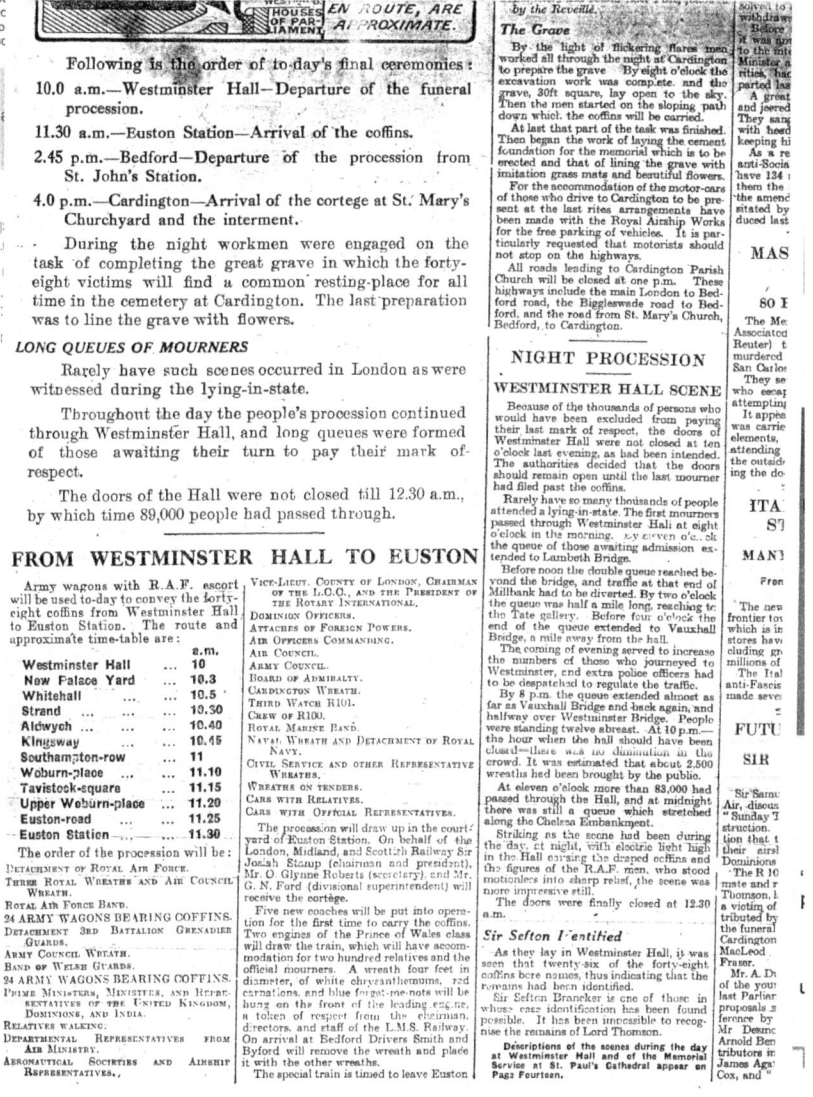

The schedule for conveying the coffins from Westminster Hall to their final resting-place was published in the daily papers. Image supplied.

The common grave

As darkness fell on the night of 10 October and crowds of people continued to queue at the doors of London's Westminster Hall, far away in Bedfordshire workmen were busy throughout the night, preparing the common grave at Cardington by the light of acetylene flares. The grave lay under open sky, and had a sloping entrance through which the bearers could carry in the coffins. It was planned that the concrete sides forming the base of a projected memorial would be hidden by masses of flowers during the solemn rites on the coming Saturday.

LONDON TO CARDINGTON

Funeral procession through London

On the morning of Saturday 11 October, the coffins were carried from the Hall, placed on horse-drawn gun-carriages and heaped with flowers. The funeral procession moved slowly from Westminster Hall to Euston Station, over a period of two hours before noon. In it marched the third watch of R101 reserve men, as well as the crew of the sister airship R100. Three military bands accompanied the procession, playing funeral marches as the gun-carriages were wheeled through the heart of London.

You can view this on YouTube: *The Nation Bows Its Head (1930)* on the British Pathé channel.

The funeral cortege of the victims of airship R 101 in Aldwych on its way to Euston station bound for Cardington 11 October 1930. Alamy ID:2BWAK5F

Funeral of R101 victims. The funeral cortege seen here passing through the Strand and into Kingsway as it makes its way to Euston Station. Where the coffins will be taken to Cardington for a final committal service. 11th October 1930. Alamy ID:ETXTBA

LONDON'. October 11.

'Another half mile to come,' whispered the officer at the gate of Westminster Palace Yard, where Mr Macdonald and the Dominion delegates stood watching the R101 funeral procession, of which a mile and a half had already flowed slowly past.

Every window of the grim grey stone buildings, from Whitehall to Westminster, was flowered with faces, and the footpaths were filled with a solid, sombrely clad mass of people, with their faces brightened with the Autumn sunshine. The while uniforms of a group of nurses on the roof of the Westminster Hospital stood out boldly against the sky, as a startling contrast.

First came the mounted police, then 500 Royal Air Force men marching in fours at funeral pace with reversed arms. Next two by two came more Air Force men, bearing the three royal wreaths and the Air Council wreath. After the band moved slowly 34 artillery limbers, each drawn by four or five horses bearing the coffins while behind these marched 100 guardsmen topped by huge bear skins. The Welsh guards band followed, then the remaining 24 coffins. Behind these fell in the motor cars, the first of which were occupied by Messas Macdonald, Scullin and Bennett, General Hertzog and others. The remaining Dominion delegates and their relatives followed walking. Thereafter came the City Council of London, and representatives of the Air Ministry, foreign powers, Dominion officers, Army Council, and Admiralty.

Not since the nation mourned King Edward the Seventh has such a spectacle been seen as that in the neighbourhood of Westminster. All day long, at the rate of nearly 10,000 per hour, representatives of all classes and ages poured sadly, with downcast heads, passed the coffins, many bringing flowers, some wreaths of hothouse blooms, and others simple posies. Two crippled British Legionnaires carried a silver tissue model of the R101 picked out in scarlet poppies. Early afternoon the queue extended half a mile, thousands giving up their lunchtime to pay their last tribute.

After that the dense ranks of steadily increased until by dusk they extended for a mile stop when Londoners were released from work everyone seemed to make for Westminster.

Conspicuous among the uniformed crew of the third watch of the R101 and the crew of the R100 which was preceded to Cardington by a wreath of quite trumpet lilies and red carnations, was the redheaded Bell, one of the survivors who was in mufti, hat in hand. The others wore dark blue caps. Behind the airmen came 100 naval men, and a band of cars with the relatives, and 12 Air Force tenders, carrying wreaths. The first one was a model of the airship. Huge crowds lined the streets during the two hours of the funeral march and at Euston Station where the procession entrained for Cardington. One man used a periscope to see the procession. Girls employed hand mirrors as reflectors.

R 101 VICTIMS BURIED WITH TRIUMPHANT SALUTES FROM THE SKY.

STARK TRAGEDY OF THE FORTY-EIGHT COFFINS STILLS THE HEART OF LONDON.

The heart of London was stilled yesterday when the forty-eight men killed in the airship R 101 were borne through the streets on the way to their common grave. The stark tragedy of those forty-eight coffins reduced tens of thousands of people to silence and to tears. The hush that fell upon the streets spread into every dwelling.

Around the little village of Cardington, near Bedford, where the burial took place, at least 75,000 people gathered, and there were many minor casualties among women who had waited hour after hour without food.

As the funeral procession moved along the country road from Bedford, two flights of Royal Air Force bombers appeared suddenly in the sky and impressively saluted their comrades — a dramatic reminder to the multitudes below of man's triumph over disaster and unknown perils.

On playing fields and racecourses throughout the land men stood silent and bareheaded for two minutes in memory of the dead.

London newspaper cutting, 1930. Image supplied.

Euston Station to Bedford Station

From Euston, a special train carried the dead to Bedford station.

```
The Register News-Pictorial
(Adelaide, SA: 1929—1931)
Mon 13 Oct 1930 Page 5
Sad, Impressive Ceremonies:
Last Scenes In Tragedy Of R101
REGISTER WORLD CABLES
LONDON, Saturday.


The Prime Minister of Britain (Mr. Ramsay Macdonald),
the Dominions Secretary (Mr. Thomas), the Australian
```

Prime Minister (Mr. Scullin) and other Ministers; stood silent in farewell on the platform at Euston as the long special train bearing the flag-covered, wreath-heaped coffins of the victims, accompanied by 200 relatives and officials slowly pulled out.

It was a mourning countryside through which the special bore its melancholy freight. At towns all along the route the villagers stood bareheaded, and railway station staffs were at the salute.

Sunday Pictorial
12th October 1930
PLANES' LAST SALUTE OVER THE GRAVE TOWN OF MOURNERS
Funeral Procession a Mile and a Half in Length

These last scenes at Bedford and in the little churchyard were unforgettable.

Slowly the train carrying the forty-eight coffins steamed into the station. With bowed heads representatives of the country's mourning, stood the Lord Lieutenant of the county and the Mayor of Bedford.

To the purple-shrouded carriage walked the bearers. The silence was intense until the first coffin was lifted to the platform.

The funeral procession formed up at Bedford station in impressive sllence.

Then came a great roar, and two squadrons of bombers shot overhead in salute. They remained overhead until the procession had been formed and was moving slowly through the densely crowded streets towards Cardington.

MOURNFUL LAMENT

At its head marched the firing party of the RAF carrying their arms reversed. Then came the first of [a fleet of] grey RAF lorries, with two coffins in it, covered by the Union Jack and almost hidden with flowers.
Marshalled at the roadside was the band of the Bedfordshire Regiment, which played a mournful lament as the sad procession passed.
The four mile route to Cardlngton, along which the coffins were borne was densely lined with people.
Through the closely packed mourning crowds the long cortege wended its way. Everywhere were women and men clad in black.

The funeral procession from Bedford Station to Cardington. Image supplied.

```
TOWN OF MOURNERS
Funeral Procession a Mile and a Half in Length

And now they come home. Nor is there aught of place or
precedence among them; they that went forth a band of
brothers, pioneers in a great enterprise. So come they
home as brothers still, peer beside peasant lad, nor
sign nor token shows them otherwise.
```

```
Rank upon rank, the long procession bears down the
wide road across the level land toward the great mast
whence one brief week since they sailed; carries them
onward, proudly yet so tenderly, towards the great and
the little church, and by the roadside one great grave.
The impulse of emotion which drew countless thousands
to Westminster Hall and yesterday packed London Streets
accompanied them to the grave.
```

Representing the king, the Prince of Wales [later to become Edward VII] had also travelled to Cardington. He walked with Prime Minister MacDonald in the procession, taking the victims to their last common resting place.

British Pathé's footage of this funeral procession can also be viewed on YouTube: "The Nation Bows Its Head (1930)"

Mourners line the route. Image supplied.

THE FUNERAL AT CARDINGTON

Near sunset, R101's passengers and crew were finally laid to rest in a communal grave at Cardington, near the Royal Airship Works and within sight of the airship sheds.

Each coffin was adorned with a small label made from the metal of R101's framework.

Fourteen of the plates bore names, but the others were never identified in the wreckage. On their plaques was inscribed: "To the memory of the unknown airman who died on October 5th."

Front page of the Daily Mirror, Monday 13 October 1930.

A burial service was held, attended by distinguished guests including zeppelin captain Hugo Eckener.

```
The Register News-Pictorial (Adelaide, SA: 1929—1931)
Mon 13 Oct 1930 Page 5
Sad, Impressive Ceremonies:
Last Scenes In Tragedy Of R101
VICTIMS LAID TO REST IN FLOWER-STREWN GRAVE
Vast Concourse, In Solemn Hush, Surrounds Churchyard In
Shadow Of Ship's Hangar
REGISTER WORLD CABLES
LONDON, Saturday.


The last sad scene in the tragedy of the R101 was enacted
this afternoon in the little cemetery at Cardington,
almost within shadow of the giant hangars from which the
airship set out just a week before.
Mourners were grouped around the huge common grave in
St. Mary's churchyard; the dark blue clad crew of the
R100 in the front rank. Mr. Bell, the sole representative
of the R101 survivors, bore wreaths from his comrades.
There was a long, sorrowful interlude as the grey-clad
Air Force pallbearers carried one by one a seemingly
interminable line of flag-draped coffins, and reverently
laid them in rows of 12 in the flower-lined grave.
```

Fainting Women and Men in Tears in Cemetery

Joint Burial Services

The burial services were jointly carried out by the Bishop of St. Albans, a Roman Catholic Bishop, and Prebyterian and Methodist staff-chaplains. The Doxology was sung to the strains of a distant band, after which a firing squad fired three volleys over the grave.

As the rifle crashed out, several women mourners, overcome by the prolonged strain, fell fainting at the graveside. The vast concourse surrounding the churchyard stood in a solemn hush. Then, just as the last rays of the setting sun illumined the scene, trumpeters sound the Last Post.

There were a few moments' sllence. And then, from a neighbouring field, the Reveille rang out.

The tragic homecoming of the men of the R101 was over. The mourners heaped in the flowers until the grave was nearly filled and left them in their comradeship of death.

Australia's Wreath On Grave

LONDON, Sunday.— [Australian Prime Minister] Mr. Scullin, who rode in the first Official car with Mr. Ramsay MacDonald, Mr. Bennett, and Gen. Hertzog, described the funeral as the most tragically impressive thing he had ever seen.

At his instructions a beautiful wreath was sent to Cardington in the name of Australia.

Mr. Forbes also sent one for New Zealand.

You can watch the Cardington funeral on British Pathé's YouTube channel @britishpathe.

The coffins in the mass grave during the service Alamy ID:KYMC9T

The funeral at Cardington. Image ssupplied.

Painted signs on the ground: "Choir", "Relatives of R101..." Image supplied.

The R101's dead were buried in a mass grave, within sight of the two gigantic airship sheds.

In 1931 a memorial tomb was completed and inscribed with the names of the victims. This memorial still dominates the tiny churchyard to this day.

This faded photograph of the R101 airship memorial in St Mary's church-yard, Cardington, is from the Palstra/Holdaway family collection.

PART XIII: AFTERMATH

Will's Family

By 11 October, all the pomp and ceremony had finished.

The communal grave had been covered with soil, and lay quiet beneath the sky. Will's life was over.

What of his loved ones?

At the time of the R101's departure for India, Will and May and the children had been staying at the house in Fawley, Hampshire, so as to be near RAF Calshot, where Will had been studying.

Will had kissed his family goodbye and left Fawley on the afternoon of Friday 3rd October.

May knew that Will would stay overnight at Charlie Harman's home in South Norwood before catching public transport to Cardington. No doubt she worried about his safety, as always. And young Margaret must have asked questions about her beloved father - "Where is Daddy going? Why can't we go with him? When will he come back?"

"Daddy's going to India on the big airship," May might have replied. "He'll be back in about two weeks."

She slept alone on Friday night and Saturday night, missing him, longing for his return.

On the morning of Sunday 5th October, May was alerted by unexpected sounds—the garden gate squeaking on its hinges, quick footsteps along the garden path, and an urgent knock at the front door. Why would anybody be rapping so insistently, so early on a Sunday morning? Her heart must have sunk, as she was gripped by a terrible foreboding.

May probably guessed what had happened, even before she opened the door and beheld the telegram delivery-boy standing on the threshold. She took the envelope from his hand and tore it open. What was typed there, on that pale yellow paper, confirmed her worst fears.

Did May's knees buckle, and did she drop to the floor, right there in the entrance hall? The newspapers reported that Squadron Leader Palstra's "wife was prostrated with grief. Flight- Lieutenant Harman, his closest colleague, motored to Fawley early on Sunday . . . He offered his colleagues' consolation."

May was too distraught to attend any of the funeral ceremonies. She was in a state of almost complete mental and physical collapse, and had no family at hand to support her. Charlie Harman and his wife did their best to help, as did Doris, the family's erstwhile maid who had become a friend.

```
THE TIMES, Saturday October 11, 1930 R.101
MRS. PALSTRA RETURNING

Flight-Lieutenant C. J. Harman, who was assistant to
the late Squadron-Leader W. Palstra, Australian liaison
officer with the Air Ministry, is arranging for Mrs.
Palstra and her three children to embark for Australia
immediately.
They will be under the care of Flight-Lieutenant Hewitt.
```

Many were the obituaries for Squadron Leader Palstra published in Australian newspapers, and in the RAAF journal "Flight". In Sydney on 15th October, and in Amsterdam on October 17, memorial services were held in his honour.

```
The Sydney Morning Herald, Tue 7 Oct 1930:
A GALLANT OFFICER
Squadron-Leader Palstra
The Royal Australian Flying Corps has lost one of its
most brilliant officers by the death of Squadron-Leader
William Palstra. In single combat in France in 1917
and 1918 Squadron-Leader Palstra shot down six enemy
machines, and as the result of other exploits he earned
advancement and was mentioned in dispatches. The Military
Cross had already been awarded him. This decoration was
won for devotion to duty and bravery during the battle
of Messines on June 6, 1917. As a second lieutenant of
the 39th Battalion, he was the only officer remaining at
the close of the engagement.
```

His career as an airman began in October 1917, when he transferred from the infantry to the Australian Flying Corps as a flying officer in the third squadron.

Enterprising and aggressive in the air, he soon earned the right to fly a Sopwith Camel, the type of machine then exclusively engaged in protecting the heavier Allied aeroplanes from the enemy formations. He then transferred to the independent air force, and was attached to several of the "circuses" of picked pilots who elected daily combat with the most skillful and resourceful of the enemy air force. Towards the close of the war he flew a Bristol Fighter with conspicuous success.

A forced landing in the burning town of Cambrai and a take- off after repairing his engine were amongst the most vivid memories that he brought home from the war. On another occasion his aeroplane was so badly holed during a successful encounter with a German machine that he was forced down, and alighted between the British and German lines. Fortunately, there was a heavy mist, and he was able to restart the engine and fly away.

A brother of the dead officer, Mr C.E. Palstra, who is connected with the Salvation Army Boys' Home at Bexley, said yesterday that Squadron-Leader Palstra had died as he would have chosen. In his last letter Squadron-Leader Palstra had written of the coming flight to India, and had put forward the view that lighter-than-air machines would never supersede heavier-than-air machines for defense purposes, whatever merits they might develop in the field of commerce. He had emphasized that the safety of the big airship and its complement of 50 or 100 men, still depended on the skill and judgment of an individual.

Squadron-Leader Palstra was born in South Africa [sic] 39 years ago. His father, Commissioner Palstra, was field secretary of the Salvation Army in Australia until 1921, and was then appointed to a similar position in China. Later he became Commissioner to Korea, and now holds a similar post in the Dutch East Indies.

FLIGHT, Oct 17, 1930:
[Article includes photos of funeral procession]
AUSTRALIA'S LOSS
In Squadron-Leader William Palstra, M.C., B.A., p.s.a.28, the Royal Australian Air Force has lost a very brilliant officer. He served during the war in the 39th Battalion, Australian Infantry, and afterwards in No. 3 Australian Squadron of the Flying Corps. He won his Military Cross while in the Infantry. During the attack on the Hindenburg line in September 26-29, 1918, he highly distinguished himself as a pilot of No.3 Australian Squadron. After the war, he went to Melbourne University, graduated B.A., and was then employed in an administrative capacity at the University. On August 10, 1925, he was commissioned as Flying Officer in the Royal Australian Air Force. He was promoted to Flight-Lieutenant in 1927 and to Squadron- Leader in 1930. Last year he went through the R.A.F. Staff College at Andover and subsequently was appointed Australian Liaison Officer at the Air Ministry until last month. He then took a course in air navigation at Calshot. He leaves a widow and three children.

Will's parents, Jacoba and Wiebe, in China, 1930, mourning their eldest son. Wearing the white Salvation Army uniforms of summer, they are seated before a photo of Will in his RAAF uniform. The photo is surrounded by Chinese vases filled with white lilies.

Poverty and Repatriation

For May, Margaret, Jocelyn and little Bill, the loss of the man at the centre of their lives, the one they loved so dearly, forever blighted their lives. He had been torn from them violently, in circumstances so horrific that decades later, in order to avoid a similar fate, people would leap from the top floors of the USA's World Trade Center.

For Will's wife and children, this was the termination of all happiness and hope. The light had gone out of their lives. Unable to cope with the enormity of their loss, they would be forever doomed to vainly seek a way to make him live again. So profound was that curse, that it would ripple through generations as yet unborn.

To add to their misery Will's young family had also lost all social and financial advantages associated with his career.

Despite the fact that Squadron-Leader Palstra had risked his life for his country during the First World War, represented Australia at high levels in the UK, and lost his life in the service of the RAAF; despite Senator Foll's public statement on October 8 that, "he was sure that Australia will not neglect her obvious duty to see that his dependents are provided for", Prime Minister Scullin did not see any necessity to provide Will's bereaved family with the financial help they would so desperately need, now that they were deprived of their breadwinner. For the rest of their lives they would be afflicted by both unresolved grief, and poverty.

Now that the family had lost Will's Air Force income, they were destitute. All the trappings of his comfortable squadron leader's income had to go—the motor-car, the maid-servant, the big house, the comfort and privileges that accompanied their old, happy life.

There had been no last viewing, no family to support May and the children, no headstone in a quiet cemetery that they could visit on weekends. After his death the authorities made Will belong to them, not to his family. He was snatched away from his loved ones utterly, in death as in life.

It was not until the last day of the year that travel arrangements were completed, and May and the children embarked for Australia.

Everything had changed. Wednesday 31 December 1930 was the final day of the old year and the old decade; the decade that had seen the rise and fall of the Golden Age of Airships.

The bitter winds of the English winter chilled the woman and her three young children as they boarded the mail-ship Moldavia at the Port of London to make the slow, lonely, sad voyage back to Australia without Will. They had made the outbound journey with such high hopes, and now all were dashed beyond repair.

```
The Australasian (Melbourne, Vic. : 1864 - 1946)
Sat 10 Jan 1931 Page 9. PERSONAL.

Mrs. W. Palstra, widow of Squadron Leader W. Palstra the
Royal Australian Air Force, who was killed in the R.101
disaster near Beauvais, France, last year, returned to
Melbourne on board the P. and O. mail liner Moldavia
on Monday. Mrs. Palstra and her three children, who
accompanied her, will reside at Surrey Hills. They were
met by representatives of the Air Force and relatives.
```

The Palstra family archives contain a photograph from the newspapers. It shows nine year old Margaret seated on a large coil of rope on the deck of the Moldavia. Her two young siblings are playing nearby. Margaret has turned her head and her gaze rests on the camera.

WIFE AND CHILDREN OF R101 VICTIM.—Mrs. W. Palstra (wife of Squadron-Leader W. Palstra, who was one of the victims of the R101 tragedy), who arrived with her children on the Moldavia this morning. Mrs. Palstra will live with her parents in Surrey Hills, Melbourne. Left to Right—Margaret (nine years), Mrs. Palstra, William (two years), and Jocelyn (14 years).

This other blurry photo was in *The Adelaide Mail*, Saturday 3 January, 1931, under the heading 'Wife and Children of R101 Victim', with 4 year old Jocelyn's age incorrectly reported as '14 years'. Brave Margaret, always trying to be the 'good girl', smiles for the camera.

Margaret (on the right) on SS Moldavia, December 1930, seated on the Christmas mailbags with her friend Joyce and the boatswain. Her polite smile for the camera hides her devastation.

The endless grief of May and Margaret

After Will's death, May changed the name of the house in Surrey Hills from "Aurunui"—her middle name—to "Zwolle", the name of Will's birthplace.

May preserved the official telegram from the Air Ministry, informing her of Will's death in the

R101 disaster. She kept copies of the newspaper articles reporting on the funeral arrangements, the tributes from France, and all the pomp and ceremony that accompanied her loss. She clung to everything that was in any way related to him.

She brought these papers back to Australia with her, along with his letters to her, and hers to him, and the journals of their holiday trips together, and the letters of condolence from all the Prime Ministers and ambassadors and other officials and dignitaries.

She carried them all back to the little weatherboard house in Surrey Hills, that safe nest where the young couple had made their first home together, and she stored them, with Will's war diaries, in a hidden compartment inside a large, wooden chest of drawers. Only the immediate family knew of their existence.

There they remained for decades.

The Enquiry

What caused the destruction of the R101 and the appalling loss of so many adventurous and talented men?

On 22 October 1930 the Air Ministry appointed Sir John Simon[84] to hold an investigation into the causes and circumstances of the accident to the airship R101. The inquiry opened on 28 October 1930 and spent 10 days taking evidence from 42 witnesses.

---

84 1st Viscount Simon, a British politician who held senior Cabinet posts from the beginning of the First World War to the end of the Second World War.

A 15-foot model of R101, about one-fiftieth the size of the airship and constructed for exhibition at the Olympia Aero Show the previous year, was suspended in the hall where the inquiry took place. Photographs show the model seeming to hover above the heads of the dark-suited scientists and engineers who occupied the rows of seats.

The chairman and assessors issued their findings from the Inquiry in 1st April 1931. They concluded that the airship's excessive weight had played an important part in the disaster, but the immediate cause, according to their report, was a sudden loss of gas in a forward gasbag at a time when the nose of the craft was being depressed by a downward current of air.

They deduced that the fabric had been torn by rough weather, sparks from a broken electric circuit had caused the fire, and pre-flight trials had been inadequate. No Government department, high official or group of individuals was held responsible, but there can be no doubt that political necessities behind the R101 affected its development.

Wing Commander Thomas R. Cave-Browne-Cave wrote to the Royal Aeronautical Society Historical Group in August 1962. "Perhaps the fatal mistake was insistence that the ship must take the Secretary of State [Lord Thomson] to India in most impressive style and get him home to tell a personal story to the Imperial Conference. Without him and without the supporting passengers and the great unnecessary weight and, if Colmore [one of the airship designers] had been allowed to choose his time of departure, R101 could almost certainly have flown to India and probably returned before the end of the Imperial Conference."[85]

The final word of judgement came from the Court of Inquiry: "The desire of all involved to achieve the flight to India before the conclusion of the 1930 Imperial Conference (at which decisions would be taken on the future of the airship programme) led to a premature flight in adverse weather conditions.

---

85   Royal Aeronautical Society Journal Paper No. 2015/02 p.66. Source: Davison 2015

"It is impossible to avoid the conclusion that the R.101 would not have started for India on the evening of 4th October if it had not been that reasons of public policy were considered as making it highly desirable for her to do so if she could."

Had there not been pressure from Lord Thomson for that October 4th takeoff to India, it is possible that corrections of the great ship might have been made and the whole history of the airship gone in another direction.

A model of the R101 hangs in the hall in which the enquiry is being held.
GettyImages-558655977

The Effect on Airship Development

The R101 disaster was one of the worst airship accidents of the 1930s. 48 people had been killed—more than the 36 who lost their lives in the dramatically publicised Hindenburg catastrophe of 1937.[86]

The shock of the tragedy was so great that it effectively ended further airship development in Britain.

In "The R.101 Story", Peter Davison says, "The loss of His Majesty's airship R.101 on 5th October 1930 marked a turning point in the development of long distance air travel. The accident stopped the development of rigid airships in the United Kingdom and heralded the development of the aeroplane for all aspects of commercial air travel.

"The emotional effect of the disaster was on a scale not seen since the Titanic. The public outpouring of grief and sympathy in the immediate aftermath and the subsequent inquiry, coupled with media and technical speculation, marked the end of the programme in 1931.[87]

The Fading of the Age of Airships.

The R101 was built of dreams, and with her end, Britain's airship hopes vanished. After she went up in flames on 5 October 1930, her sister airship R100 never flew again.

The Air Ministry ordered R100—ironically the more successful in design and performance—to be grounded. She was deflated and hung up in Shed No. 2 at Cardington for a year while the Ministry contemplated her fate.

On 31 August 1931 the British Cabinet decided to abandon airship development altogether. The desire to banish all thought of airships was so intense that in November 1931, the Air Ministry decided to sell R100 for scrap. She was wheeled out of her shed, and

---

86   LZ-129 Hindenburg was under construction in 1933 but was not completed and flown until 1936.

87   Davison, 2015

steamrollers were driven back and forth over her metal framework until it was crushed beyond recognition. The flattened girders[88] were sold to scrap metal dealers for less than £600.[89]

```
Mirror (Perth, WA : 1921 - 1956)
Sat 13 Dec 1952 Page 9
The sister ship of the doomed vessel, the R100, was sold
for scrap and a 'no airship' policy was brought in. Five
years' planning and work had been wrecked in ten minutes
on that stormy October night.
```

Proposals for the planned R102, R103 and R104 airships were now given up completely. The loss of R101, the deepening world depression, and doubts about the optimistic financial forecasts, were all factors in these decisions.

So many talented men died in R101 that the development of civil aviation in Great Britain was set back for years. Arguably, no comparable disaster has hit any industry in quite the same way, before or after the R101.

Instead of airships pioneering the Empire's network of international air routes, aeroplanes took over. Imperial Airways, the early British commercial long-range airline, had begun using flying boats in 1929 and later, they employed planes that were designed to take off from land.

Nonetheless, both the US Navy and the US Army continued to be interested in acquiring and developing dirigibles. Between September 1931 and April 1933 the Navy operated the USS Akron (ZRS-4). A helium-filled airship, she was the world's first purpose-built flying aircraft carrier.

---

88   C.P. Hall: "I believe that R.101's longitudinals were 100% stainless steel, mainframes had steel and duralumin parts, and reefing girders were duralumin."

89   Popular Aviation, 1932, p. 225

On the morning of 4th April 1933 a thunderstorm off the coast of New Jersey destroyed the Akron, killing 73 of the 76 crewmen and passengers. Never before had so many lives been lost in any airship crash.

The wrecking of the Akron triggered the demise of airship development in the US Navy. Notwithstanding, the US Army's interest in airships persisted well into the 1930s. In the mid 1930s the American Air Corps began to grow rapidly, and competition for funding grew fierce. That spelled the decline of the Army's airship program, and it was officially terminated in mid-1937.

Zeppelins

In 1933, the same year the Akron was destroyed, a new hydrogen-lifted airship entered passenger service. Manufactured by the Germans, it was called the Hindenberg (Registration D-LZ 129). On the Hindenburg, stringent fire precautions were adhered to. The crew wore hemp-soled shoes and anti-static asbestos overalls without buttons or any kind of metallic surface. All matches and lighters were removed from passengers before they boarded. The smoking room was especially insulated, pressurised to prevent hydrogen entering, and fitted with a double door. A steward lit cigars and cigarettes from a special lighter and ensured that no fire left the room.

Infamously, on May 6, 1937 the Hindenberg was destroyed by fire in the United States, during its attempt to dock with its mooring mast at the Naval Air Station in Lakehurst. Thirty-six people died, including thirteen passengers, twenty-two crew-members and one man who worked on the ground.

Confronted with the filmed scenes of flaming catastrophe, the public lost all confidence in passenger-carrying airships. This marked the sudden and final end of the era of the great airships, world-wide.

The Age of Airships had been short-lived—a mere three decades long. Its end was hastened by a series of horrific accidents including that of the R101, and by the late 1930s airships were completely deposed by aeroplanes.

Vale R101

The Airship Heritage Trust's website proclaims, "The wreck of the R.101 lay where it had fallen until well into 1931, becoming a haunt for air accident investigators and day trippers who wanted to see the near perfect skeleton of the largest airship in the world. Thomas William Ward, scrap metal contractors from Sheffield who were specialists in stainless steel were employed to salvage what they could."[90]

Eventually, workmen using oxyacetylene blow torches and metal saws broke up the wreckage of the R101. Caterpillar tractors had already hauled out the heavy engines. The eight tons of girders were compacted, before being freighted by rail and ship to the steelworks of Sheffield. There, it was melted down for scrap.

An urban myth arose that materials from the R101 were used in the construction of the Hindenberg airship, but this has no basis in fact.

Memorials

A masonry monument commemorating the memory of the R101 victims was unveiled in Cardington Cemetery on 21 September 1931. In 1933 the French finished building a smaller permanent memorial on the crash site near Beauvais in France. It is a tall, rectangular monolith rising from a massive block of stone, upon which are engraved the words, "A la memoire des victimes de la catastrophe du dirigeable R101 5 Oct 1930". In Beauvais, at 33 rue de Paris, there exists a private museum called "Musée Souvenir du Dirigeable R.101" (Museum in Memory of the R.101 Airship).

A memorial tablet to William Palstra was unveiled at the Wyclif Church in Surrey Hills on 28 July 1935. This was the church he and his young family attended, near their home in Australia.

There are R101 memorials on the Internet, too, such as the page by "Cardington Sheds," which hosts photographs and information about the R101.

---

90   The Airship Heritage Trust "R101"

The two enormous airship sheds remain standing at Cardington,[91] once the home of the Royal Airship Works (RAW). The remains of the mooring mast site can be seen, although the mast itself is long gone.

See also: (1) YouTube: "R.101: Ship of Dreams (BBC, 2001)" Alejandro Flores-Ibarra. Uploaded Oct 6, 2020

(2) The YouTube channel Air and Space '46 and Beyond has made a short but poignant video of the R101 with her lights on, flying through a storm: "R 101 VIDEO". When you watch it, turn on the sound.

(3) Read more about the R101 at Airships Online, the website of the Airship Heritage Trust. Their journal is called "Dirigible". https://www.airshipsonline.com

The Years that Followed

Eternal Love

Will was the great love of May's life.

When she heard what had happened, she wanted to die.

After she lost Will she never married again, never loved another. She spent the rest of her life alone, though surrounded by a network of loving friends and family. So profound was her trauma that she could not speak to her grandchildren about what had happened. Her religious faith helped her struggle through the years of grief.

The tragedy had, perhaps, the opposite effect on her daughter Margaret as she grew to adulthood. After May passed away, Margaret stopped going to church. It was as if she could have no faith in a God who could take her father away.

In 1930 there was little or no counselling available for the bereaved. People were expected to "get on with it". After all, hundreds of thousands of families were still suffering from the loss of sons, fathers, brothers, husbands, sweethearts, nephews, friends in the Great War.

---

91 In the year 2020, Google Maps showed the erstwhile location of the Royal Airship Works as "Cardington Studios, Hangar 2, Cardington Airfield, Bedford MK42 0TF, United Kingdom." It's about four miles from Bedford Railway Station, along Cardington Road.

May Palstra, nee Holdaway, continued to live in the same house where she had lived with Will, until she died in 1964. She raised their three children there.

The house in Surrey Hills became like a shrine to Will's memory. Nobody intended for this to happen. Nobody even realised it was happening. It just happened. Until the time of writing this, the year 2023, that humble weatherboard house has never been sold out of the family.

Margaret was permanently damaged by the death of her beloved father and the ensuing, prolonged grief of her mother. "My mother used to cry every day," she told her children. May mourned for the rest of her life.

Margaret was only a child, vulnerable, sensitive, trapped in a horrifying nightmare of inexplicable, unspeakable sorrow and desolation. The world was awry, out of control, and there was nothing she could do about it. The mental scars of her bereavement and her mother's distress remained with her forever.

Sometimes, as she grew up in that house, Margaret would take the letters and diaries and newspaper cuttings out of the secret drawer and read them.

Until she knew them by heart.

In 1990, when once again looking through the boxes of letters, some of which have been published herein, Margaret wrote to her sister; "This is a fairly depressing experience. Time present seems to stand still, but when one looks at it as time past, one regrets lost opportunities and mourns over people gone forever from one's life..."

Throughout the years of her life, without really being aware of it, Margaret kept vainly trying to bring her father back.

As a young woman, Margaret chose a boyfriend who was an RAAF pilot. His plane crashed over the English Channel, and he did not survive. In her twenties, Margaret travelled through England and France, perhaps following her father's footsteps. In later life she became secretary to the vice chancellor of LaTrobe university, echoing Will's clerical job at Melbourne University.

What happened to her siblings?

Her sister Jocelyn married, and had four children.

William "Bill" Palstra, Will's son, went to live in France in the 1960s. He lived there for most of his adult life, and his own son was born there. Why France, of all places in the world? Was he, too, seeking the ghost of his father?

Margaret lived in the Surrey Hills house all her life, surrounded by all the marvellous souvenirs and antique mementos brought back from far-flung lands by her missionary ancestors. A gum tree she had planted in the garden when a small child, helped by her father, grew tall and venerable, arching its branches protectively yet destructively over the roof. At the age of 72, Margaret died in the back room of the house, having been born in the front room. As someone said, "Her whole life was a journey through that house."

So intense was her terrible longing for all that had been lost, that unintentionally, she passed it on to her children.

One of her granddaughters was born in the same front bedroom where Margaret was born. So profound was the impact of Will's loss that it continues to ripple through the generations, close to a century later. Some of Will's descendants, through his three children, also spent years trying to "find" him, or bring him back to life, or replicate his life, or somehow "live his life for him". Some journeyed from Australia to France, as if seeking him. Some formed associations with aviation, or universities, or gave birth to their children in significant locations. One became haunted by airships and wrote his biography. Other saw themselves as curators for the museum of curios and traditions that the house in Surrey Hills—stuck in time—became.

Down the years: What happened to the family afterwards.

On 28 November 1931 Wiebe and Jacoba returned to Australia on the Taiping. They retired to Australia in 1932 and lived at 28 Middlesex Road, Surrey Hills. Four of their children also settled in Australia.

Charles Palstra

Charles Palstra managed to survive the arsenic poisoning, but after his war experiences and other ordeals he had endured throughout his life, he (like so many returned veterans) become an alcoholic. In 1939 he married a young woman named Flora Sproston and settled down in Melbourne.

```
The Argus (Melbourne, Vic. : 1848 - 1956)
Monday 5 June 1939 Page 5
PALSTRA-SPROSTON

Deep cream velvet cut on classical lines, was chosen
by Flora, younger daughter of Mr Charles E Sproston of
Ford street Ivanhoe and the late Mrs Sproston for the
wedding to Charles Engelbert second son of Commissioner
W Palstra of Middlesex Road, Surrey Hills and the late
Mrs Palstra at St James's Church of England Ivanhoe on
Saturday. The Rev T Howard Whitworth officiated.
The bride was attended by Misses Pat Sproston and Jean
McPhie who wore cyclamen taffeta frocks . . .
```

Flora was Charles's saviour, according to family members. She was proud of him. She gave him the love, understanding and support he so badly needed, to cope with the horrors life had thrown his way. She transformed his life for the better. Charles and Flora had two sons.

In a cruel twist of fate, it was not until five years after Charles's death that the Australian government belatedly decided to honour those brave men who had endured the nightmare of Gallipoli in 1915.[92] One could wish that the medal had been awarded to Charles during his lifetime, and the lifetime of his father, who would have been so proud of him.

Next of kin were entitled to receive the medallion on behalf of their relatives. As soon as Charles's widow Flora heard the news of the medal, she wrote to the Central Army Records office requesting the Gallipoli Medal for her late husband. No doubt it is still in the possession of his descendants.

Paranormal claims

A wave of spiritualism swept through English-speaking countries during the 1920s.

Spiritualists believe that the spirits of the dead exist, and can communicate with the living through people called 'spirit mediums', who have the gift of being able to undertake such communication. The popularity of this movement reached its peak between the 1840s and the 1920s. Arguably the First World War played a major role in perpetuating it, because so many families were desperate to 'contact' their loved ones who had been killed in the fighting.

In 1926, ghost-hunter Harry Price established the "National Laboratory of Psychical Research" in London. On Tuesday, 7 October 1930, two days after the R101 disaster, a séance was held at the rooms of the NLPR, the psychic being Irishwoman Mrs. Eileen Garrett, a well-known trance medium. Garrett was attempting to contact the deceased Sir Arthur Conan Doyle when suddenly she claimed to have made contact with Flight-Lieutenant H. Carmichael Irwin, captain of the R101, who was giving her information about why the airship had crashed.

---

92   "The Anzac Commemorative Medallion was instituted 1967. It was awarded to surviving members of the Australian forces who served on the Gallipoli Peninsula, or in direct support of the operations from close off shore, at any time during the period from the first Anzac Day in April 1915 to the date of final evacuation in January 1916. Australian Defence Force [https://www.defence.gov.au/medals/imperial/wwi/Anzac-Commemorative-Medallion.asp]

The event attracted worldwide attention, thanks to the presence of a reporter. Immediately after the séance, the reporter's shorthand notes were transcribed and copies of the transcript were distributed to various people, including some at the Air Ministry. Its existence was even brought to the attention of Sir John Simon, who had conducted the public inquiry into the R101 disaster.

Major Oliver Villiers, a friend of Brancker, Scott, Irwin, Colmore and others aboard the ship, participated in further séances with Garrett, at which she claimed to have contacted both Irwin and other victims.[93]

Understandably, May Palstra hated these spiritualist claims, which upset her greatly. Imagine how she must have felt when a woman she'd never met claimed to be able to speak with those who had been aboard the R101, or when journalists labelled the dead as "spooks".

The jargon-filled technical information Garret presented at her séances, which she claimed Irwin's spirit gave to her, appeared very convincing. Since then it has, nonetheless, been debunked.

The image opposite is from *The World's News* January 1947.

---

93   See also "The Airmen Who Would Not Die" John G. Fuller, G. P. Putnam's Sons, New York (1979)

Dead Men As Radio Stars
BBC PLAN TO SHORTWAVE THE VOICES OF SPOOKS

Britain's staid Broadcasting Commission, held up by critics as the world's most perfect example of Victorian conservatism, has defied convention with an attempt to broadcast a spiritualist seance. The ambitious plan was the most startling in radio history; interest in it exceeded even that aroused by the famous American "Invasion From Mars" broadcast, that threw prewar New York into a panic.

By PETER HILDRETH—From London.

WHILE Britain's leading spiritualists were sitting around a table in Broadcasting House, London, waiting for the red light to flash that they were on the air in an attempt to contact victims of the 16-year-old R101 disaster, the BBC lost its nerve and cancelled the programme.

The cancelled programme, widely publicised as "The Dead Witness Of The R101," and one of a series titled, "Do You Believe in Ghosts?" was taken by Britain's very active spiritualist group as an official vindication of their beliefs.

The cancellation was made not because the august BBC commissioners doubted the ability of mystics to raise echo voices of the R101's passengers and crew. The programme was called off at the last minute because it was considered an abuse of a public service for even such interesting experiments, if it caused grief to relatives and friends of the victims.

Special Investigator

Script for the programme was written by Harry Price, the BBC's Investigator of Psychic Phenomena, and closely followed the lines of a seance held on October 7, 1930, two days after the giant airship crashed at Beauvais, France.

That seance was one of the most dramatic and convincing in the history of modern spiritualism, and because of interest in the tragedy and its perfect conditions for the recapture of spiritualistic influence, the BBC hoped to repeat its thrills.

The seance was conducted by Mrs. Eileen Garrett, who claimed she raised the voice of the dead captain of R101, Flight-Lieutenant Irwin. Mrs. Garrett's claims to have spoken with the flight-lieutenant were scoffed at until she reported his conversation word for word, using phrases that were typical of Irwin.

Mrs. Garrett repeated a conversation with Irwin in which he described technical faults in the airship that caused it to crash.

The seance was held two days after Irwin was killed; an inquiry headed by Lord Simon, sitting for 38 days, upheld most of what Mrs. Garrett reported.

The official finding was that R101 lost a part of its gas when the ship was thrown about by a sudden storm, and that the lack of lift made it unable to rise above hilly ground at Beauvais.

Spiritualists have always regarded the R101 tragedy as a perfect subject for contact with the "other side." For the last 16 years there have been repeated attempts to speak with victims, the majority of whom were learned men and specialists whose brains, it is claimed, would have fitted them for spiritual contact.

When she crashed, the airship had 53 men aboard—five officers, 37 crewmen, and 11 passengers, including men like the Air Minister (Lord Thomson), the Director of Civil Aviation (Sir Sefton Brancker), Squadron-Leader Palstra, of the Royal Australian Air Force, Wing-Commander Colman, Major Scott, Lt.-Commander N. G. Atherstone, all well known in Australia, and the designed of the R101, Col. Richmond.

The Right Type

Those men, who had keen and inquiring minds during life, are considered by spiritualists to be the kind who, if existing in a spirit world, would be eager to regain contact with the earth world. In addition, the last flight of R101 is considered specially favorable for the promotion of spiritualist contact.

R101 left her mast at Cardington, Bedfordshire, with friends and relatives waving good-bye from the base. This, it is considered, left a train of thought and remembrance between those on the ground and those in the ill-fated airship.

Over France, the great gas bag struck a sudden storm, and as the crew and passengers felt themselves in danger, mediums reckon, their thoughts would return to loved ones in England.

The experiences of the six people who got away alive from the crash is held as the greatest point in favor of spiritualist contact.

Most of the six men were trapped momentarily in the gondolas before breaking their way out. It is likely that others of the crew were similarly held alive, but burned to death when the gas bag exploded.

It is reasoned that the minds of those trapped but still alive for the moments between the crash of the ship and the terrifying flash of flame as she blew herself to pieces, would be directed to loved ones in England.

Secrets Of The Crash

Success in contacting Flight-Lieutenant Irwin is attributed by spiritualists to the fact that if he knew what had caused the disaster, his mind would be striving to tell his superiors the secret he alone could reveal.

Spiritualists attach much importance to the action of the mind before death, so that persons trapped and with a sure knowledge of death are considered easier to contact through mediums than persons killed instantaneously.

In the meantime, the BBC has shelved the idea of its attempt to recapture the drama of Mrs. Garrett's "speech" with Irwin. Spiritualists are hopeful, however, the wonder of radio will be called in to solve man's most interesting query—are there spooks?

The great British airship, R101, which crashed to complete destruction at Beauvais, France, while on a flight to India. The BBC planned to broadcast a seance seeking to capture the spirit voices of dead passengers and crew from R101.

THE WORLD'S NEWS, January 4, 1947.

Voices from the past

Long after I thought I had found all the family letters, I received, from relatives in Canada, copies of two hitherto unseen letters that deeply moved me. They were written by May to her mother Agnes, not long after the disaster, and they are filled with grief and pain. She wrote this first letter a mere three days after learning of the catastrophe.

Ashlett Meade Fawley, Hants. 8/10/30

Dearest Mother,

My heart feels just broken, but I must send a few lines to you. I did long to have you with me & it's such a comfort to feel you'll be able to be with me soon. I've thought of your shock & hoped it wasn't too severe for you. The shock of the telegram from the Air Ministry on Sunday morning nearly drove me crazy for awhile. Even now I find it so hard to realise that my darling Will isn't coming back again. The children, thank goodness, don't realise it, although Margaret does at times I think. But I've had a wonderful feeling that he is very near me. We both dreaded the separation & the last week we spent together was just perfect. We had just heard of May's death [May, née Bensley, was May's sister-in-law], & we had several very solemn conversations about life after death. Will told me (as he has several times) that ever since he was a little boy he has felt that God had some great destiny for him. I think he has gone to that now. He also told me that he looked on death as the beginning of a splendid adventure and had no fear of it. Of course he would not have chosen to leave me & the children just now, but somehow even when I felt most desolate I have never thought of rebelling against it. All the colour seems to have gone from my life, but I must try to do as Will would have wanted me to & look after the children.

I feel that I want to get home as soon as I can. We may be sailing by the "Ulysses" on Nov. 8. I'll be calling. Everybody has been just wonderful to me. I'll be able to tell you more next week. Just now my hand is so shaky and my brain so dazed that it is hard to write. Mrs. Ewart came on Sunday & is staying this week with me.

My love to you & all the others,

May.

It is Will's birthday today.

* * * * * *

Letter from May: Ashlett Meade Fawley

15/10/30

Dearest Mother,

I seem to have been living in a ghastly nightmare these last days, from which alas there is no awakening. My only comfort has been the sense of my Will's nearness to me, but I do so long for his physical presence.

I went up to London one day to see if I could identify any of his belongings. It was a dreadful ordeal, but I couldn't bear to think of anything of his being just thrown aside if I could prevent it. The only thing I could identify was his razor (Wilkinson sword Co.). I have been so near physical collapse with shock that I couldn't risk going either to the Memorial Service or funeral. I feel I would gladly welcome death tomorrow but I mustn't risk sickness or what would our children do.

My date of sailing is still uncertain. I was hoping to get away with the Ewarts on Nov. 8th, but now hear that Will's father & mother expect to land in London on Nov. 9th so feel I must see them for a few days, as I know what Will would wish me to do. I feel I hate this place now.

My present plans are to leave here on the 31st. I will take the two little ones with Doris [the maid] to her home where they will stay while Margaret & I go to Mrs. Riggall at Bowne, Lincolnshire. On the 7th of Nov. I will return to London, stay with Mrs. Powley for a couple of nights & then stay wherever Mum & Dad are staying till we sail. I'm longing for my "ain folk".

Everybody has been so very kind. I've been overwhelmed with letters & telegrams. Mrs. Ewart has been wonderful. She stayed with me for ten days & has done everything to help me. Her dressmaker is running up some frocks for me for the trip home. Of course I know Will would hate me to wear black. I can just hear him saying, "Don't waste your money on such nonsense Maisie."

Mrs. Harman has been a tower of strength to me. I may have to have the Will proved here to get our money from the bank, but am hoping to avoid it somehow. Can you find out if Frank has our A.M.P. Policies. I cannot find them here, & think they must be in Aust. somewhere. Perhaps in our spareroom in a box. You might be able to have a look. Mr. Harman is tackling the Directors here about Will's policy as there just might be some difficulty about the type of risk. I hope not as I will want it all in the future. I don't know quite what to decide about where to live. I keep wondering what your ideas are. Perhaps we ought to go back to our house, but I'm a bit afraid of the garden. I thought you might be thinking of our going into 58.[94] Perhaps we had better just stay with someone for awhile till we talk it over, although

---

94 The house next door to May and Will's house at No. 60.

with all our luggage it might be better to go straight into our own home. Since you are on the spot I think I'll leave it to you to do what you think best after consultation with Frank [Will's brother, the banker] & our crowd. I'll be quite pleased to abide by your decision. I feel so dazed and weak that my brain isn't functioning properly yet. The doctor from the camp came to see me & has given me some medicine. The very sight of food makes me want to vomit.

I'll have a pension as Will has been contributing to the fund. It'll be quite sufficient to manage I think. This has been a terrific spiritual experience for me— death & the after life wear a very different aspect for me now. The children are all well but Bill & JoJo have had hives. They all send love. I'm longing to get home to you. Love

May.

Doris has been a brick.

* * * * * *

May and the children at Healesville in the Dandenongs (Victoria, Australia) circa 1931

May and the children - Margaret, Jocelyn and Bill - visiting family in New Zealand, 1936,

Margaret and Jocelyn ready for school, circa 1937. At the front gate of
No 60 Guildford Road, Surrey Hills.

May with her son Bill, who appears to be in his 20s. Probably in Australia in the 1940s.

The legacy

I'm one of Will's eight grandchildren. I grew up in that Surrey Hills house, too. As a young teenager, I used to visit my Auntie Blanche (Will's sister, née Palstra) and Uncle Arthur Holdaway, who lived next door at No.58. We'd sit together in their living-room and pore over the old sepia photographs in their albums. I'd ask them question after question. Even in those days, I was fascinated with family history.

That history permeated the lives of myself and my sisters, for it had soaked into the very fabric of our house. It was in the antiques and curios brought back by our globe-trotting Salvation Army grandparents on both sides—the Chinese and Dutch ornaments, the Maori artefacts. It was in the photograph albums, the wooden aeroplane propeller, the boxes of slightly tarnished A.I.F. "rising sun" buttons and badges, the handful of shrapnel, the old upright piano, the derelict chicken coop at the bottom of the garden, the old wooden sea-trunk (probably Will's) in my bedroom … Some frugal housekeeper (probably Granny) had covered that trunk with padding and thick curtain material to serve as a combined storage box and seat, but when I lifted the fabric away, and peered underneath I was enthralled at the sight of the many old unexplained and deteriorating steamship company stickers, plastered over the surface. They spoke of long-ago journeys to exotic places...

That history, those memories—those ghosts that never fade—silently pervaded the existence of the adults who surrounded us—unspoken, but immutable and eternal as, in hindsight, we know.

Using the letters and diaries that were concealed in that hidden drawer, I have told the story of my grandfather, Will Palstra. I have finally completed the duty that seemed to be laid upon me at birth. I have (I hope), after more than a century, immortalised him.

"A man's not dead while his name is still spoken," Sir Terry Pratchett once wrote.

Speak his name!

William Palstra.

The last word belongs to Will's daughter Margaret.

MEMORIES

Memories, by Margaret Thornton, née Palstra, July 1991:

A few memories of childhood float past like feathers in a soft breeze. Is it I who was there?

Perhaps I entered someone's dream, so cloudy are the beginnings and endings.

A drift of bluebells in a hazy mist on the floor of a wood bursting into leaf; small fields of wheat laced with scarlet poppies; the intricate mystery and fascination of the hedgerows.

These lingered like paradise lost in my mind; for seventeen years after I returned to my birthplace I felt alienated and repulsed by the Australia landscape.

Looking back I realise this was my way of rebelling against the miserable circumstances of our return - my adored father dead on the brink of a brilliant career; the family income reduced from twenty-two pounds and ten shillings to three pounds and three shillings a week; my mother often weeping and trying to adjust to bringing up three little children on her own and in poverty; the fantastic and marvellous two years in England gone forever.

The shadow of the Depression hung heavily over all grown-ups, and to one nine-year-old girl it seemed life would always be gloomy and hateful.

The Scar, by Margaret Thornton, née Palstra:

Elusive memory.

The hunter scans the years and finds a moment of such pain, that like a sea anemone, sensing corrosion in the tide, awareness shrinks from confrontation.

Loose the caged monster? Face bravely till excised? Did this really happen? Is it true?

Only the heart knows, in secret chambers, the demons of the past.

***

Maisie Margaret Palstra Thornton passed away on 23 November, 1992.

May
Will
Margaret

THE END

Memories

A few memories of childhood float past like feathers in a soft breeze. Is it I who was there? Perhaps I entered someone's dream, so cloudy are the beginnings and endings.

A drift of bluebells in a hazy mist on the floor of a wood bursting into leaf; small fields of wheat laced with scarlet poppies; the intricate mystery and fascination of the hedgerows. These lingered like paradise lost in my mind; for seventeen years after I returned to my birthplace I felt alienated and repulsed by the Australian landscape.

Looking back I realise this was my way of rebelling against the miserable circumstances of our return - my adored father dead on the brink of a brilliant career; the family income reduced from twenty-two pounds and ten shillings to three pounds and three shillings a week; my mother often weeping and trying to adjust to bringing up three little children on her own and in poverty; the fantastic and marvellous two years in England gone forever.

The shadow of the Depression hung heavily over all grown-ups, and to one nine-year-old girl it seemed life would always be gloomy and hateful.

I had to return to England in 1947 before the demon was exorcised.

. . . . .

My father, Squadron Leader William Palstra, was one of the seven passengers on the Airship R101, which crashed in Beauvais, France, on 30th September, 1930. He was representing the Government of Australia on the Airship's maiden voyage to India.

He had been due to return to Australia in two months' time to become Commanding Officer of Laverton Air Base.

Margaret Thornton.

BIBLIOGRAPHY

Books:

Barker, Anthony. What Happened When: A Chronology of Australia from 1788. Allen & Unwin, 1992.

Chisholm, Hugh, ed. "Chapelle Ardente." Encyclopædia Britannica, 5 (11th ed.), Cambridge University Press, p. 851, 1911.

Jackson, Ashley. The British Empire: A Very Short Introduction. OUP, 2013. ISBN 978-0-19-960541-5.

Kingston, S., & Lambert, M. "Catastrophe and Crisis." Bloomsbury Books, 1979.

Masefield, Peter G. To Ride the Storm: The Story of the Airship R.101. William Kimber, 1982. p. 337, 1982.

Journal Articles:

Davison, Peter. "The R.101 story: a review based on primary source material and first-hand accounts." Royal Aeronautical Society Journal Paper No. 2015/02, 2015.

Scott & Richmond. "A detailed consideration of the effect of meteorological conditions on airships." R.38 Memorial Prize paper, Royal Aeronautical Society, London, 1923.

Newspaper Articles:

"34 Squadron Air Training Corps–History of Cardington Airship Sheds." 134.org.uk. Accessed May 16, 2012.

"Mr Rose in Sir Samuel Hoare's Statement." Hansard, UK Parliament, March 12, 1928.

"The Age" (Melbourne, Vic.: 1854—1954), October 6, 1930, p. 9.

"The London Illustrated News," March 9, 1929.

Online Resources:

"Airship Heritage Trust 'Interiors R101." https://www.airshipsonline.com/airships/interior/R101Interior.htm

"Flight International (UK)*. DVV Media Group, 1909.

"How to Moor a British Rigid Airship." Airship Heritage Trust's YouTube channel.

Long Branch Mike. "Empire of the Air: The Imperial Airship Service." 2016. https://www.londonreconnections.com/2016/empire-of-the-air-the-imperial-airship-service/

Meager, G. "Leaves from My Logbook." Wingfoot Lighter Than Air Society, Akron, Ohio, 1961.

"R100 Meets End." Popular Aviation, October 1932, p. 225.

Royal Airforce Museum UK. https://www.rafmuseum.org.uk/about-us/our-history/Hendon-cradle-of-aviation.aspx

"Unit history, RAF Hendon." National Archives UK. https://www.forces-war-records.co.uk/units/599/raf-hendon.

Wallis. "Some Technical Aspects of the Commercial Airship" R101. Box B Masefield Archive, Brooklands, February 10, 1926.

Other:

Callanan, Tim. "'Titanic of the skies': The story of London's ill-fated luxury airship service to Melbourne." December 29, 2018.

Hall II, C.P. Correspondence with the author, Jan-Feb 2024.

Leech, Harry. Foreman Engineer, Statement AIR5/903. Source: Davison, 2015.

McAuley, Rob. "The Story of Airships." Film Finance Corporation Australia. Rob McAuley Productions, 2004.

The British Newspaper Archive. https://www.britishnewspaperarchive.co.uk/viewer/bl/0002130/19301006/095/0004.

Watch video footage of the R101

Visit the Airship of Dreams channel on YouTube @AirshipofDreams

Enjoy looking through the "playlists" collected for you from across the YouTube platform. There's historical footage of the R101 in flight; the airship leaving on the fatal voyage; the aftermath of the tragedy, and also films of other zeppelins and airships. Don't miss the "walk-throughs" of British airships created by the Airship Heritage Trust. Playlists include:

#1 R101: His Majesty's Airship	#7 Zeppelins
#2 R101: The story	#8 US airships
#3 R101: The crash	#9 The Hindenburg
#4 R101: The aftermath	#10 Other airships
#5 R101 down the years	#11 Airships in general
#6 British airships	#12 Future airships

Write a review

If you enjoyed Airship of Dreams, please write a review. Even a short sentence is welcome! This can help others find the book, and it means the world to the author. To find a place to write your review, visit any of the following websites . . .

- Amazon.com (USA)
- Amazon.co.uk (UK)
- Amazon.ca (Canada)
- Amazon.com.au (Australia & New Zealand)
- Goodreads
- Barnes & Noble

. . . and type into the search box any of these terms:

- **Airship of Dreams**
- **C.M.S. Thornton**
- **ISBN: 9781923212008**
- **ISBN: 9781923212015**

THE CALL TO ARMS

The Office Clerk Who Dared the Great Adventure

VALIANT HEART 2

This is the biography of First World War hero William Palstra between 1914 and 1917. An office clerk in London sails across the sea in a steam-powered ship and becomes an office clerk in Melbourne, Australia. The Great War commences and his younger brother enlists in the Australian Imperial Force (A.I.F.), becoming an Anzac. Will Palstra enlists in 1916, trains at Ballarat in Victoria, and voyages back to Britain with the 39th Infantry Battalion. They complete their training at Stonehenge on Salisbury Plain and cross the English Channel to begin active service on the infamous Western Front.

"The Call to Arms" is Book #2 of the VALIANT HEART trilogy following Palstra's well-documented life story as he comes of age, maturing from a mild-mannered office clerk to a commissioned officer in the Australian Army.

Valiant Heart Trilogy

Book 1: Airship of Dreams
Book 2: The Call to Arms
Book 3: Blood and Fire

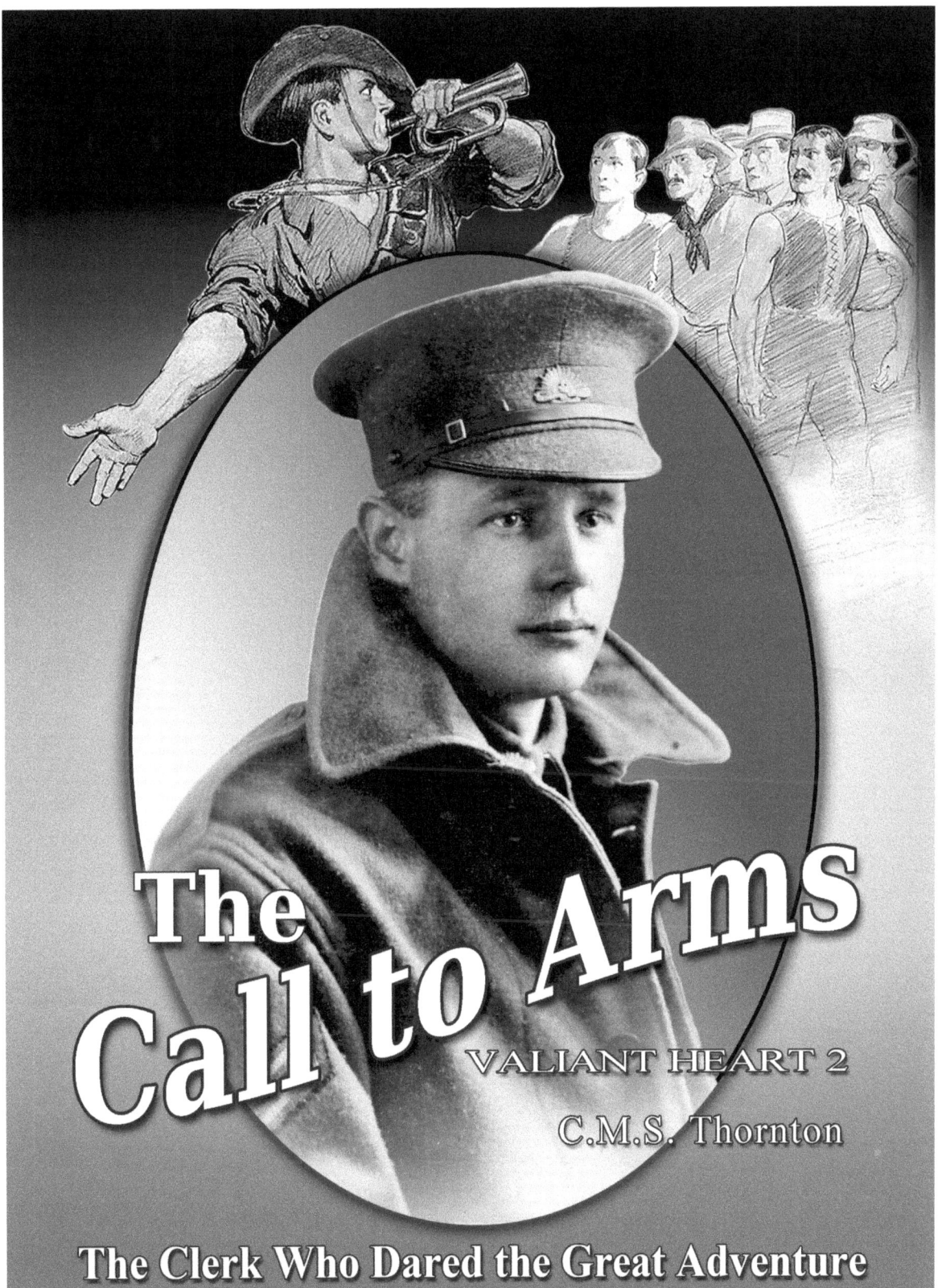

The Call to Arms

VALIANT HEART 2

C.M.S. Thornton

The Clerk Who Dared the Great Adventure

BLOOD AND FIRE

The Hero Who Conquered the Skies

VALIANT HEART 3

This is the story of First World War hero William Palstra between 1917 and 1919. Fighting the trenches on the Western Front with the 39th Battalion AIF, the Battle of Messines, being awarded a Military Cross by the King at Buckingham Palace, joining the Australian Flying Corps and learning to fly biplanes, braving artillery fire and enemy planes while flying over enemy lines, Armistice Day 1918 and the celebrations in Paris, the happy and victorious homecoming.

"Blood and Fire" is Book #3 of the VALIANT HEART trilogy following Palstra's story as he walks through the valley of death and emerges a hero.

Valiant Heart Trilogy

Book 1: Airship of Dreams

Book 2: The Call to Arms

Book 3: Blood and Fire

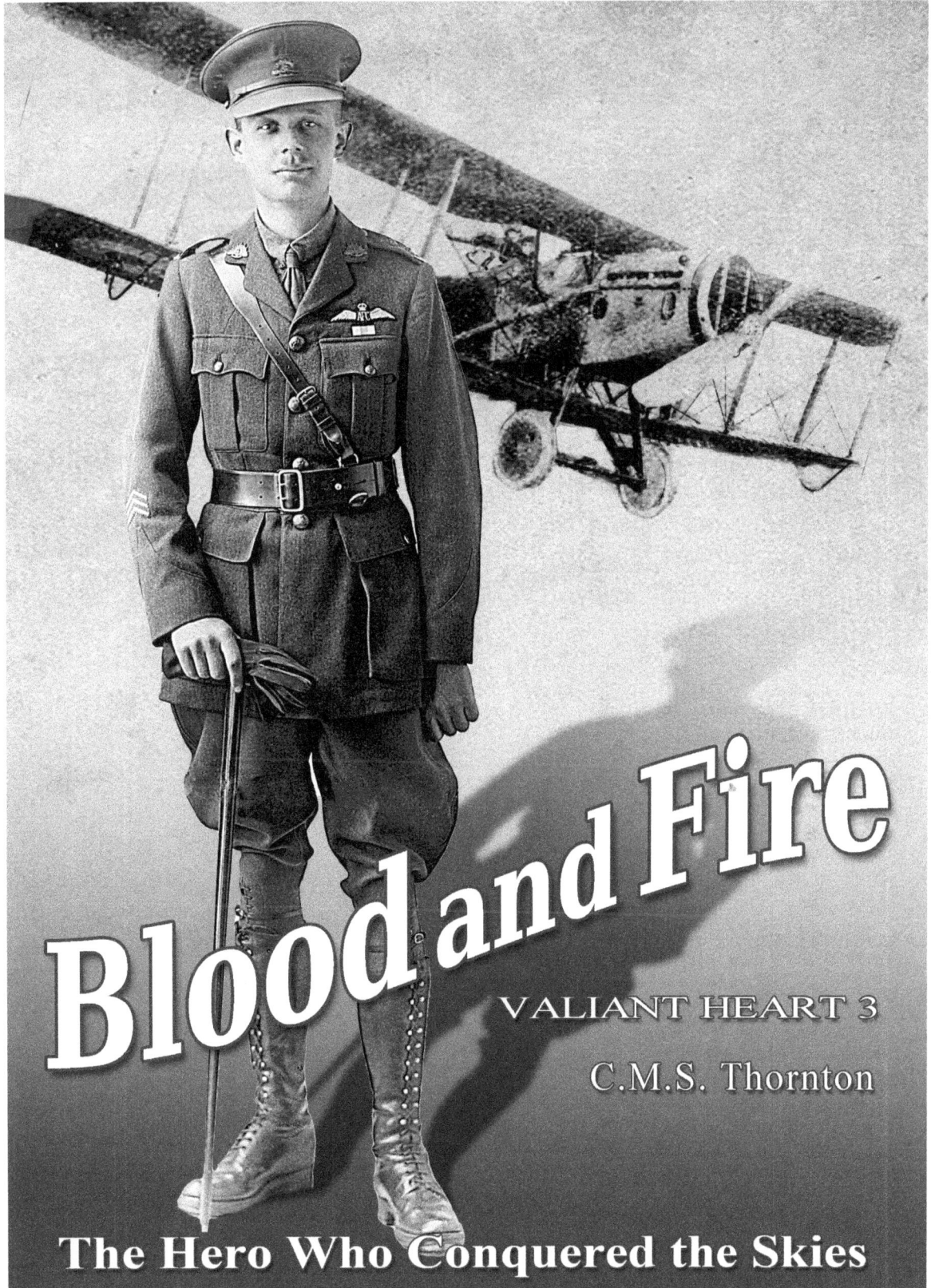

Blood and Fire

VALIANT HEART 3

C.M.S. Thornton

The Hero Who Conquered the Skies

www.ingramcontent.com/pod-product-compliance
Lightning Source LLC
Chambersburg PA
CBHW061924290426
44113CB00024B/2817